THE
DETERMINANTS
OF
FREE WILL

PERSONALITY AND PSYCHOPATHOLOGY
A Series of Monographs, Texts, and Treatises

David T. Lykken, Editor

1. The Anatomy of Achievement Motivation, *Heinz Heckhausen*. 1966°

2. Cues, Decisions, and Diagnoses: A Systems-Analytic Approach to the Diagnosis of Psychopathology, *Peter E. Nathan*. 1967°

3. Human Adaptation and Its Failures, *Leslie Phillips*. 1968°

4. Schizophrenia: Research and Theory, *William E. Broen, Jr.* 1968°

5. Fears and Phobias, *I. M. Marks*. 1969

6. Language of Emotion, *Joel R. Davitz*. 1969

7. Feelings and Emotions, *Magda Arnold*. 1970

8. Rhythms of Dialogue, *Joseph Jaffe* and *Stanley Feldstein*. 1970

9. Character Structure and Impulsiveness, *David Kipnis*. 1971

10. The Control of Aggression and Violence: Cognitive and Physiological Factors, *Jerome L. Singer* (Ed.). 1971

11. The Attraction Paradigm, *Donn Byrne*. 1971

12. Objective Personality Assessment: Changing Perspectives, *James N. Butcher* (Ed.). 1972

13. Schizophrenia and Genetics, *Irving I. Gottesman* and *James Shields*, 1972°

14. Imagery and Daydream Methods in Psychotherapy and Behavior Modification, *Jerome L. Singer*. 1974

15. Experimental Approaches to Psychopathology, *Mitchell L. Kietzman, Samuel Sutton,* and *Joseph Zubin* (Eds.). 1975

16. Coping and Defending: Processes of Self-Environment Organization, *Norma Haan*. 1977

17. The Scientific Analysis of Personality and Motivation, *R. B. Cattell* and *P. Kline*. 1977

18. The Determinants of Free Will: A Psychological Analysis of Responsible, Adjustive Behavior, *James A. Easterbrook*.

In Preparation

19. The Psychopath in Society, *Robert J. Smith*.

°Titles initiated during the series editorship of Brendan Maher.

THE
DETERMINANTS
OF
FREE WILL

A Psychological Analysis of
Responsible, Adjustive Behavior

JAMES A. EASTERBROOK

Department of Psychology
University of New Brunswick
Fredericton, New Brunswick, Canada

with the assistance of
PAMELA J. EASTERBROOK

ACADEMIC PRESS   New York   San Francisco   London   1978

A Subsidiary of Harcourt Brace Jovanovich, Publishers

ACADEMIC PRESS, INC.
111 Fifth Avenue, New York, New York 10003

United Kingdom Edition published by
ACADEMIC PRESS, INC. (LONDON) LTD.
24/28 Oval Road, London NW1

Library of Congress Cataloging in Publication Data

Easterbrook, James A
      The determinants of free will.

      (Personality and psychopathology series)
      1.   Adjustment (Psychology)   2.   Free will and deter-
minism.   3.   Autonomy (Psychology)   I.   Easterbrook,
Pamela J., joint author.   II.   Title.
BF335.E2   153.8   77-2028
ISBN 0−12−227550−0

PRINTED IN THE UNITED STATES OF AMERICA

Contents

Preface

This book develops the concept of personal adjustment as freedom of will, and consequently as personal responsibility. Its principal contributions to the literature on adjustment are that its terms provide an historical context for psychological doctrine on the topic and that it shows the necessity of morally acceptable behavior for the attainment of ideal relationships with one's environment. To the literature on freedom of will it adds a survey of information on the environmental conditions that affect it, and a review of evidence that two important classes of determinants are implicated, one concerned with intelligence and intention, the other with emotion and freedom of choice.

The text is split into four interdependent parts. The first two chapters introduce working definitions and establish the rationale and general framework for what follows. Many of their propositions are of the nature of claims that are substantiated in later chapters.

The second part of the book sets out basic arguments on will, causal responsibility, and personal adjustment. Inspired particularly by the thought of Kurt Goldstein, it differentiates behaviors that are determined by what is immediately "given" from those which are shaped by, and serve to attain, the "possible" or ideal. One fundamental chapter is devoted to the impelling, choice-reducing, effects of distressed biological and emotional conditions, and to the sources of resistance against their driving influence. Another reviews evidence on the differences in content of thoughts by people who often produce forward-looking, situation-shaping behavior and others whose actions are commonly shaped by their situations.

The third part of the text takes up the problem of independence in a social context. One chapter focuses on the maladjustments produced by societies that require obedience to the commands or examples of others. Another surveys evidence on the childhood determinants of self-discipline, introduces the concept of self-rewarded self-instruction, and raises the issue of its validity. The final chapter pursues the themes of motivational and informational independence through the literature on attitudes as mechanisms of behavioral autonomy. It recounts evidence of both maladjustment and restricted freedom of will in "closed-minded" persons and of similar disabilities in gullible individuals. Different conceptual systems, different criteria of truth, and different instructional histories seem to distinguish the attitudinally free from both the attitudinally rigid and the situationally driven.

The four final chapters of the book are concerned with conditions in which freedom of will and good personal adjustment can be shared by interacting and interdependent persons. An account of laboratory studies into the development of cooperation reveals how freedom of will promotes social harmony and depends upon relative equality of power. This theme is followed into the socioeconomic field, with a description of recent theory and evidence about the sociological determinants of free will and adjustment. A subsequent review of research into moral concepts justifies considering the interactional systems that promote freedom of will in large numbers of people as ethically more advanced. It is contended that higher ethical beliefs are in fact concerned with the promotion of freedom of will for all as a matter of right. The book concludes with a résumé of the necessary social conditions for the maintenance and propagation of free will, and brief synoptic descriptions of the responsible personality and the good life.

To place all of this in the context of philosophical history, it is convenient to refer to the eighteenth-century work of Immanuel Kant, whose views on freedom of will seem to have dominated European conceptions of human potentiality for at least a century. There are, in fact, important similarities between Kant's views and those described here, if one thinks metaphorically. Kant maintained that "to will . . . is to choose a course of action" and that "independence from the determining causes of the world of sense is freedom." This is analogous to what stands out in the behavioral evidence I have reviewed. It seems clear, too, that rational man, as a collectivity, has indeed displayed autonomy in developing his "conceptions of laws"—the determining causes of behavior that is shaped in the "world of understanding"—and that actions taken in accordance with some of those conceptions do indeed promote the independence we are concerned with.

It is at this point, though, that Kant's and the following thesis first diverge. In postulating self-legislation in the "world of understanding" as the principal condition of freedom—in order to reconcile freedom of will with determinism—Kant seems to have misjudged the importance of accuracy or objectivity in that understanding. It is true that he mentioned the value of "moderation in the affections and passions, self control and calm deliberation" to freedom of choice, and clearly stipulated that their maintenance should be regarded as a matter of duty. Yet, in the course of his grand argument, he focused upon autonomous intelligence, to the apparent neglect of effectiveness in maintaining the relations with the environment that facilitate "calm deliberation." When he specified mere autonomy in the world of understanding as the source of freedom for the will, he seems to have dignified subjectivity at the expense of effectiveness. It is evident, however, that actions which bring environmental events under their author's control, and accordingly produce autonomy, also differ from impulsive, situationally stimulated (or inhibited) actions in being more objectively appropriate, as if determined with a more objective understanding.

The following reconciliation of free will with determinism agrees with Kant's that freely willed behavior is determined and that the contribution of "understanding" to its determination differentiates it from other sorts of action. However, it follows Goldstein in viewing accurate abstraction and imagination as sources both of will and of freedom. The "world of understanding" creates freedom of will in persons who are competent to shape their actions by its "laws." Over the long term, then, it does so because those laws represent reality *better,* and facilitate a superior adjustment, than do the "determining causes of the world of sense." It does so because those "laws" reconcile and serve to predict the evidence of that world, not because they ignore it, nor yet because they are newly invented.

Another way in which Kant's thesis seems inadequate by contemporary standards has to do with the importance of cultural influences upon the development of freedom of will. When he discussed autonomy in the creation of laws of the "world of understanding," he did not distinguish man, the individual, from man, the collectivity. Accordingly, of course, he was able to elide the fact that much of our world of understanding is provided by others. We have more and better evidence today. In fact it seems to be true, in large measure, that freedom of will develops when it is cultivated in us by influential others in favorable social and economic conditions.

ACKNOWLEDGMENTS

I am particularly conscious, at this moment, of the favorable social conditions in which this book has been produced. Many persons have contributed to it. Some of them are cited. I fear, though, that the help of many persons will not have been acknowledged. It seems to me that much psychological and sociological theory and research has been moving for some time in the directions I have outlined. One cannot be confident of having identified every important influence on such a trend.

Of course I have had local support too. Pamela J. Easterbrook's assistance is recognized on the title page. Her work on self-discipline yielded Chapter 7 and exerted an important influence on my thinking. She helped in many other ways as well, not least by buoying my faith in the project. Sergio Sismondo, then director of research for New Brunswick Newstart, Inc., and Satrajit Dutta, one of my colleagues at the University of New Brunswick, performed similarly supportive functions. Their criticisms of my drafts were extremely valuable; our discussions were often exciting, commonly provocative, and always enjoyable. The patience of others who examined the text is also appreciated, notably that of the students who endured a term with an inadequate draft and helped me identify faulty passages in it. Finally, as every writer knows, the whole enterprise would have been impossible without the patience and support of my wife and other members of our family.

I

FREEDOM, RESPONSIBILITY, AND RELATED CONCEPTS

Free Will in Psychology and Human Affairs

Sigmund Freud was studying hysteria and Karl Marx was writing *Das Kapital* when William Ernest Henley, under treatment for tuberculosis in the 1880s, produced a short poem that ended with the lines,

> *It matters not how strait the gate,*
> *How charged with punishments the scroll,*
> *I am the master of my fate;*
> *I am the captain of my soul.*

Henley's belief in freedom of will was widely shared in Victorian Europe, but the theses Marx and Freud were developing at the time have seemed to contradict it. Those great works showed how social affairs and human thoughts and actions are influenced by forces outside the individual mind, by economic and cultural circumstances and biological instincts. They went further and said those forces *determined* human affairs. Their authors had adopted the scientific assumption of *determinism,* and their arguments proved very persuasive. Indeed, as many writers have noticed, they were so persuasive as to change some men's views of the nature of man. In the words of Rollo May, "The image that emerged was of man as determined—not *driving* any more but *driven* [1969, p. 183]." They brought about revolutions in modern thought about psychic and social affairs that have led to a widespread rejection of the Victorian belief in willpower.

More than that: in the opinion of a number of philosophers and psychiatrists cited by May, the social sciences that Freud and Marx pioneered have created new problems of human existence. They have led some people to believe that individual choices do not matter and that enterprises involving personal imagination, effort, and fortitude cannot prosper or succeed. If world events in general and human behavior in particular are determined, how can private choices or endeavors be either possible or effective? How can individuals be responsible for the outcomes of their actions, good or bad? Some social science students speak this way, as if pride, guilt, and responsibility were out of date; these students are alienated instead. Rollo May regards thoughts like theirs as "neurotic":

> Indeed the central core of modern man's neurosis, it may be fairly said, is the undermining of his experience of himself as responsible, the sapping of his will and ability to make decisions. The lack of will is much more than merely an ethical problem: the modern individual so often has the conviction that even if he *did* exert his "will"—or whatever illusion passes for it—his actions wouldn't do any good anyway. It is this inner experience of impotence, this contradiction in will, which constitutes our critical problem [1969, p. 184].

This book is addressed to these conflicting views of man's nature and condition, to the reality they reflect, and to the associated problems of human well-being they regard as solvable or not. Its central thesis holds that the kinds of human behavior men have meant by the term *freedom of will* are commonly evident today, though often under other names. They are now called "purposive," "deliberate," "enterprising," "skillful," and so on; and the personalities who produce them reliably are known as "competent," "well-adjusted," "mature," "self-actualizing," or something of the sort. Moreover, it holds that these sorts of behavior are properly contrasted with the anxiety, depression, impotence, and "neurosis" that May and others associate with lack of "will."

PRELIMINARY DEFINITIONS

As an initial definition, freely willed behavior is considered to have been demonstrated whenever an individual has planfully created preferred changes in his environment. These are also the conditions in which one is held, and holds himself, responsible for his actions. Driven behavior, by contrast, arises when action is impelled by immediate external circumstances or events, and the actor is not considered responsible. When the behavior of human beings is "driven," it and they are often described as "maladjusted," and sometimes this is attributed to a disorder of the *psyche*. Freely willed behavior, on the other hand, produces and thrives upon the personal satisfactions that develop in harmonious social and economic conditions and is comparably described as "well adjusted."

These crude preliminary distinctions and definitions are developed in later chapters, each of which elaborates on them while describing relevant theory and fact. Nonetheless they will serve here as context for a crucial proposition: The driven and freely willed types of behavior are equally subject to the "causal" principle that underlies the notion of "determinism," although their determinants seem to differ in both their numbers and their nature. This is not to say that the determinants of a given choice can be fully specified; it is to claim that the possibility of making a choice is determined and that determined components enter the choice.

The alleged incompatibility of free will and determinism, discussed on the opening page, involves a misconception of will. It is based on a biased question—one that implies that will must work in a causal vacuum. A better question focuses on the concept of will and carries the opposite implication: "If events in the world are *not* determined, how might anyone produce any of them at will?" This sort of consideration recurs in the following chapters, in reference to the effects of experience on human behavior. It refers as much to the definition, as to the psychology, of will. For present purposes, an old definition of that old concept is acceptable. It is one of Kant's. *"The will is conceived as a faculty of determining oneself to action in accordance with the conception of certain laws. And such a faculty can be found only in rational beings* [Kant, (1785/1910, p. 358)]." Thus will (and its freedom) refers to the type of, not the lack of, determination shown in action.

In turn, the concept of freedom is understood as referring to a relationship between an individual and his environment, in which freedom varies as a function of the individual's ability to govern what happens to him. Of course competence by a person depends upon predictable responsiveness in the environment and the person's possession of appropriate knowledge or power. Individual competence counteracts the restraints, impulsions, or compulsions that oppose freedom. Indeed its various determinants come into focus in various dictionary definitions of freedom.[1] Thus "exemption from arbitrary, despotic or autocratic control" emphasizes the importance of environmental predictability and individual knowledge of it. And "exemption or release from slavery or imprisonment" focuses on relative power. So does the more general definition, "the state of being able to act without hindrance or restraint." Each of these statements has a weakness, however, in its use of a dichotomous term ("exemption," "release," "without") that depicts freedom as an all-or-nothing matter. It is clear that the restraints, impulsions, and compulsions that oppose it can vary in strength. The same is true of a person's ability to govern what happens to him. Freedom, like restraints and the rest, varies in degree.

Although there is no more freedom than will in movements or wishes that occur in reflex reaction to environmental events, both are evident in all projects

---

[1]From *The Compact Edition of the Oxford English Dictionary.* Oxford: Oxford University Press, 1971. It will be seen later that the general definition of freedom in the opening sentence of this paragraph is also consistent with Kant's (1785/1959) statement that "independence from the determining causes of the world of sense . . . is freedom [p. 71]." It is consistent, too, with the main conclusion of M. J. Adler (1958, p. 616) that "A man . . . is free in the sense that he has in himself the ability or power whereby he can make what he does his own actions. . . ," but perhaps not with the corollary that completes Adler's statement, ". . .and what he achieves his own property."

involving creative imagination. This is true even if those projects are influenced by the wishes and knowledge of their authors.

The latter statement is notably and amusingly true even of imaginative arguments that deny the possibility of free will. Such self-contradictory works have been produced by others beside social scientists and amateur philosophers. There are ancient precedents. Thus, for instance, Ulysses and mankind at large were portrayed in the *Odyssey* as pawns in the games of the gods. Following that view of man, no consistent person could logically undertake any novel enterprise, like creating an ode. Indeed if a man were to plan a project and carry it through to remarkable accomplishment, then he would be considered either a favorite or an agent of a god or goddess (as Ulysses was). Or, conceivably, he could be regarded as a god himself, a view some later Greeks are thought to have taken of Alexander the Great. Yet the Homeric epic, like Freudian theory, was in fact composed by man.

While some men have speculated on human impotence and others have imagined mankind as molded in the image of God, still others have demonstrated creativity by changing their environments. "What except imaginative power," one writer has asked, "lifted inert mud into the fantastic ziggurat with its crowning temple or the resistant mass of rocks into a gleaming pyramid [Hawkes, 1973, p. 4]?" Some philosophic speculation might deny its possibility, but human creative imagination long ago built monuments both to itself and to the fallacy of those speculations.

FREE WILL AND ADJUSTMENT

Powerlessness, neurosis, and failures of will may be rife today, and denials of human willpower may indeed be contributing to this state of affairs, although determinism is not. Certainly there is evidence that such denials are becoming increasingly commonplace (Rotter, 1971). There is also evidence that belief in one's impotence creates impotence in one (Rotter, Chance, & Phares, 1972). But, it is logically possible, and psychologically reasonable to believe, that feelings of impotence and denials of will both result from other causes. Accordingly, plausible as it is, May's hypothesis that the teachings of Freud and Marx created modern man's neurosis is *not* adopted in what follows. The "neurosis" is assigned instead to the ways in which human beings deal with one another and to the complexities of modern life. Nonetheless, many of May's recommendations are compatible with the facts and theories that have to be presented here.

In May's conception, stated in gross terms by paraphase of the foregoing quotation, the cure of modern man's "neurosis" is the reorganization or reconstruction of an experience of himself as responsible, the reconstitution of his will and ability to make decisions. The facts, arguments, and assumptions to be described here should aid in this process by revealing the range and limits of the free will that determinism permits and its absence prevents.

Probably because they refer to the same realities, there are resemblances between May's and some other modern conceptions of ideal relationships between man and his environment. Each advocates one or more aspects of free will as the criteria of "mental health," optimal "personal adjustment," or "maturity." Thus Goldstein (1939, 1940) and Maslow (1954) wrote of "self actualization," Freud (1927) and others of "integration" among subsystems of personality, Fromm (1941, 1947) and Riesman (1955) of "autonomy" as opposed to dependence, and still others of "environmental mastery" (Jahoda, 1958), "competence" (White, 1959, 1972; Smith, 1969), "objectivity" (Jahoda, 1958), or the "positive self-regard" (Rogers, 1951) that is associated with such conditions. Critical reviews of these and other concepts of mental health or adjustment have been published elsewhere (e.g., Jahoda, 1958; Sechrest & Wallace, 1967; Lazarus, 1974; DiCaprio, 1974). Although the present thesis is remarkably influenced by Goldstein and Maslow, it also comprehends the conditions that some other writers have regarded as criteria of good adjustment. That is, the concepts of this book integrate such conceptions by treating them as features, components, or functions of free will.

FREE WILL IN PSYCHOLOGY

The "Situationalism" Bias

The ideas of freedom and of personal will and responsibility have been used for centuries in social philosophy, but not in recent psychology. Yet the situation is changing. Psychological knowledge has advanced to the point at which investigators are discussing "perceived freedom" (Steiner, 1970), "personal causality" (Heider, 1958; de Charms, 1968), and even "the illusions of control and freedom" (Lefcourt, 1973). Scientific psychology is waiting for the old concept of free will to organize such evidence, but hesitates to use it.

Two related factors seem to account for the reluctance of psychologists to discuss freedom of will. One is the philosophical error about determinism already mentioned, the other is a related bias of thought. Both are evident in a well-known monograph by B. F. Skinner (1971), an outstandingly successful student of behavior.

Experimental psychologists invariably assume that mental events and behavior are determined. Otherwise their aspirations to create a positivistic science would be unthinkable. Unfortunately, some have also supposed that freedom of will and determinism are competitive explanatory principles. To such persons, accordingly, the term *free will* means a kind of magic. For them it is not a descriptive name for some kinds of mental or behavioral events that differ from others in their determinants and in their relation to subsequent events. So they have failed to recognize that the assumption of determinism is no less applicable to free will than it is to stimulated responses.

The pertinent bias in thought has been designated "situationalism" (Bowers, 1973). This is the assumption that environmental events shape or control an organism's behavior. It has been an extraordinarily fruitful assumption for psychology, having facilitated countless experiments which show in detail that what an individual does depends (partly) upon what happens to him just before, and/or upon what happened in earlier similar situations just after, an action. These findings in turn support the assumption and those who have made it. It is "true," and every psychologist knows that. If situations shape or "control" behavior, it must be nonsense to speak of freedom of will or of personal responsibility!

Yet it is also true, and no less true though some psychologists overlook it, that actions by people and animals shape or control environments. Organisms and environments interact. They influence one another. Indeed, of the two, no doubt the organism ordinarily exercises more control over his physical environment than vice versa. He is more active, smarter, and more adaptable, and physical environments are more predictable. Indeed, it seems likely that well-educated adult humans might truthfully claim that, 9 hours out of 10, they meet nothing new or surprising in their environments, but are easily able to control what happens to them.

Free Will and Competence

If the "situationalism" bias of some psychologists looks unacceptable, the bias of many writers who take freedom of will as an ideal is no less so. And it is equally alarming. Based, in part, on related misunderstandings, the position these "defenders of freedom" take actually threatens freedom of will. They argue strenuously, even contemptuously, against some of the sorts of social actions that will be shown necessary to develop it. We must not arrange to reward people for taking correct actions, they contend: What Skinner wants us to do will reduce their freedom. This position has some intuitive appeal and is accordingly dangerous. Its error and its danger lurk in the negative relation it presumes between freedom and training and the positive relation it presumes between freedom and unpredictability. Both notions are diametrically opposed to the truth.

Freedom of will depends upon competence. Competence in turn depends upon learning and upon the structure and predictability of the learner's environment, among other factors. Among the main constituents of competence are known relations between individual actions and desirable environmental reactions. These are control relations, in which each component is indispensable. They cannot be established in chaotic environments, nor by erratic or capricious individuals. The relation between competence and freedom is one of the main topics of discussion in what follows.

Most human and animal actions are clearly shaped to suit their environments. There is no debate about that. The issues concern the nature and locus of the control that brings this about. Extreme situationalists ascribe the control to the environment. According to Skinner, for instance, "A scientific analysis of behavior dispossesses autonomous man and turns the control he has been said to exercise over to the environment [1971, p. 205]." Others have somewhat different views, but still accord major influence to the situation. The present (and public) view treats the environment as the object of knowledge. And, because experience clearly accumulates across environments and may even be reorganized in the process (Inhelder & Piaget, 1958), it ascribes both the knowledge and the control that experience creates to the individual. It ascribes competence to people.

The relationship of competence to freedom has been seriously neglected by many psychologists in recent years, at least since Goldstein's important lectures of 1940. Even more serious, however, has been the related misconstruction by many people, including some psychologists, of the importance to freedom of contingencies between acts and rewarding outcomes. For instance, Brehm (1966) reviews evidence that some people react negatively when offered rewards for changing their customary behavior, and he interprets this phenomenon as showing a preference for "freedom over reward" (rather than indicating suspicion, for instance). Skinner (1971) urges that the benefits of reward for the development of desirable social behavior are so important that society ought to go "beyond" freedom to employ them. And, though vehemently rejecting his proposal, many of his critics fully accept Skinner's contrast of freedom with the use of rewards for "control." The same opposition is explicitly asserted by another psychologist: "To the extent that the person expects reward for his task he is unfree . . . the source of the reward is an external causal locus for his behavior [de Charms, 1968, p. 329]." The contrast these writers have drawn is fallacious, and it is apparently associated with misunderstanding of the relations of free will to control, to determinism, and to competence.

It is alarming that this erroneous thinking appears to be gaining acceptance by those Skinner called "defenders of freedom." If it should produce advice about public actions in the interests of freedom, that advice could be self-defeating. Although given in the service of personal freedom, it could in fact undermine it. The reason for this statement is at once simple and complex. It concerns one of several instances of paradox that becloud the topic.

Behavioral freedom is not possible without behavioral control. The statement is left in this form, because it must be understood that control cuts both ways. Indeed, Skinner (1971, p. 169) noted as much, citing Sir Francis Bacon. When the environment has been constrained to respond consistently and predictably to an action, then that action controls the environment, as much as the environment controls it, and more directly. The fact that psychologists deal with this point in an old trade joke—"The rat has the experimenter trained"—makes it no less true. Purposive actions, and the freedom to produce their effects, depend upon a predictable environment for their very existence.

Few people seem to doubt that rendering the physical environment predictable increases one's freedom within it. It is principally when consideration of the social environment arises that errors of reasoning creep in. If one thinks that social reality is relatively fixed and that individual behavior alone is changeable, then it is perhaps understandable if he believes social sanctions act solely to control the individual. Though understandable, such reasoning is faulty. When we, as the social environment, agree to reward socially desirable behavior, we are agreeing to a constraint on the number of possible actions that we, the environment, might take when a person behaves that way. In short, we are rendering our actions more predictable. The constraint here is not upon the person who is rewarded but, rather, upon our own freedom of choice. He achieves prediction, the option of commanding our rewards and the possibility of designing actions to attain them if he will. Instead of reducing it, knowing how to attain a reward one desires can only increase what Goldstein (1940) called his "capacity for freedom."

Control and Punishment

Escape from punishment or the threat of it is a special sort of reward, and has a special relation to freedom. It is possible, as Skinner has suggested, that many people fear the "behavioral control" he advocates, because they associate control with punishment. Certainly we need to be free of fear or anxiety, and the actions we learn to relieve these states can serve to increase freedom of choice, as will be shown. However, punishment or threat of punishment for an act are not always useful in preventing that act in the future. And, as will be shown, frequent intensive use of such sanctions by parents seems to be associated with the development of conforming, apathetic, and submissive sorts of behavior in place of "self-reliant" initiative. The case against punitive control techniques, in the interests of freedom, will be shown to be quite strong.

Yet this issue, too, is more complicated than it first appears. For instance, Haines (1966) argues persuasively that power to punish another person is a necessary precondition for allowing freedom of action to that person and for wresting the same concession from him. And the facts of several experiments, to be described later, indicate that Haines is at least partially correct is some circumstances. Punishment and the threat of it *can* have liberating effects. Whether they do or not depends on how and when they are employed. So Skinner's point that our society's use of punishment and threat of punishment is what people object to in their aversion to "behavioral control" may be incorrect. What they find objectionable may be his situational psychology.

SITUATIONALISM IN THE PSYCHOLOGY
OF ADJUSTMENT

A psychology that says in effect that the pyramids caused men to build them is here considered to be wrong, both technically and ethically. The ethical error is the one pointed out by May. And it is particularly dangerous in a psychology of personal adjustment. Pure situationalism implies there is nothing man can do about environments that make him uncomfortable, frustrated, or frightened, except act as circumstances demand, get used to the distress, or escape to more acceptable settings. However, books on the psychology of personal adjustment are represented as showing how personal "problems" can be solved and situationally induced stresses reduced. This poses a difficulty for the authors of such books.

Only three consistent courses of action seem to be open to writers on the psychology of adjustment. First, they might adopt the situationalism bias, review the relevant experimental evidence, and accordingly teach fatalism by implication—in contradiction of the general point of such texts. Second, they might reject situationalism and the evidence of situational influence, concentrating instead on showing how people can and do change environments. Or, finally, they might avoid either bias, review evidence of both kinds, and attempt to understand the differences between the situationally shaped and the situation-shaping sorts of actions. This is the strategy and aim of this book.

Another important ethical consideration deserves notice. When two people are interacting, situationalism implies that each determines the behavior of the other but has no direct control over his own. This is because the presence and actions of each define the social part of the situation that controls the other. At the opposite extreme, of course, one might assume with the defenders of freedom that each of two interacting persons controls his own actions but (ideally) has no direct influence over the other. The first of these viewpoints considers the social system as affecting people, while the latter does not. But both ignore the fact that individual actions affect social systems. So neither accommodates the notion that ethical behavior promotes personal adjustment. One's ethics are thus regarded as a matter of *value,* outside the domain of scientific psychology.

The case is different, however, when the truth of both extreme views can be recognized—when one understands that *each of two interacting persons may participate in shaping not only the other's actions but also his own.* Then it becomes clear that the social harmony of good adjustment and the social discord of bad adjustment result from actions to which ethical concepts have traditionally been applied. "Truth," "justice," "trust," and the rest are then understood not only as value judgments about individual actions, but as referring to characteristics of social relationships that can be created by individual actions for common welfare. Reconciliation of the two extreme views of how human behavior is controlled makes the determination of some aspects of moral behavior a central concern for the psychology of personal adjustment.

People familiar with conventional textbooks on "adjustment" will find additional novelty in what follows. The basic terms in which evidence is construed here are meaningful and familiar to the traditional disciplines of law, philosophy, and theology. In addition, stress is laid on the importance to human behavior of the social, economic, and political conditions that concern other social scientists, and some reference is made to evidence on changing those conditions. Personal adjustment is not usually treated in such an interdisciplinary context; instead, the important contributions of other disciplines to the topic are too often ignored.

FREEDOM AND SOCIAL DEVELOPMENT

Although the defenders of freedom may be confused over the use of rewards in relation to freedom and behavior control, they have not exaggerated the importance of their topic. A free person is one who strives to master his environment in accordance with personal standards and recognizes his responsibility for his deeds. By contrast, a "pawn"—to use the neat term of de Charms (Carpenter & Kuperman, 1965) for a person who lacks the freedom of an "origin" to produce desirable changes in his environment—yields to the forces and structures that he perceives in his situation, regardless of his personal ideals, and denies personal responsibility for his actions or inaction. Free individuals are responsible. They are also inventive. When society makes errors that threaten the future of mankind, it is not the pawns who produce solutions. Impotence, demoralization, ritualism, and other sins of omission, like liability to accidents, can be shown to be the lot of the driven and the drifting. So perhaps are such positive evils as bigotry, hypocrisy, and complicity in genocide (Fromm, 1941). Invention, poetry, art, and science are all the work of free wills. It is the free who break trail on the path of human progress.

Those whose desirable actions have been inconsistently rewarded do not. They are pawns and lack freedom of will. Some evidence for this statement concerns the social and psychological conditions and behavior of poor and underprivileged people, who are distressed by, and wish to escape, their poverty. For the past two decades or so, governments all over the world have been engaged in programs of economic development, with a view to assisting such persons. As a result, some people have prospered but others have not, among them the most deprived.

According to a literature review by Easterbrook and Fuller (1969), those who prospered from such opportunities did so by means of three sorts of advantages over others. They had easier access to money, were better educated, and had more of the abilities and dispositions required for independent initiative. To put it briefly (and hypothetically), they had more freedom of will.

Many poor people lack the personal characteristics necessary to exploit opportunities to obtain the benefits they desire. Important among these are the initiative and enterprise associated with belief in personal autonomy. Discussing success, such people accord maximal importance to luck, social acceptance, and power or status, and they assign minimal importance to personal initiative, independent judgment, self-control, and competence. Their views have been called fatalistic and may contribute to their failure to plan actions that could gain them personal control over events. That is, the poor report believing, and act as if they believe, they are driven by events and have no freedom of will.

The fatalism of the poor is commonly justified. Experience in certain types of social environments produces beliefs of that sort. Experience in other types of environments produces independence, self-control, enterprise, autonomy, and a belief in free will. Situational psychology has a good deal of information to contribute toward understanding the freedom of will it hesitates to acknowledge. For this reason it has a contribution to make to the "social development" programs that societies are now operating to enable fatalistic people to take advantage of economic and cultural opportunities.

The Issue of Freedom in Current Public Projects

The existence of social development programs raises important questions for public debate. Who is to be developed? Into what? How should the development programs be designed and executed? How do they affect freedom? This book takes a position on these issues. The aim of social development must be to increase freedom of will for the driven, and the necessary means are implicit in the nature of people and of freedom. The following chapters present relevant evidence and theory.

Similar kinds of questions are raised by various new psychotherapeutic enterprises that involve modifying the environments of people with "psychological" disorders. These include "family therapy," "behavior modification," and "remedial social work," and all are demonstrating the utility of "situationalism."

In terms of freedom, the "maladjustments" to which the psychotherapeutic and social development programs are addressed are identical. Both amount to, *are,* simply the inability of some people to control events for the satisfaction of their needs. According to the new remedial hypotheses, these defective relations between individuals and environments can be corrected by altering the environments. This analysis may also apply to the powerlessness and alienation that seem to afflict other segments of the population. By contrast, freedom of will refers to satisfactory relations between persons and situations. When it is acquired under appropriate conditions, it reduces the impact of later misfortunes and so counteracts the development of later maladjustments. It contributes to subsequent freedom. The bases for these statements must be appreciated if public reactions to the novel therapeutic programs are to be fully informed.

The theory and evidence that follow have some applicability to political affairs as well. Some driven personalities are compliant and can be readily managed by powerful people. It seems indeed that autocratic governments have come into existence because of support from driven persons (Fromm, 1941; see Chapter 6). It will be argued that the risk of totalitarian control is *reduced* in social environments that consistently reward suitable actions—the very contingency that the freedom defenders have attacked Skinner for advocating. On the other hand, environments that foster fatalism and powerlessness in many people set the conditions for coercion and exploitation by a few. The reasons for these statements need to be known if freedom is to be defended intelligently.

So the following chapters are not merely designed to show the utility of the old concepts of free will and responsibility to psychology. They are also intended to summarize psychological and related knowledge on those topics, to show the relation of individual well-being to responsibility and freedom of will, and to review their organismic and situational determinants—which include social beliefs and customs. In these respects this text attempts to treat its subjects like any other psychological phenomena. Yet they are not. Both responsibility and freedom of will are highly valued. Their promotion and maintenance are liable to be taken as ideals in the planning of social action, and so they should be. This fact gives the topic added importance. It also means that the reading of what follows should be approached with unusual critical vigilance.

SUMMARY

Philosophical men over the centuries have taken opposing views of human responsibility for human well-being. Recently, the assumption of behavioral determinism seems to have led to an erosion of belief in freedom of will and of belief in personal responsibility for the effects of one's actions. The results of these changes have been described as a modern neurosis. This book addresses the contrasting views of willpower in the context of personal adjustment, which is also concerned with ideal relationships between persons and environments.

Episodes of behavior differ in the degree of control the actors attain over the consequences of their actions. The concepts of responsibility and free will refer to actions by which people attain the greatest control. The belief that freedom of will is somehow incompatible with the causal–analytic assumption of determinism is false.

Freedom is not possible without control. Environments have been said to control human or animal behavior when they consistently reward particular kinds of action. However, in responding thus predictably, they actually promote an actor's freedom whenever he needs pertinent rewards.

Various distressing conditions that afflict individuals or groups exist where freedom of will is restricted. Promising methods of alleviating these maladjustments are being advocated and tested. Paradoxically, however, some resistance to them has been expressed in the name of freedom. A survey of pertinent fact and theory is evidently required to aid the enlightened development of public policies and to facilitate personal adjustment.

Responsibility and Freedom
in Folk Psychology

AN IMPLICIT THEORY OF RESPONSIBILITY

Suppose that on two different days you see:

1. A 2-year-old boy bend over, grasp a stone in his fist, stand up, and awkwardly fling his arm around, with the result that the stone goes through a basement window of your house
2. A 16-year-old boy pick up a stone between thumb and fingers, expertly cock his arm, and shy the stone through your basement window

What would you do about these similar sequences of action and effect? Would you try to arrange punishment for both of the hurlers? For one of them only? Why? How would you justify doing so in one case and not in the other?

Perhaps your thinking would be something like this: "Oh, the little kid was just *trying to throw a stone*. He didn't even notice the window. Maybe he didn't even know that stones can break windows. I'd make sure he knew what had happened but I wouldn't do any more about him. It was *an accident*. I'd get after the big fellow though, probably through his parents, and I'd see that he fixed the window at least. You could tell *he knew what he was doing*. There was no good *reason* for throwing a stone toward my house. I guess he's angry at one of us. I can't think why. The stone went right where he was *aiming* it. He *intended* it to go there."

In these thoughts, the emphasized words and phrases refer to judgments about the responsibility of a person for his actions and their effects. Our language has a large set of such terms and concepts, including, as other instances, *can, would, culprit, purpose, thoughtless*. Indeed, approximately one-quarter of all the English words and phrases in *Roget's Thesaurus* (Roget, 1939) are relevant to decisions of this kind.[1] These terms refer to an organized set of categories for classifying behavior with respect to personal responsibility. *Accidental* and *impetuous* are different from one another, and both differ from *deliberate*. That such concepts constitute a set, each with different implications and different criteria, means that together they *imply a theory*. We learn this theory as we learn our language, and we use it when we have to decide what to do about someone's actions. So it can be designated an *implicit theory of responsibility* (ITR). It may be widely shared by human beings, perhaps at least by all cultures that use Indo-European languages. The controversial concepts "will" and "free will" belong to it.

Some of the concepts of our implicit theory of responsibility are compared and contrasted by A. R. White in a linguistic–philosophic monograph entitled *Attention* (1964). According to White's analysis, the first thing we do in judging other people's actions and their outcomes is to distinguish *intentional* from *unintentional* deeds (deeds being actions and their effects, taken together). Some unintentional actions are *impulsive*—reactions to environmental events. What we call intentional actions, by contrast, are those that we think were undertaken *by plan, on purpose,* or *willfully* to produce one or more of the effects resulting.

Some intentional actions are directed toward effects that seem attractive to their authors, and these are the actions that are classified as *willing* or voluntary. By contrast, it may happen that one is forced into some intentional deeds to avoid unpleasant effects, and thus undertakes them unwillingly, driven, as it were, by circumstances against one's inclinations. For instance, a person may have to go out of his way to pay a traffic fine he considers unjustified. *According to the ITR, thus, actions that advance a person's well-being develop from different motivational roots than do actions that merely prevent a loss of well-being.* The one seems to involve attraction to a chosen one of a number of *possible positive benefits* that improve an acceptable relation to the environment; the other, aversion to one *actual or incipient negative condition* that attests an unacceptable relation to the environment. This second important distinction of the ITR refers accordingly to the *degree of choice* a person's actions are regarded as displaying.

The psychology of motivation does not ordinarily make this distinction. Much more commonly, all motives are assumed to be oriented both ways—away from an unpleasant state and toward a more pleasant one. All are assumed to have the same sort of base in current distress. The basic distressed state may, it is true, be accorded a slight priority in time over the expectation of the preferred condition. That state is supposed to act as the stimulus to the expectation. However, the two sorts of referents are also usually supposed to exist in essentially the same material sense, as reactions by the organism to immediate or imminent environ-

---

[1]Entries referring to "volition" and to "personal affections" occupy approximately 115 of 386 pages.

mental conditions. That these are tenable and useful assumptions for cases of elementary, experimentally induced motives seems to be clear; however that fact does not necessarily invalidate the ITR.

Subsequent chapters will show in some detail that the ITR differentiation of *possible positive* from *actual or incipient negative* states is a very useful one, particularly in reference to freedom and adjustment. The behavioral differences between enforced and chosen acts can be quite considerable. So can the motivational differences between their determinants. It seems indeed that freedom of choice arises to the degree that aversive motives are reduced, and vice versa. Thus it is possible that the ITR's view of motivation has even more general utility than the customary psychological view of elementary motives.

When a person's actions seem to advance his private interests directly and are simultaneously intentional, he is judged to have willed them (freely). They are called *voluntary,* according to White, and their agent is held accountable for their effects. The definition of free will in terms of these basic distinctions is summarized schematically in Figure 2.1.

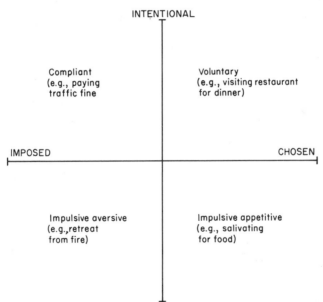

Figure 2.1. The place of free will among varieties of action according to the implicit theory of responsibility. The two distinctions depicted in the figure, intentional–unintentional and imposed–chosen, are made by people in our culture when deciding whether the person whose actions brought about specified effects is praiseworthy or blameworthy. An action that is judged to have been executed intentionally and by choice is regarded as having been freely willed.

The implicit theory of responsibility is more elaborate than Figure 2.1 shows, of course. It recognizes that some unsatisfactory effects of intentional acts may have been intended without proper understanding of all the consequences of the intended results. These are called mistakes. It also recognizes that some effects of intentional actions may be unintended: the accidental ones, caused by unpredictable events, and others due to inadequate foresight or to inattention. Despite this we *blame* a person for an injury to another that occurs as an unintended by-product of some other, intentional deed. We do this if we judge him to have acted voluntarily to the neglect of reasonable precautions against foreseeable danger to others (or against foreseeable benefits to others). This is to say we may blame a person for the unintended ill effects of voluntary actions in which he seemed to show inadequate concern for, or *responsiveness* to, the needs of others.

THE ITR AS A POLICY FOR SOCIAL SANCTIONS

Normally, we reserve our censure for the willing authors of intentional injuries to others. By contrast, one who has been coerced into harmful action may be exonerated, depending on the threat. "Criminal intent" seems to involve personal desire. And we hold a person praiseworthy under comparable conditions; that is, responsibility earns credit as well as blame. We believe that beneficial effects must have been voluntarily intended before praise or gratitude is warranted. No credit or affection is thought to be due to anyone who was coerced into beneficial actions. Nor do accidental benefits count.

In point of fact, a slight modification to all these statements seems needed to account for irrational biases that we feel in favor of anyone associated with the good things that happen to us and against anyone associated with the bad (Bramel, 1969; Burnstein, 1969). Culturally, however, we justify reward and punishment rationally, in accordance with our implicit theory. That is, we deliberately try to respond in kind to good and bad deeds we judge to have been voluntarily produced.

The ITR in Person Perception

The management of social sanctions and the determination of personal sentiments are not the only functions of our ITR. We use it to understand our fellows, that is to recognize their dispositions in order to predict their future actions, according to Fritz Heider (1944, 1958).

Heider was the first psychologist to consider the relationship of the ITR to person perception. His discussion of the topic concentrated on three concepts: *can, try,* and *want. Trying,* he argued, refers to intentional action in progress.

When one judges that a person *can* produce a given kind of event and sees him exerting himself in making appropriate actions, then one judges him to *intend* that event, and to *want* it. If he is further thought to want it for personal reasons, and not because of external pressure, he is also understood to have a *disposition* toward such deeds. The responsibility and will thereby accorded to the agent, Heider described as a perception the agent had *personally caused* the effects in question.

Jones and Davis (1965) developed a theory of the inference of dispositions, which they said was inspired by Heider's. It did not speak of the perception of personal causation, however. It spoke instead of freedom of choice. This was said to be imputed to the author of a remarkable deed when it was understood that his situation, knowledge, and abilities would have permitted him to have acted differently than he acted in fact. Theoretically, it is only when such freedom is perceived that inferences about intentions and dispositions are made. Then they are made only if the agent is also believed capable of having purposely brought about the events of interest. "Knowledge and ability are preconditions for the assignment of intentions [p. 221]." The wants we imagine to be served by the effects we see attained, then, define the intentions and dispositions we infer.

Of course the subsidiary judgments are difficult. Which of a number of effects were probably intended? Which other wants might have been served at the time of action but were not? For this reason, Jones and Davis argued, actions producing unusual effects are most likely to lead us to impute dispositions to their authors, and the resulting dispositions are correspondingly unusual. In support of their theory, these writers have described original experimental results, and further substantiation is found in evidence from comparable experiments reviewed by them or produced by others (e.g., de Charms *et al.*, 1965; de Charms, 1968). According to this evidence, it appears true that people in our culture are most readily known by their deeds when the deeds are unusual and their authors are judged to have been competent, free of external compulsion, and pursuing personal rewards.

A variety of influences short of compulsion may induce purposive behavior by humans. Many of these are social. A person may, for instance, undertake a particular course of action because his role in an organization calls for it— perhaps on explicit orders from another (whom he may like or dislike) or perhaps on instructions implicit in a job (which he may like or dislike). Or, he may act under the influence of a small group. According to the interesting investigation by de Charms and his associates (1965), one is more likely to be judged responsible for actions induced by a small group than by a large organization. In addition, one is more often considered responsible for the effects of action when one likes the source of influence or enjoys the job which calls for that action, than when one does not. In short, the more nearly a person seems to be acting on his own, or for his own interests or enjoyment, the more probable it is that we will judge him personally responsible for his actions and their effects. These facts seem to confirm White's analysis, as displayed in Figure 2.1, and those of Heider and of Jones and Davis.

The Challenge for Psychology

These, then, are the modern referents of the concept of free will: voluntary actions, intentionally and willingly executed for personal satisfaction, whose agents we hold personally responsible for their effects. A complete psychology will account, as many do not, for the differences between intentional and impulsive actions. It will also account for the differences between actions that are chosen and those that are imposed, that is, between actions oriented toward *possible* positive *benefits* and those that merely avoid *actual or incipient distress*. It will account for "freedom of will."

It is now apparent that willingly intended behavior reflects more will than unintended behavior and more choice than either it or unwillingly intended behavior. It may be just as lawful, though, however different its determinants. It cannot be either ungoverned or erratic. The freedom of the will that is revealed in willingly intended behavior has to do with choice and plan, not with chaos or magic. The differences between the types of behavior encompassed by the ITR are matters of the "how," not the "whether," of causal and control relations between organism and environment. They have to do with competence, not determinism.

DETERMINANTS OF FREE WILL

Freely willed action must have specifiable kinds of determinants—although their precise specification may be impossible in any given instance. So must the personal responsibility and initiative that accompany it. What are they? What is meant by "strength of will"? Some hypothetical answers can be derived from the implicit theory of responsibility.

In the ITR, it seems, freely willed action sequences are those that bring results their authors are regarded both as wanting and as having the knowledge and ability to produce on purpose. No inducing or impelling *external* influences are apparent, so the causes are supposed to be internal, which is to say, their authors are considered to have caused the effects of the actions concerned, to be responsible for them. People who often produce such actions and effects ought, thus, to differ in specifiable ways from others who seldom do. They ought, first, to be remarkable for a wider range of knowledge and ability. And, second, they ought to differ from less competent persons in being less afflicted by persisting environmental pressures or correspondingly biological needs. Probably they should also differ in having greater faith that future needs will be met. For these reasons, their "personal adjustment" ought to be superior. All of this is deducible fairly directly from the ITR.

Are these deductions correct? On a certain assumption, the answer seems to be yes. The assumption is that people use the ITR criteria of responsibility relatively accurately in reporting judgments about their own responsibility for relations with their environments. The evidence comes from a study conducted by the writer for quite another purpose, but its pertinence to the present context is striking (Easterbrook, 1972).

In answer to questions formulated by Rotter[2] and his associates, some people say they are able to control the rewards and punishments they receive in life, that is, that they produce these effects and so are responsible for them. Others say such events are controlled by luck or powerful others, thereby denying personal responsibility and the freedom to fulfill their own wishes. In experimental situations, the two contrasting groups tend to act as they might be expected to if they actually held such beliefs. They act, respectively, as if they were dealing with situations calling for skill or for luck (Rotter, 1966; Lefcourt, 1966; de Charms, 1968; Joe, 1971). A person who claims personal or "internal" control and responsibility is also more likely to hold others accountable for *their* deeds than is one who claims external control (de Charms *et al.*, 1965). Apparently the former understands that the effects of an individual's action are generally controlled by the individual himself. So this "locus of control" questionnaire evidently assesses belief in personal responsibility and personal freedom of will.

Rotter's questionnaire was administered to 174 coal mine workers, varying widely in age and education. So were 53 other tests and measures, and another set of questions with the same purpose as Rotter's, compiled by Haller and Miller (1963). Statistics expressing the relations between resultant scores were then subjected to a more complex analysis—a so-called principal components (factor) analysis. This procedure reveals independent patterns of relationships between sets of test scores that are hypothetically due to the operation of hidden determinants or general "factors." Theoretically, each such determinant is a contributing factor to, or component of, scores on related tests. So, each specifies an inferred dimension, measuring a general attribute of skill, that differentiates those to whom the tests are administered. The two primary general dimensions on which the miners differed from one another are pertinent to the appraisal of deductions from the ITR.

The first of these dimensions (Factor 1) was formal, that is, educated general intelligence, assessed with the appropriate scales of the General Aptitude Test

---

[2]For instance: "Please select the *one* statement of each pair which you more strongly *believe* to be the case as far as you are concerned. (*a*) Many times I feel I have little influence over the things that happen to me. (*b*) It is impossible for me to believe that chance or luck plays an important role in my life." (See Rotter, 1966.)

Battery (GATB) of the United States Employment Services (USES Staff, 1967). Closely associated with differences in GATB scores were differences in scores on vocabularly tests, educational achievement tests, and three nonverbal tests of spatial aptitude or "perceptual intelligence." One of the latter, called the Hidden Figures Test (HFT)[3], will be the subject of some later discussion, as will those assessing verbal proficiency.

The second factor to differentiate the sample (subsequently referred to as Factor 2) was defined by Factor scores from the Sixteen Personality Factor Questionnaire, Form E, of the Institute for Personality and Ability Testing (IPAT Staff, 1967), most strongly by two that the authors (Cattell & Eber, 1967) claim as assessors of boldness and self-confidence. According to the same source, it distinguishes men whose answers reflect self-control—or "will control," as the relevant factor was once designated (Cattell, 1964, p. 90)—confidence, imagination, readiness to venture, and satisfaction of personal needs, from men whose answers indicate they often feel frustrated, apprehensive, timid, emotional, and driven by circumstances. The one cluster sketches a venturesome, imaginative, independent will, while the other suggests an anxious, frustrated, driven personality. The differences between them can be understood as referring to the choice aspect of voluntary behavior: differences in the impelling *pressure of prevailing needs,* on the one hand, and in preparedness to pursue various *possible rewards,* on the other. Conceivably they refer jointly to past success and current motivational freedom.

The naming of this second dimension is a matter of taste, because of the nature of the evidence. The original investigators, who have repeatedly discovered it (Handlesby, Pawlik, & Cattell, 1965), wrote of "good adjustment" as opposed to "high unbound anxiety." This concept is similar to the "sense of competence" discussed by Stotland and Canon (1972) as the opposite of anxiety. These writers assume that a sense of competence develops from specified sorts of experience, including successes arising from freedom of choice among behavioral options. Related theoretical concepts are also available, such as Rotter's "freedom of movement," which is supposed, if low, to constitute anxiety (Rotter, Chance, & Phares, 1972). "Freedom of movement" may be loosely translated as behavioral flexibility, a direct function of the number of optional acts a person can produce in a given situation, or of the size of his behavioral repertoire. As explanatory rather than descriptive concepts, both "sense of competence" and "freedom of movement" may be preferable to "good adjustment" or "anxiety." However, neither is specifically justified by the evidence; so, for reasons that will emerge later, the term *efficacy*[4] is adopted here, instead.

---

[3]The HFT is a modification by Philip E. Vernon of the Gottschaldt figures. It is used in this study with his permission, which is gratefully acknowledged.

[4]Without the connotation of "efficacy motivation," which was suggested by R. W. White (1959). See Maslow's (1954) concept of "gratification health."

The word *efficacy* denotes satisfactory experience. The idea it is to convey resembles those suggested by the terms *effectiveness* and *potency*—or even Freud's (1938) *ego strength*. But it does not attribute as much causation to the individual as they do. It takes more notice of influence by the environment, being consistent with the fact that different frequencies of satisfactory experience can arise from differences in environmental response to individual actions, as well as from differences in the actions themselves. It is used, thus, to suggest that the observed venturesome, independent will and good adjustment (which are classically associated with a strong *ego*) all developed because the consequences of actions often proved to be satisfactory, and that the contrasting emotionally driving pressures of frustration and apprehension arose from unsatisfactory experiences.

Factors 1 and 2, and the principal test scores defining them, are set out as the axes of Figure 2.2. That figure also displays the relations of the two "locus of control" scores to these factors.

According to Figure 2.2, both their intelligence and their efficacy influenced what the miners said about their personal responsibility for their fortunes. Comparably, it will be remembered, our culture demands evidence of the requisite knowledge and ability, and of freedom from compulsion, before it ascribes responsibility and freedom of will to the person who produces any action. Thus, what is now evident is that men who claim or admit more responsibility, that is, freedom of will, answer tests in ways that suggest both the capacity for intentional actions and prior success in pursuit of personally attractive ends. One possible interpretation of this coincidence is that intelligence and efficacy merely determined the *answers* to the responsibility questionnaires and do not refer to any real differences in freedom of will. Other interpretations are also possible. The most exciting is that the dimensions of Figure 2.2 confirm deductions from the ITR and represent components of mental freedom.

In the following presentation of psychological evidence and theory, it is assumed that the determinants of educated intelligence and of efficacy are indeed the determinants of free will and responsibility. It is assumed that the intentional aspect of voluntary action demands intelligence, in various forms, like knowledge of processes and ability in causal analysis and planning. Presumably, the greater a person's intelligence, the wider is the variety of situations in which he can produce streams of intentional actions. It is also assumed that the choice aspect of voluntary behavior depends similarly upon the constellation of efficacy attributes in Figure 2.2, especially the freedom from driving motivational pressures, the confidence, and the disposition to "imaginative" activity. That is, it is supposed that these characteristics not only result from satisfactory person–environment relations, they also tend to facilitate their future creation. Further justification of these assumptions is the object of most of what follows.

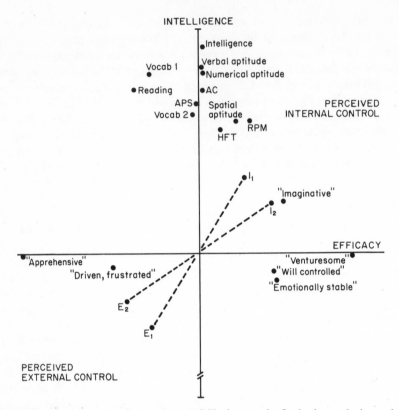

Figure 2.2. The components of personal responsibility in a sample of redundant coal mine workers. The heavy dots indicate the loadings of the measures on the two dimensions. The intelligence, verbal, numerical, and spatial aptitude tests are from the USES General Aptitude Test Battery. The names of other relevant tests and measures have been abbreviated as follows: Vocab 1; Reading, AC, and APS are, respectively, the vocabulary, reading, arithmetic computation, and arithmetic problem-solving tests of the Adult Basic Learning Examination; Vocab 2 is Ammons's Full Range Picture Vocabulary Test; RPM is Raven's Progressive Matrices (not corrected for age); HFT is Vernon's Hidden Figures Test; I_1 and E_1 refer to Rotter's questionnaire for perceived internal or external control of reinforcements; I_2 and E_2 refer to that of Haller and Miller. All of the other scores are from scales of the IPAT Sixteen Personality Factor Questionnaire, Form E. The maximal factor loadings were .93 for the intelligence dimension, .81 for the efficacy dimension. [Adapted from Easterbrook (1972).]

It is thoroughly established, of course, that a person's intelligence is a major determinant of his ability to establish satisfactory or well-adjusted relations with his environment (Matarazzo, 1972, p. 145). Freud's "ego strength," which has long been regarded as crucial to mental health, was not clearly differentiated from intelligence, and intelligence may be a component of it. So, of course, may efficacy. This is to say that strong arguments can be produced to show that the main dimensions of Figure 2.2 are components of good personal adjustment or mental health. What is hypothetical, and remains to be substantiated, is the suggestion that they are also important determinants of free will and responsibility, and that these in turn produce optimal relations between an individual and his environment.

SUMMARY

The concept of free will belongs to a theory of responsibility that is implicit in the terms of our language. Its focal referents are willingly intended, voluntary deeds. For these, people are considered, and consider themselves, to be responsible, causal agents, and either praiseworthy or blameworthy. They are actions and effects of action that humans understand themselves able to control. The contrasting, nonvoluntary deeds, for which responsibility is not assumed or imputed, are supposed to be generated either impulsively or, in response to driving pressures, unwillingly.

People differ in the freedom of will they claim. It can be deduced from the implicit theory of responsibility that those who do so more consistently should have a greater range of knowledge and abilities, suffer fewer frustrations and display greater confidence. In a relevant study, men who more consistently reported themselves responsible for significant events in their lives made higher scores on tests of information and intelligence. They also presented themselves as more satisfied, confident, and self-disciplined, and as less anxious and driven by circumstances. Apparently they had enjoyed need-fulfilling relations with their environments. This constellation of attributes is accordingly designated "efficacy." The two characteristics, educated intelligence and efficacy, can be regarded as determinants of mental health or good personal adjustment. Hypothetically, they are also components of mental and behavioral freedom.

II

THE GIVEN AND THE POSSIBLE
IN GOVERNMENT OF ACTION

Freedom from
Stimulus Control

SEGMENTAL ACTS AND INTEGRATED ACTION

Your task is to trace a simple visible maze with a pencil, without going "off the path" or "into blind alleys." You know this, but all you can see now is a small circle of white paper, displaying a little arrow and totally surrounded by a black mask. The mask overlays a piece of clear plastic so you can see part of the maze. Your pencil point sticks through the plastic so it and the mask will move when you move the pencil.

Your task is rather difficult. You have to move the pencil slowly, because you would like to be neat. Still your tracing is jagged, made up of short lines with untidy junctions and it sometimes takes the wrong direction. You have to look, move your pencil a bit, look again, move again, and so jerkily on.

Now you are set to do the same sort of thing again, but this time you can see much more. The hole in the mask is bigger. Go! This is easy! Your tracing is almost as neat and smooth as you would wish, a continuous economical line with neat sections and smooth elbows. And you do it much more quickly, because you can look and design the next element of action as you are completing the last, and so make longer, smoother movements.

You have been an imaginary subject in a simple experiment devised at Cambridge University (Bartlett, 1951). No doubt your tracings would have resembled those displayed in Figure 3.1. They were produced by an adult to illustrate this chapter, using one mask with a ½-inch diameter hole and one with a 3-inch diameter hole.

The masks experiment demonstrates some of the benefits of foreknowledge to the government of action; these benefits were particularized in other, more sophisticated experiments, notably by E. C. Poulton and J. A. Leonard (Bartlett, 1951). Two points about it are particularly remarkable.

31

Figure 3.1. The effect of foresight on maze tracing proficiency. These tracings were made through masks that moved with the pencil. The lower one was drawn first, with a field of view 3 inches in diameter. The upper one was drawn 1 minute later with a ½-inch field of view. Thus the order of the tracings differed from that described in the text in a way designed to *minimize* the demonstrated effect.

The person who uses foreknowledge in tasks like this gathers and deals with it while he is acting on the prior information. The action the foreknowledge leads to is integrated with action based on the prior information (the junctions are smooth). Or one might state the fact in other terms: The actions taken with foreknowledge are developed in reference to larger pieces of the maze pattern. However described, the tracer's actions when foreknowledge is available are serially integrated. Those without, or with very little, foreknowledge are segmental responses. With foreknowledge, the determination of behavior is thus more "abstract," that is, the pertinent information is more highly selected and better integrated.

The quality of performance with adequate foreknowledge can be described, secondly, as improved, because it more closely approximates some *ideal*. In the mazes experiment, the ideal was partly specified in the task instructions, but not wholly so, for we have all learned to prefer neat work. Evidently the abstraction permitted by foreknowledge enabled the shaping of behavior toward the ideal.

Even when a task is defined in relation to a tangible environment, for instance a maze, human performance of it can become free in these two important senses. It can be liberated from influence and pressure by segmental features and irrelevant aspects of the environment. And the actor can shape it—responsibly— toward match with a criterion he brings to his task or is asked to meet in it. Both of these achievements are due to the availability of advance information and to the ability of people to make constructive use of it, to impose serial integration on their actions. By this integration, *one's movements become one's own actions*, not simple consequences of environmental events. So a person achieves what Adler (1958) and perhaps Haines (1966) regard as a fundamental condition of freedom at the same time as he achieves responsibility for the effects of his movements.

The differences between the performances of a skilled automobile driver and a beginner parallel those demonstrated in the maze tracings. The beginner "steers" his vehicle; his movements are responsive to conditions in the segment of the road just in front of his wheels. By contrast, the expert "aims" his car, adjusts his actions to deal not only with the further and nearer sections of road but also with dangers—events that might occur but have not, that is, with possible events. In a sense that many of us can recall, the novice is controlled by the situation as it comes to him; he reacts and feels driven. The skilled performer drives with greater foresight, anticipating future circumstances, actively selecting and dealing with relevent cues. Making adjustments and avoiding stimuli, he remains responsibly in command. He can even safely look at and converse with his passengers, because his method makes economical use of his time. His performance is *serially integrated* and free of pressure from immediate events.

INTENTION AND PURPOSE

When a person is engaged in some serially integrated activity, he is executing a "plan," whether he be conscious of it or not, and so has an intention, according to Miller, Galanter, and Pribram (1960). It can usually also be said that he then knows what he is further doing in being occupied as he is at any given moment—which is Anscombe's (1958) definition of an intention. The object of an intention is, of course, to make the actual effects of ongoing action correspond to some conception of ideal effects. Serially integrated behavior is thus the objective counterpart of intentional action. It can also be described as purposive, if work toward an ideal is purposive.

Intentional actions are probably "motivated," but they are not necessarily distinguishable from unintentional actions in those terms.[1] The succession of segmental responses and the series of integrated actions in the mazes experiment were equally and similarly motivated. The essential difference between intentional and unintentional actions is a matter of the control, not the impetus, of action. Gordon Allport (1947) seems to have had a similar conception in mind when he urged the development of a psychology of intention. He described an intention as a guiding idea that may be in or outside of awareness and that deals with the direction of action. It is not motive, in the sense of energy arousing stimulation, that distinguishes intentional from unintentional actions.

Some purposive behavior has another important feature, which is no more valid as a criterion of intentionality. It is that many different successions of acts, under the impetus of a given need, arrive at the same end state, which is accordingly known as the purpose of the action. For instance, some of a wolf's forays over different pieces of ground on successive days end with a kill, eating, and rest, so we infer that all of those actions had that purpose. This phenomenon has been called "equifinality" (Heider, 1958) and occurs in a variety of circumstances when disturbed systems return to their equilibria. It was described more than 40 years ago (Humphrey, 1933) in a resolution of the problem that behavior must be purposive, because it maintains life, and yet determined—if there is to be a science of behavior. While such sequences of action may be intentional, they are not necessarily so. They may be mere chains of segmental responses to stimuli under recurrent stimulation, such as can be produced by fairly simple machines (Ashby, 1960). It is the serially integrated feature of purposive actions, not their equifinality, that makes them intentional.

PROACTIVE SERIAL ORGANIZATION AND WILL

However it comes about, the imposition of serial order upon behavior demonstrates the adoption of a definable strategy of information processing. The operator looks ahead, collecting information and dealing with it in larger chunks than those that guide simple reactions. Of course "looking ahead" can be regarded as "working behind" (Woodworth, 1938). But that term obscures an essential characteristic of the relationship to his situation that the integrating operator achieves in "aimed" action. It is a *proactive* one.[2] This means that his actions

---

[1]For recent psychological discussions of intention in relation to motivation that do not always coincide with the present one, see Irwin (1971) and Ryan (1970).

[2]The term "proactive" in this usage was suggested by an expression of S. A. Pizer in McClelland and Winter (1969, p. 382). However, the essence of the concept of a proactive relationship between agent and environment comes from very old sources. The psychology that was abandoned when the study of behavior replaced the study of consciousness distinguished active or voluntary attention from

are particularly remarkable for their organizational relationship to designed effects, rather than for simplicity of relationship to unanticipated situational causes. Movements that are especially notable for simple relation to earlier causes may be called reactive movements. The information processing that produces them may be known, for contrast, as *reactive*.

Proactive information processing, it should be reiterated, involves an active search for *possible cues,* important features of the environment that might be encountered. It amounts to a state of (informed) vigilance to ensure that future movements will synchronize with oncoming environmental circumstances in the manner demanded by some ideal or ideals. Its use of incoming information is mediated by the extemporaneous development and application of an ongoing series of plans. It is by such plans that the movements required by successive events along one's path are integrated with one another into smooth actions.

The importance of the concept of proactive information processing to the topic of free will is obvious. Immediate situational influences do not monopolize the determination of behavior by those who practice it, as they do in the reactive case. And internalized standards of performance (ideals) are more influential.

Other studies of maze tracing proficiency have provided additional knowledge about it. So, for that matter, have many other lines of investigation; but the maze tracing research is simple and convenient for expository purposes.

More than 60 years ago, S. D. Porteus (1950) introduced a graduated series of visible mazes as a test of intelligence, claiming that the essence of intelligence is ability to act with "foresight" and that this ability could be assessed with his mazes. A simple and a complex maze from one of his series are presented in Figure 3.2.

Before being tested with the Porteus mazes, a person is given essentially two kinds of instruction and later assigned two different scores. First he is told his objective, to find and mark by pencil the route from the indicated beginning to the indicated end of the maze. His task then starts with simple and proceeds to complex mazes, that is to those in which false courses are longer and more circuitous so the correct one is more difficult to find.

The first score is calculated according to detailed rules, but may be regarded as roughly the difficulty level of the most complex mazes a person can consistently

---

passive or involuntary attention. One of the distinguishing features of voluntary attention was that it was prepared. See Titchener (1908) and Kulpe (1909). The present discussion of will accords with William James's (1890) conception of will as active attention. However, this account—like earlier contributions by Easterbrook (1959)—focuses upon the mechanisms of complex attentive behavior as evident in studies of the determinants of skilled action. Proactive information processing is, of course, the counterpart of voluntary attention, referring to behavior, rather than awareness. Woodworth (1938, pp. 156–175 and 730–734) was one of the first students of behavior to review scattered evidence on this aspect of skilled activity.

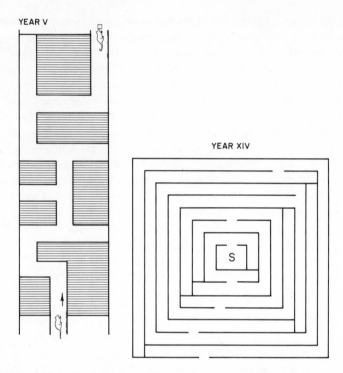

Figure 3.2. Examples of Porteus mazes. [These samples from an early series are from Porteus (1950, pp. 169 and 177). Reproduced by permission. Copyright 1933, 1946, 1950 by S. D. Porteus. Published by The Psychological Corporation, New York, N. Y. All rights reserved.]

trace in a limited number of untimed trials without entering a blind alley. To trace mazes successfully in terms of this measure, one must be able to discover and consistently orient himself toward each correct path at each of a number of choice points. He must, so to say, produce a serially integrated tracing, that is, use foresight accurately. Maze level scores have been shown throughout the years to be fairly closely related to many standard measures of intelligence, and this is still so with the more refined modern tests. They are particularly closely related to scores on two groups of tests that seem to measure what have been called "perceptual intelligence" and "attention concentration," or "freedom from distractibility" (Cohen, 1959). What we mean by intelligence, especially in these aspects, is evidently involved in proficient performance of this analogue of intentional behavior.

The Porteus maze testee is secondly instructed in the rules to be followed in his tracing, that is the *ideal*. Specifically, he is told to trace a continuous line, not to lift his pencil nor cross any of the printed walls of the maze. The second score developed by Porteus, the so called qualitative (Q) score, is derived from the number of violations of the ideal by the testee. A tally is kept of the occasions on which he lifted his pencil, crossed lines, or cut corners, and each tracing is also scored for "waviness" of line. Each fault is then assigned a standard numerical weight, and the total score is the sum of frequency–weight products for the mazes attempted. High Q scores have been shown repeatedly to be frequent among neurotic and delinquent children and rare among their "well adjusted" peers.

The signs of faulty performance from which Porteus derived his two maze test scores are, of course, marks of the reactive movements that have here been called segmental action. The entries into blind alleys, the cut corners, crossed lines, lifted pencils, and so-called wavy lines are all reminiscent of the jagged tracings without foresight in the masks experiment. Such errors are not evident on the simplest mazes, however; they increase in frequency as maze complexity increases.

Every testable person produces evidence of serially integrated (proactive) behavior when the task is sufficiently simple, and some signs of segmental (reactive) movement when it is sufficiently difficult. But people differ in the level of task complexity at which segmental reactions begin to appear. It is as if each person has his own mental window which permits him to deal proactively with certain amounts of information in simple open mazes but is too small to accommodate the larger amounts of information required for more complex ones. People differ in their capacity for proactive information processing.

The total number of environmental cues in any situation that an organism observes, maintains an orientation to, or associates with a response has been discussed as the *range of cue utilization* (Easterbrook, 1959). Cues are those events in, or features of, a display that an organism may use to guide action, and that are not necessarily disturbing or motivating as "stimuli" are. This latter is the crucial difference between cues and stimuli. It refers to the source of initiative in action and, of course, to the proactive–reactive distinction. So, the range of cue utilization describes the complexity of proactive information processing.

Some cues in the maze tracing case are the positions and orientations of the printed lines and of the tracer's pencil marks, the positions of his pencil, hand, and arm muscles, and the instructions he has been given. A person whose tracing never enters a blind alley or crosses a printed line on a complex maze has used a large number of relevant cues. This is so even—indeed, especially—if he has been engaged at the same time in some other, distractive activity (using irrelevant cues). Low proficiency, of course, may be due either to considerable distractive activity or to a small range of cue utilization. The span of the mental window varies according to the relevance of the information processing, as well as according to the testee's total range.

The amount of task-relevant information in process at any given moment can be roughly measured in a fairly direct manner. For instance, in the oral reading case, it is proportional to the number of words of text that can be spoken after the text has been covered unexpectedly. In general it is the number of units of task material between "receptor" input and "effector" output and so has been called the "receptor–effector span" (RE span) by Bartlett (1951). Of course it represents the amount of task relevant information being processed proactively.

RESPONSIBILITY AS PROACTIVE PROFICIENCY

When the number of task cues a person can deal with at any moment falls below the number that must be integrated for proficient performance of a given task, he has met his limit of integrative ability. Because he can no longer process all the necessary cues, he may be said to *neglect* or *forget* to check whether an alley is open at its far end. This is the most common type of error on the Porteus mazes. He may check, but *inadvertently* lift his pencil as he does so. Or he may check frequently, remembering not to lift his pencil, but *inadvertently* leave "wavy lines" instead. He may rush, lest he forget what he saw when he last searched, and *carelessly* or *heedlessly* cut corners or cross lines. These various *accidental* effects of action, though counted toward different scores on the Porteus test, can thus be construed as alike in one respect. They are all signs of segmental action, signifying that task complexity has exceeded the operator's RE span. Of course in the ITR of our culture they are all classified, by means of the italicized or similar names, as unintentional, or due to inattention.

Imagine the RE span as variable between one and many. At the low end of this dimension, when a single cue is used, no serially integrated behavior or intentional action is possible. Integrated action is necessarily governed by a plurality of cues. At the high end, complex behavioral sequences with stipulated effects can be produced and described as intentional. Between these extremes, if the task being performed is always complex, the number of intended effects will increase as the RE span rises, and the number of unintended effects will fall. Task complexity varies among tasks, however. So, for each person, there will be some enterprises in which all effects are intended and some on which accidents will occur (Drew, 1963). The number of operations at which a person can "make what he does his own actions" (Adler, 1958, p. 616), the degree of his basic freedom and responsibility, is set by his proficiency in proactive information processing. If his proficiency is high, he should often achieve effects that match the ideals he was striving to attain. Accordingly, he should often be able to claim to have produced those effects. If it is low, however, many of his actions will be less well controlled and he will not achieve responsibility for all their effects. This may explain why people do in fact appear to claim responsibility for successes more often than for failures (Rotter, 1966; Wolosin, Sherman, & Till, 1973).

If graded maze tests really assess the ability to produce intentional effects in situations of varying complexity, then the more competent a person is with mazes, the more likely he is to have had experiences showing him that he controls his own fate. Evidence of the utility of this assumption was obtained in one experiment with university women and another with rural French housewives (Leger, 1972). The investigator assessed belief in personal responsibility with the Rotter scale or a translation of it. To test maze tracing proficiency, he used a dot maze with a complex, concealed pattern. In that task, foreknowledge had to be gained by trial and error, and to be remembered over a long period of time—much longer than is the case with visible open mazes. Proficiency scores were average times and errors in both the simpler and the more difficult halves of the maze, and the total number of steps learned in the whole maze. The two measures referring to the simple part of the task were unrelated to the questionnaire responsibility scores. However, in each case, at least two of the other three measures were reliably related to reports of responsibility.

The results of these experiments demonstrated the relation under discussion, albeit with considerable error. The women who performed more proficiently on the complex section of the maze tended to be the same women who had earlier and most consistently expressed the belief that they control their own fates. Even so, this relationship did not account for much of the variation in responsibility scores. Nor should it, if the results displayed in Figure 2.2 are generally true. Variations in efficacy also affect judgments of responsibility, and they occur independently of variations in ability to produce intentional effects. Although it is not the only component of freedom, the mental competence manifest in a large RE span is clearly associated with reports of personal responsibility for the effects of action just as it would be if it measured general ability to produce environmental changes intentionally.

Factors That Affect RE Span

What sets one's limit in proactive information processing? In broad terms, the answers to this question are clear enough from studies of the RE span. Facility in distinguishing relevant from irrelevant cues and in dealing appropriately with each both increase the RE span up to a point. These are the recognized components of skill. In addition, however, the upper limit seems to vary with what may be thought of as cerebral competence. Damage to the brain reduces it, whether the damage be permanent or temporary, due to physical or to chemical abnormalities.

Proficiency of maze tracing is so sensitive to the effects of brain damage that two of the most useful tests for it have been variants of visual maze tests: Reitan's Trail Making Test (Reitan, 1955) and Elithorn's dot maze (Elithorn, 1955;

Elithorn, Kerr, & Mott, 1960). The same deficit also develops with emotional stress; this has been observed with various kinds of maze and other tasks at which high proficiency theoretically depends on a large RE span. Consideration of this effect must be deferred to a later chapter, however. For the present it is sufficient to note that a necessary condition for the freedom one attains by intentional behavior is a healthy brain.

Cerebral disorder reduces the number of task-relevant cues used together in operations that demand serial integration of what would otherwise be many disparate acts. It should accordingly increase the probability of unintended effects in action and reduce the proportion of all deeds that can be regarded as intentional. At the ultimate end of the process, when only a single cue can be dealt with at a time, action will appear to depend upon that cue. If that cue can be regarded as stimulating, then an observer might be tempted to say, as many behaviorists do, that it had "stimulated" a "response." The freedom won by an actor with foresight and abstract functioning would then have disappeared and his actions would be *reactive,* driven by circumstances. As the RE span falls from sufficiently high to unity, the government of action comes more and more nearly under the control of a succession of singular events in, or aspects of, the concrete situation. Accordingly, any condition that reduces the RE span, as brain damage does, can be said to increase stimulus domination and to reduce freedom of will and responsibility.

THE CAPACITY FOR FREEDOM

Years ago, reporting on the actions of men who had suffered gunshot wounds to the head in World War I, Kurt Goldstein wrote

> The reactions are bound to the stimulus in an abnormal way. We call this phenomenon abnormal *stimulus bondage, or forced responsiveness to stimuli....* Thus *isolated processes within the organism may determine the reactions of the sick individual in an abnormal, compulsive way* [1940, pp. 16–17].
>
> actions in isolation are simpler or, as we say, more 'primitive' [1940, p. 18].

And he conceived these characteristics of behavior by brain-damaged persons to be due to impairment of processes that normally give adult human behavior an *abstract* quality.

It is notable, and illustrative, that many of the men studied by Goldstein would previously have been diagnosed as having lost ability to use words, that is, as *aphasic.* Goldstein found, however, that this was not their central problem. They might fail to provide the right answer when asked to define a word or display marked inadequacies when attempting to answer or ask some questions or tell about something intangible (i.e., in propositional speech). Still, they would often produce the correct names for things they were shown, words they had been unable to produce when not so stimulated. Their difficulty, accordingly, had more to do with "the capacity to deal with that which is not real—with the possible [1939, p. 30]" than it had to do with lack of words.

Depending on which sort of task the patients were set, different features of their disorder came into focus, Goldstein noted. So various writers have described disturbances of "symbolic expression," "representational function," or "categorical behavior"—each of which Goldstein regarded as dependent upon "the capacity to comprehend the essential features of an event [1939, p. 30]"; that is, to use relevant cues. Among the normal abilities of adults, which were impaired in these patients, are those of being able to analyze and resynthesize parts of wholes, to abstract common properties of different objects or events, to hold various aspects of a situation in mind simultaneously, to shift attention from one aspect to another, to deal with the possible, and to plan ahead. As a result of impairment in these abilities, "voluntary performances are particularly affected while activities directly determined by the situation remain relatively intact [1939, p. 30]."

In Goldstein's view, the functions lost by his patients normally also enable individuals to control their own life careers, to effect what he called "self-actualization." He later described these functions as constituting "the highest capacity of man, the capacity for freedom [1940, p. 238]."

Goldstein suggested various ways of construing the basic psychological disorder of his brain-damaged subjects. In one context he wrote

We might point to the patients inability to emancipate and withold himself from the world, the shrinkage of his freedom and his greater bondage to the demands of the environment. The most general formula to which the change can be reduced is probably: the patient has lost the capacity to deal with that which is not real—with the possible [1939, p. 30].

In another context Goldstein used the concept of *dedifferentiation*. As a function changes under that disturbance it *"proceeds from the highly differentiated and articulated state to a more amorphous total behavior* [1939, p. 31]." For instance, dexterous use of a pencil by fingers disappears and it is operated clumsily by the whole hand. Or, diplomatic niceties of speech are replaced by blunt, crude talk. The behavior reveals use of fewer environmental cues.

Used in this way, the term *dedifferentiation* has two meanings. One is descriptive and the other is hypothetical, and Goldstein seems to have intended both. The descriptive one refers to the loss of precision or skill in action. The hypothetical one refers to the loss in facility at analyzing things or events, which is presumed to underlie the clumsiness and other symptoms. This sort of facility is related in two different ways to the notion of abstraction, and again Goldstein seems to have been referring to both of them. One relation is that the ability to discover common properties in different things or events depends upon the ability to analyze their respective properties. The other was described earlier, in the discussion of determinants of the RE span. Up to some limit, the greater a person's facility in dealing with relevant and irrelevant cues and associated actions, the larger can be his RE span. The possibility of developing integrated or abstract patterns of action to deal with multiple cues and produce skillful performance thus depends upon this facility in perceiving basic cues.

DIFFERENTIATION

The relation between speed in the perception of stimulus elements and the development of integrated action patterns was first demonstrated three-quarters of a century ago in a study of learning to transcribe telegraphic signals (Bryan & Harter, 1897, 1899). Initially, the learners concerned were involved in translating patterns of dots and dashes into corresponding letters. The rates at which they could do so improved with practice up to a point, but their learning curves then showed a "plateau." For a while, further practice produced no improvement. Then, apparently suddenly, the number of letters they could translate per minute shot up. They reported they were beginning to "hear" words in the code. Their perception of the basic units had been reorganized into larger units. After further practice and another plateau, they finally improved again and entered an even higher stage, as they began to "hear" phrases rather than words or letters. This sort of abstraction seemed to depend directly upon the learner's familiarity with the basic signals and their meanings. It seemed to depend upon the readiness with which he could differentiate the lower-order signals and interpretations. Such ability has been regarded as an attribute of the operator and designated "differentiation." In these terms, learning and practice increased the operator's differentiation—more accurately, they improved his facility at differentiation.

Although originally described in the telegraphic context, the integration that emerges with increasing facility in differentiation is known to occur in many tasks, such as reading aloud, piano playing, typewriting, and maze tracing, and it is presumed to occur in the development of all complex skills. Ability to use a plurality of cues seems to underlie recognition of more abstract patterns. And it seems to depend upon speed in the component cue–action processes, that is upon "differentiation." The more rapidly particular cues can be dealt with, the more cue–action processes can overlap with one another and the greater is the probability of their being integrated into more efficient, more abstract patterns—like those that effect intentional behavior.

Investigations of differentiation have been done by H. A. Witkin and colleagues (Witkin, Dyk, Faterson, Goodenough, & Karp, 1962; Witkin, Faterson, Goodenough, & Birnbaum, 1966). Among a number of tests they use for its detection, the so-called Embedded Figures Test (EFT) is the most convenient for the brief synopsis of those works required here. In the EFT, the testee is shown a card bearing a simple geometric form. He is then given a colored card on which that form appears again, sharing some of its boundaries with alternative visible organizations. The time to find the embedded figure is recorded and averaged over a set of problems. The more highly differentiated personalities are those who find the embedded figures more rapidly. They also tend to be more skillful at adjusting a tilted rod to vertical, despite conflicting cues in the visual field, and to make higher scores on tests of perceptual intelligence. Slowness in finding embedded figures is of course associated with the tendency to have one's judgments of the vertical distorted by the interfering visual cues, and the tendency is accordingly described as (visual) "field dependence."

The Hidden Figures Test (HFT), which loads on the intelligence dimension of Figure 2.2 is related to the EFT, having been adapted by Philip Vernon from the same Gottschaldt figures as was the EFT. The Gottschaldt figures and a considerable number of related tests have been shown to assess ability at "perception through camouflage" (Roff, 1952), which is closely related to speed of perception (Thurstone, 1944).

In Witkin's theory, differentiation refers to the ease with which stimulus materials are *analyzed* (from stimuli into cues), a skill that increases with maturation of the nervous system. Such analysis presumably underlies recognition of common attributes in different objects or events, the process known as *abstraction*. Indeed, in reporting a now thoroughly confirmed deficiency of schizophrenic patients, which extends to the brain-damaged as well, Weckowicz and Blewett discussed proficiency at locating figures in the Gottschaldt series *as* abstraction in Goldstein's sense. For them abstraction is "simply described as paying attention to certain characteristics and disregarding others... some information is used, other is suppressed [1959, p. 929]." Another group of investigators wrote of differentiation in terms of the "field articulation" it accomplished, and construed it as ability to give "selective attention in situations that contain compelling relevant and irrelevant cues [Gardner, Jackson, & Messick, 1960, p. 108]."

Speed of learning can be predicted from perceptual differentiation scores (e.g., Gollin & Baron, 1954; Elliot, 1961; Gardner & Long, 1961; Long, 1962; Longnecker, 1962). Why this is so has not been established in detail. One experimenter found finger mazes to be learned more rapidly by more highly differentiated people, and suggested the association was due to a tendency in some persons toward disorganization of learning ability in the face of strange stimulus configurations, such as the differentiation tests and the mazes (Elliot, 1961). Another found that anxiety did indeed reduce differentiation scores on several tests (Longnecker, 1962), and thereby confirmed an earlier generalization that emotion reduces differentiation (Barker, Dembo, & Lewin, 1943). However, still others have demonstrated that some of the "learning" disabilities of mentally retarded persons are not attributable to the faulty registration or storage of information received, but to a failure to differentiate (abstract) the information to be learned from other information that was associated with but irrelevant to the task (Zeaman & House, 1963).

Perceptual Freedom of Choice

All of the considerable body of research into perceptual differentiation reveals that healthy adult humans recognize a variety of features in a given display, so as to be able to select any one of them for special treatment. In a sense this amounts to *perceptual freedom of choice*. As in the maze tracing case, which presumably also involves perceptual articulation, such freedom is evidently reduced by brain damage. It appears to depend, as nearly as any skill yet studied, on physiological health in the nervous system (and sensory apparatus).

Normally, many detectable features of environmental objects and events are disregarded. One learns which cues to use in steering one's actions. And much of the education involved is guided by other people, perhaps especially when the child is learning his language. Words are responses to (or stimuli for) abstract concepts. In day-to-day life, stimulus information is encoded and processed in terms of selected environmental cues and associated responses or cognitive categories such as word names. What is encoded is abstracted from what is given.

The number of categories a person has available for use while registering or encoding his experience—his coding repertoire—is an important determinant of his freedom. It is the simple sum of the perceptual differentiations he makes, with or without associated names, and the nonperceptual discriminations he learns with his language. Part of it, conceivably a major part, is represented in his vocabulary and can be appraised with tests like those Figure 2.2 shows loading the intelligence dimension. As in the case of intelligence, cultural factors as well as physiological factors limit it.

The greater the number of different ways in which a person may encode his experience in a given situation, the greater the selectivity he must display in registering and dealing with it and the less can either his behavior or his experience be considered determined by outstanding objects or events (i.e., stimuli) in the situation. The size of a person's coding repertoire also sets a logical limit on the total amount of information he can deal with in a unit of time (Ashby's, 1958 "law of requisite variety"), and thereby limits his ability for proactive use of information. Although it does not seem to be a sufficient condition of mental freedom, a large, well-differentiated coding repertoire is accordingly an essential one.

WORDS AND POSSIBILITIES

Some of both the perceptual and the cognitive categories a person uses gain their prominence during communications with other people. This is plain enough in the case of words, like *gray* or *speed* or *oxygen,* which are names for attributes or entities. But language consists of *sets of words,* standing in organizational relationships to one another that parallel relationships in the world. An example is the set that includes *father, mother, aunt, uncle,* and others. Hearing any of these words presumably reminds one of the others, and thereby conveys some meaning. Thus language embodies a system for designating relationships between things or events, a system for analyzing nature, a "semantic system" (Brown, 1965). Basil Bernstein has suggested that, when they are being learned, "forms of spoken language elicit, reinforce, and generalize distinct types of relationship with the environment and thus create particular dimensions of significance. Speech marks out what is relevant—affectively, cognitively, and socially, and experience is transformed by that which is made relevant [1961, p. 283]." Thus, according to Bernstein, what a child's attention is directed to, what he accordingly learns about, and how he consequently understands the world, depends to an important degree on the way his associates communicate with him and with one another.

This quotation from Bernstein may seem to be a statement of fact, but it is also a fundamental proposition of an interesting theory that touches on mental freedom. According to that theory, the considerable differences that exist between systems of communication used by speakers of English (for instance) cause in those who use them either acquisition or failure to acquire a number of important skills. Among these are skills required for development of self-control and self-satisfying intentional behavior. Lack of them is theoretically associated with impulsiveness and liability to being driven by circumstances. How could this be?

Remember the way conversations used to run in the gang you belonged to as a youngster? You used a good deal of slang and short sentences with few qualifications and fairly simple explanations. You pointed a lot and made other gestures. Bernstein has designated this a "restricted" communications code and suggests that it is commonly employed in some adult societies. Nowadays, probably, you often talk, read, and write formal English, which discourages use of gestures, is grammatically complex, and accommodates elaborate explanations. This, by contrast, is the "elaborated" code; its differences from the restricted code are the bases of Bernstein's theory of personality.

Nonverbal signals generally refer to concrete events in the here and now. So do the earliest verbal communications of children, even those they hold with well-educated adults (e.g., Brown, 1965, pp. 286–304). They are reactive and resemble the verbal exchanges of Goldstein's brain-damaged patients. However, the talk of normal, educated adults ranges much more widely through time. It may refer to events in the recent or distant past or future, prospectively or retrospectively. It may even refer to events that were in the future at some time in the past, and to predicted events that will probably have become past at some future time. To understand and use this way of speaking, one needs a semantic system in which such different signals can be decoded or encoded. One needs a mind that is aware of the *possibility of other time references* and is prepared for and alert to temporal discriminations. Temporal discrimination is basic to sequential and causal analysis. "Elaborated" communications are supposed to stimulate the development of semantic systems that make fine temporal discriminations and comprehend many possible points in time. So they are supposed to promote development of skill in causal analysis. "Restricted" communications, by contrast, are not.

A smile, as a simple nonverbal message in the present, is restricted in another sense. Like all messages, it derives some of its meaning by stimulating awareness of *possible alternatives* that might have been used but were not, a frown, say, or a poker face. The number of alternatives to a smile is not great.

The statement: "It's good to see you" also has a small number of alternatives. "I am very pleased to see you today" implicates considerably more options, more possibilities. It not only implies pleasure and its alternatives of indifference or displeasure, like the smile, but also suggests that degrees of pleasure and displeasure are possible. It implies further that others might feel differently and that even I might do so on another occasion. The elaborated code states the given in reference to a greater range of possibilities than does the restricted code. It demands and stimulates more alertness toward the possible.

The elaborated code makes more distinctions, involves more precise analysis and description of events. Analytic precision often requires registration of personal experiences as distinct from the consensus of a group. It often requires registration of what Bernstein calls "the personal qualification," which he assumes to be suppressed by the consensus-oriented public code. Like the analytic precision and the alertness to the temporal sequence of events that are required for use of the elaborated code, awareness of private feelings seems to Bernstein to be essential for appreciation of sequential and causal relations. These include relations between a person's needs and emotions on the one hand and his actions and their effects on the other.

Without attending to his private feelings, a person may never be aware of his wishes or of the intentions of his acts. So, people raised with the restricted code are expected not only to ignore feelings and sentiments (to be "tough") but also, in consequence, to be ignorant of, and so to deny, any relation between their needs or unrecognized wishes and any actions they may take. They should be, and act as, irresponsible fatalists. By contrast, those raised with the elaborated code should discover their own responsibility and become interested in planning for it. Their developing skills at causal analysis should facilitate their recognition of cause–effect relationships in behavior. So they should be equipped for self-control and for inferring the intentions and dispositions of others.

The elaborated linguistic code is thus conceived to trade in precise, qualified, analytic statements, that are ''imaginative'' in alluding to possible but absent states of affairs. Being raised to use such a code hypothetically stimulates development of the abilities required for proactive interchanges with the environment, the abilities needed for production of intended events.

The observation recorded in Figure 2.2, that miners with high verbal proficiency scores reported themselves more responsible on Rotter's questionnaire and tended to be slightly more ''imaginative'' than those with low scores, is the sort of fact that supports Bernstein's theory. So is the observation that university students with excellent reading comprehension test scores reported themselves more responsible on the same questionnaire than did others with lower scores (Nauss, 1972). Further evidence of the same order has been reported (e.g., Hess & Shipman, 1965, 1967)—evidence that provides only inconclusive support for Bernstein's theory because it does not rule out alternative explanations. However, if the theory is indeed more useful than competitive theories, that fact seems likely to become known only through similar empirical research. The chances are infinitesimal that any investigator would attempt, let alone be allowed, to manipulate children in the manner required for experimental test of a theory that encompasses events spanning years of life and deals in such important human attributes as this one does. Weak, nonexperimental evidence must be used, and so far it supports those implications of Bernstein's theory that are important here.

Goldstein's general conceptions of the differentiation and abstraction aspects of capacity for freedom are provided with appropriate elaborative detail in the work of Bernstein and of Witkin and associates. And additional contributions to the topic are later reviewed, especially in Chapters 7 and 8. But, even together, these details are not sufficient for a complete account of ''the abstract attitude'' that Goldstein conceived to be impaired or destroyed in the patients he studied. That phrase referred to more than the normal use of abstract categories in dealing with the environment and events in it. It referred also to a sort of withholding of oneself from the world, which Goldstein found exemplified in the experience of giving oneself instructions.

It appears that, in withholding oneself from the world and giving oneself instructions, one is doing what has been described above as using the proactive strategy of information processing. That concept was introduced there only in the most general way. It must now be described more fully and formally.

PROACTIVE INFORMATION PROCESSING

The proactive strategy of information processing is manifest in proactive information transfer. Behavioral information transfer is evident when informative variations in the environment are associated with corresponding or compensatory variations in behavior. It is illustrated in the mazes experiment by *both* the tracings with foresight and those without. Information transfer has become recognizably *proactive* when performance is serially integrated, that is continuous, without recognizable junctions between discrete movements, and acceptable by some criterion of excellence. Such criteria presumably exercise a determining influence in shaping the actions that meet them. The mechanism that promotes their fulfillment by a variety of specific functions is the postulated *strategy*.[3]

Information processing, in pursuance of this strategy, must then be accorded the following minimal features:

1. It is *prospective* or anticipatory, because it serves to guide actions toward some ideal relationship to future environmental events or circumstances.
2. It is *protracted,* in that it continues through a longer time period than reaction to a single stimulus.
3. It is *sequentially selective,* being discriminatively biased toward a sequence of events and circumstances that could determine the outcome of a *course of action,* either promotively or antagonistically, and away from others that could not. The attentive behavior involved is known as concentration or voluntary attention.
4. It is *integrative,* in that it promotes (a) perception of large patterns among events; (b) development of smooth sequences of action, rather than rough chains of discrete, segmental movements; and (c) matching of consequences of action to ideals. Presumably it depends upon the effective operation of a mechanism for the ongoing evaluation and correction of actions.

Certains effects on behavior of the postulated proactive strategy have been discussed in other terms. These include:

1. Removal of action from immediate control by the environment and prevention of impulsive reactions to events in it. This effect was classically ascribed to a condition called "cortical inhibition"—of impulsive reactions

---

[3]The term "strategy," as used in psychology, seems to refer to some sort of higher order plan, such as Miller *et al.* (1960) discuss as a metaplan (see pp. 129, 169, 178, and 179).

(Diamond, Balvin, & Diamond, 1963). It can be removed by damage to the higher brain and can be interrupted or weakened by some drugs, like ethyl alcohol, that are classically described as "disinhibiting."

2. The reorganization or translation of incoming information into relevant conceptual categories, involving (a) abstraction of relevant features; and (b) integration of a number of them into larger units, as when one speaks of "traffic" instead of "other cars" on the road. This is what Goldstein called "categorical behavior."

3. The organization of outgoing movements into complex, serially integrated sequences, such as those used in accurate tracing of complex mazes or in utterance of the grammatically correct sentences that Goldstein called "propositional" as distinct from "emotional" speech (Scheerer, 1954).

4. Generally the shaping of action in reference to "the possible." This term refers not only to the possibility of matching performance to a standard of excellence but also to the possibility that counteracting influences may arise and have to be dealt with.

Quite possibly, the proactive strategy of information processing could be identified with "the attitude toward the possible." However, like Goldstein's concept, that strategy involves more than the capacity for the sort of relation between individual and environment to which it refers. There is a dispositional component to both.

Individuals certainly differ from one another in the amount of information they can use proactively in a given task. Nonetheless, virtually every "testable" person—generally everyone who understands instructions—displays proactive information transfer on some tasks. And this statement applies also to brain-damaged people like Goldstein's patients. It means that a disposition (or "attitude") toward proactive information processing is common, and that it is not this inclination the patients have lost, but the capacity to effect it. This disposition and its relation to "the attitude toward the possible" are treated in all ensuing chapters, but perhaps particularly in the next two.

SUMMARY

Intentional deeds are those in which actions are guided for effect by foreknowledge, including a conception of ideal effects. Component movements are serially integrated in accordance with an abstract plan and in deference to actual, foreseen, and possible environmental events. Unintentional deeds, by contrast, result from impulsive movements, which are stimulated by current events, or from lapses of skill.

The importance of foreknowledge and of ideals in the development of intentional actions and their consequences justifies construing those deeds both as willed and as free from domination by immediate environmental events. It also justifies treating the authors of intentional actions as having created the ensuing effects, as responsible for them, whereas that policy cannot usefully be applied to those who emit unplanned, impulsive movements.

The amount of information a person can process integratively in a unit of time sets a limit on the complexity of task at which he can control all of the effects of his actions. This limit is influenced by knowledge and by organic health, and it is related to intelligence. Evidently it is higher for people who more consistently claim personal control over events.

The importance of abstract mental functioning to human freedom was first pointed out by Kurt Goldstein, who found this "capacity for freedom" seriously impaired in brain-damaged men. Abstract processes involve selective use of relevant features of a varying and diverse environment. Such cues are differentiated from unimportant aspects of, or events in, the situation and are the referents for concepts. Goldstein used the term *dedifferentiation* to describe the loss of precise conceptual control of behavior due to brain damage.

To an important degree, human independence from domination by situational stimuli is due to the fact that interactions with environments are mediated by mental categories or concepts. Such interactions involve the use of cues, rather than responses to stimuli. Yet people differ in the degree to which their actions reflect analysis of their environments, that is in the *differentiation* they display in action.

The determinants of varying degrees of differentiation in and by human minds are being investigated. Two different lines of research have focused on perceptual and linguistic skills. Corresponding theories refer to physiological and social influences.

In discussing freedom of action from stimulus domination, Goldstein emphasized various features of relevant ability. A compatible, novel concept has proven convenient for specific consideration of the forward-looking characteristics of serially integrated, abstract behavior. "Proactive" information processing is differentiated from its "reactive" counterpart in being prospective, protracted, sequentially selective, and integrative. Its attainment seems to depend upon capacity to process multiple elements of information at any moment in time. However, it appears to have a dispositional component as well.

Efficacy and
Freedom of Choice

During the latter part of World War II, 36 young men voluntarily submitted to a diet of less than half their normal food intake for a period of 6 months. In an earlier 3 months of baseline observations they had eaten as much as they wanted, while University of Minnesota scientists made records of their normal health and behavior. Afterward, they returned to normal diets in slow stages over 3 months and were briefly reexamined again 20 weeks and 42 weeks after the end of the semistarvation period. Despite considerable personal liberty during the diet, like being allowed to dine out at a friend's home, only 4 of them gave evidence "direct or indirect . . . of non-adherence to diet [Franklin, Schiele, Brozek, & Keys, 1948, p. 33]." So, 32 men carried through their intentions, obeyed regulations for 9 months, and lost an average of 24% of their body weight in an impressive demonstration of "willpower."

The Minnesota "guinea pigs," as they inevitably called themselves, had been selected from more than 100 volunteers, not only for absence of physical disability and of marital or family obligations but also for demonstrated freedom of will. Specifically, they had been chosen for mental health and for ability to cooperate and get along with others. That is, they were chosen for proven ability to govern the effects of their actions so as to avoid adverse reactions from others. They were sociable, good humored, well mannered, well educated, effective personalities with a variety of cultural interests and academic ambitions. All of this they displayed during the baseline observation period. But the experiment altered their personalities.

After the 6 months of semistarvation and the 3 months of rehabilitation, the remaining 32 volunteers were changed people. They had become *distractible,* unable to study effectively. Indeed, they had generally abandoned their earlier studies, hobbies, and self-development projects. They had become *inefficient* in other tasks as well. They were *irritable,* unable to control their actions for social

51

acceptability, although somewhat recovered in this respect from a nadir during semistarvation. A number of them had become addicted to activities that had not figured in their earlier lives—to drinking tea and coffee, smoking tobacco, and chewing gum. Most of them had also become addicted to eating as much as possible and had ceased to display earlier discriminative tastes in doing so. Their table manners were *neglected*. Over a final celebratory weekend they generally *overate* so much that they became ill, uncomfortable, or unable to sleep. Moreover, 5 months after the experiment ended, the body weight of some of them had risen above baseline levels. In ways the italicized words indicate, they had temporarily lost control of some of the effects of their actions.

HUNGER AND SELF-ACTUALIZATION

The narrow range of interests, the lack of ambition, the failure to engage in self-expressive and self-developmental hobbies, the living for the moment, the distractibility, the crude manners, and the emotionality of these food-deprived young men all amount to failures of self-controlled enterprise. Similar sorts of behavior are often ascribed to persons of "low social class" (e.g., Rosen, 1958). Such persons, commonly the poor and deprived, are said to act in these ways. Of course the Minnesota experiment clearly indicates that food deprivation can produce such behaviors. Food deprivation reduces a person's *efficacy*.

Incidentally, although hunger did not affect intelligence test performance in this experiment, it is otherwise established that inadequate nutrition in childhood is associated with reduced proficiency on such tests later (Matarazzo, 1972). This relation is generally supposed to be due to a direct nutritional effect on brain development, and that may be so. However, similar effects can arise solely from the reduced variety of activities caused by the constriction of interests due to hunger, as shown in the Minnesota experiment. Young rats that do not explore and play because their cages lack facilities grow up less intelligent and with smaller brains than litter mates that have had such stimulation (Rosenzweig, 1966). This interesting implication of the Minnesota observations is a side issue to the main purpose of the illustration.

The semistarvation experiment shows how extreme biological need subjects a person's behavior to *external* control, even in those cases in which the deprivation was assumed and sustained voluntarily and the need existed internally. Details on this effect will be provided later in excerpts from the original report. The quotations will also serve to illustrate several important propositions about the interaction between need, learning, and freedom of will.

The pertinent theoretical points have to do with the fact that a vital class of internal states may "command" behavior. Such conditions arise when an organism's interactions with its environment have left it seriously deprived of a vital input, like food, water, or oxygen, or have caused upset of a necessary balance, like body temperatures. These are emergencies, and the individual's time and resources are automatically preempted by a physiological imperative that such threats to existence be removed. These states are known in psychology as *primary drives*. Though they operate within the animal, they do so because the external environment has denied it access to needed resources.

The term *drive* refers to the effect of need states in energizing or activating animals (Hull, 1943). This effect is readily apparent when an animal first encounters a particular need. If the need has a sudden onset, like that brought on by immersion of the head in water, for example, "frantic," energetic activity starts immediately. Different sorts of rapid movement may then quickly follow one another in what looks like "helpless" or "random" action. Such energetic "trial and error" activity continues until the organism either subsides in exhaustion or accidentally brings about relief-giving changes in the environment that culminate in what behaviorists call *drive reduction*.

The energizing effect of drive is also evident on later occasions in the behavior of animals that obtained relief relatively early on the first occasion. They will then go quickly to the place where relief occurred and energetically repeat actions they were performing at that time. However, the timing of earlier relief is crucial to this effect.

Drive states are not so clearly activating in the case of animals for whom drive reduction on the first occasion occurred only after their initial activities had subsided. Later onset of drive then produces only brief striving. This difference has been ascribed to *learned helplessness* (Seligman & Maier, 1967; Seligman, 1968, 1973; Hiroto, 1974).

Although the influence of drive states in activating overt behavior is conditional on prior experience, two other effects occur unconditionally. One is the neurochemical energy arousal of emotion, which occurs covertly. The other is the suppression of certain kinds of action by the drive state.

Whether or not an animal has had previous experience with a given drive, and regardless of whether earlier relief came soon or late, the existence of a state of high drive dominates its behavior. Certain actions that it normally produces do not then occur unless they have previously brought about drive reduction. Any tendencies to such previously *irrelevant* actions are inhibited, as if, in mentalistic terms, irrelevant ideas were inconceivable.

The Minnesota volunteers had prior experience of hunger and of eating. During the experiment, accordingly, the state induced by food deprivation acted preemptively on their overt behavior in two ways. First, it reduced their involvement in activities unrelated to hunger that had occupied them during the baseline period. Moreover, it seems to have increased their distractibility while engaged in such pursuits. Specific descriptions from the original report are quoted in Part A of Table 4.1. Second, hunger compellingly increased the volun-

TABLE 4.1
**The Driving Effect of Hunger on Volunteers in a Semistarvation Experiment,
as Described in the Original Report**[a]

A. Inhibitory Effects of Hunger

The persistent clamor of hunger distracted the subjects when they attempted to continue their cultural interests, hobby activities, and studies.

Complaints of inability to concentrate for any period of time and of difficulty in developing thoughts became numerous.

The men became indecisive, unable to make personal plans, and unwilling to participate in group activities.

The men rated themselves in comparison with their normal condition as . . . subject to indecisiveness, restless . . . unable to concentrate and markedly "nervous."

In general, fewer and fewer things were capable of stimulating overt action.

Things which would arouse their interest tended more and more to fall within the complex of "guinea-pig" life; loss of body weight, hunger, and food. In discussing these, the men would often become animated.

Personal appearance and care began to deteriorate as the stress progressed. The men often neglected to shave, brush their teeth, and comb their hair.

Their earlier interest in having a voice in the making of policies and rules for the conduct of the non-scientific aspects of the experiment dwindled.

The educational program, designed to prepare the men for foreign relief work and followed at the start with enthusiasm, in time quietly but decisively collapsed.

Social initiative, and sociability in general, underwent remarkable change.

The subjects spent more and more time alone. It became "too much trouble" or "too tiring" to have to contend with other people.

Narrowing of their interests, apathy, and lack of initiative in carrying on conversation and study . . . led the men to conclude that they had suffered actual decline of intellective powers.

B. Excitatory Effects of Hunger

In eating they were, for the most part, silent, deliberate, and gave total attention to the food and its consumption.

All food was consumed to the last crumb.

Frequently the men complained of hunger immediately after eating a bulky meal.

Although the subjects were restricted to three rather monotonous menus, the taste appeal of the diet increased rather than diminished throughout the six months of semistarvation.

It was often reported that vivid vicarious pleasure was derived from watching other persons eat or from just smelling food.

The men dreaded waiting in line while their meals were measured and weighed, each man defensively guarding his place in line.

Food in all of its ramifications became the principal topic of the subjects' conversations, reading, and day dreams. More dreams about food were reported as the stress continued.

When subjects read books and attended movies, they were deeply impressed by the frequency with which food and eating were mentioned.

Some men went so far as to re-plan their lives according to their newly-acquired respect for food.

Cook books, menus and information bulletins on food production became intensely interesting reading matter.

The subjects exhibited a possessive attitude toward their food. At the table some hovered closely over their trays with their arms placed so as to protect their ration.

[a]These statements are quoted from Franklin *et al.* (1948, pp. 30–35 and 38).

TABLE 4.1 (cont.)

The men devoted much time and energy to the collection of recipes, studying of cookbooks, and contemplation of menus. The acquisition of coffee pots, hot plates, kitchen utensils, and the like on shopping "sprees" appeared reasonable.

In order to maximize the pleasure of eating, there was much planning done by the men as to how they would handle their day's allotment of food.

The subjects were often caught between conflicting desires to gulp food down ravenously or to consume it slowly so that the taste and color of each morsel would be fully appreciated. Toward the end of starvation some of the men would dawdle for almost two hours over a meal.

Large quantities of water were consumed with and between meals, and the subjects increased the bulk of their food by "souping." For example a man would drink the fluid from his soup, then fill the bowl with hot water, salt it heavily, drink the fluid off again, and repeat this process before eating the solid part of the soup.

Some chewed up to forty packages of gum per day.

Several men who had not used tobacco prior to participation in the experiment acquired the habit of smoking during semistarvation.

About a half dozen subjects who never drank coffee or tea before the experiment became habitual users of both.

Because some of the men increased their consumption to fifteen or more cups daily, it became necessary to limit all subjects to a maximum of nine cups per day.

teers' overt and fantasy involvement in behavior directly and indirectly related to eating and drinking. Details are presented in Part B of Table 4.1.

In both of the respects documented in Table 4.1, hunger acted on these men in the way drive in general is supposed to act—exciting previously relevant actions and inhibiting previously irrelevant ones. However, in this case there was the important exception that blatant food-seeking activities had been constrained by their resolutions to adhere to the diet.

According to the stimulus–response theory that popularized the drive concept of Hull (1943), hunger had created these effects by impelling use of previously relevant, as distinct from previously irrelevant, habits. Various alternative interpretations are possible, however. One of these, due to A. H. Maslow, would have hunger operating to supplant other motives, not other habits.

In this very influential work of the early mid-1950s, *Motivation and Personality,* Maslow represented the differences between hobbies and food-seeking activities, for example, in terms of a hierarchy of motives.

It is quite true that man lives by bread alone—when there is no bread. But what happens to man's desires when there *is* plenty of bread and when his belly is chronically filled?

At once other (and higher) needs emerge and these, rather than physiological hungers, dominate the organism, and when these in turn are satisfied, again new (and still higher) needs emerge, and so on. This is what we mean by saying that the basic human needs are organized into a hierarchy of relative prepotency [1954, p. 82].

According to this view, hunger created its behavioral effects in the semistarvation experiment by supplanting higher motives.

Uppermost in Maslow's proposed hierarchy is the need for *self-actualization,* which he defined as "man's desire for self-fullfillment, namely . . . the tendency for him to become actualized in what he is potentially. This tendency might be phrased as the desire to become more and more what one is, to become everything that one is capable of becoming [1954, pp. 91–92]." Maslow's book was accordingly concerned with the motivational or emotional aspect of self-actualization in the broad sense proposed by Kurt Goldstein (whom Maslow— see 1954, p. ix—credited with having "very profoundly" influenced his thinking). It made the point that self-actualization requires something beyond the neurological integrity that Goldstein had shown necessary for abstract functioning. According to Maslow, this sort of autonomy also "rests upon prior satisfaction of the physiological, safety, love, and esteem needs [1954, p. 92]" that constitute the lower levels of the proposed hierarchy. The lower needs can enslave a person; their satisfaction can liberate him to engage in other sorts of interaction with his environment in pursuit of higher "needs."

Either Maslow's formulation or the simpler habit theory can account for the restriction in variety of activities by the Minnesota volunteers. Of the two, however, only Maslow's can easily account for voluntary adherence to the diet. It proposed that "living at the higher need level can be relatively independent of lower need gratification. . . . The higher develops only on the basis of the lower, but eventually, when well established, may become *relatively* independent of the lower [1954, p. 154]." In this view, fasting may be self-actualizing behavior. Theoretically, the men who willingly imposed this punishing constraint upon themselves were able to do so because their personalities had been shaped appropriately during earlier years, when hunger was rare. Their ability for self-starvation, their freedom of will, was a demonstration of the "will control" that can develop only when a person is well fed and free of other lower needs. Of course, simple stimulus–response theory does not even address the possibility of intentional self-starvation.

Nevertheless, reports of the Minnesota volunteers' behavior make it clear that the characterological control of their actions had been less than perfect. Current hunger evidently attenuated the liberating value of whatever self-controlling mechanisms accounted for their earlier activities. This is shown by two sorts of facts. Not only had the men "rated themselves in comparison with their normal condition as lacking in self-discipline and self-control [Franklin *et al.,* 1948, p. 34]." They had also been observed to display less self-discipline and self-control in their actions, as described in the general statements reprinted in Table 4.2. Hunger had reduced the efficacy component of their responsibility.

THE RELATION OF DRIVE TO FREEDOM OF CHOICE

According to the information in Table 4.2, the number of aspects of their behavior that were under the control of the volunteers' ideals had fallen as a result of semistarvation. Their table manners, their consideration of others, their diligence and their equable tempers had all deteriorated. In the terms of Figure 2.2, their reported emotionality and irritability suggest they were operating with lower efficacy. Over a period of 274 days and nights they had made their way through a series of choice points without entering the "blind alley" of taking

TABLE 4.2
Loss of Self-Control by Volunteers in Semistarvation Experiment
as Portrayed in Excerpts from Report[a]

The use of subjects on food-handling jobs was discontinued at their request because the temptations under these circumstances became too great; they had found themselves inadvertently licking gravy off their fingers or picking up crumbs.

The men were cultured and refined, yet they routinely licked their dishes in order to obtain every vestige of food.

Even those who had been careful or even particular in their grooming now dressed carelessly and presented a slovenly appearance.

In the later part of semistarvation, housekeeping chores were neglected and nonexperimental laboratory duties were carried out less and less effectively.

They were not altogether able to control their emotionally charged responses.

The smooth temperedness, patience, and tolerance evidenced during the control period gave way under stress to the converse. Irritability increased to the point where it became an individual and group problem.

Humor and high morale . . . characteristic of the group during standardization, gradually disappeared.

They quickly became intolerant of food waste and were visibly upset when they caught others discarding food. There were many bitter comments that any spoilage or wastage of food was prodigal and criminal in a starving world.

They tended to become irritated when the serving was slow or those who served the food gave any evidence of not taking their business "seriously."

The men became self-centered. The egocentricity and associated heightened irritability, of which the subjects were well aware, required at times a real effort to maintain socially acceptable behavior.

Outbursts of temper and periods of sulking and pique were not uncommon, and a few had strong urges to violence but these were not carried out.

The men reported annoyance when hosts or others tried to persuade them to take just a little extra food.

Some men toward the end of the experiment became annoyed by discussions of food and related subjects. One man expressed disgust at this "animal attitude"; another referred to such engrossment as "nutritional masturbation."

[a]These statements are quoted from Franklin *et al.* (1948, pp. 30–35 and 38).

extra food. They had executed their intentions and honored their promises. Yet, according to the reports of inadvertence, they seem to have "cut corners" and committed other "qualitative errors." The complexity of "maze" they had been able to "trace" without departures from the ideal had fallen.

This is another evident effect of high drive. It reduces the number of cues a person uses at any moment in time in the production of behavior (Easterbrook, 1959). As shown in the previous chapter, the ability to deal with multiple cues in a single course of action is fundamental to the development of intentional behavior. As receptor–effector spans fall toward unity, *under the influence of great biological need, actions become simpler, approximate more and more closely to impulsive stimulated responses,* and reveal fewer characteristics of proactive information transfer or intentional behavior.

The patterns of action just described can also be construed as less well *differentiated* than the normal actions of the same men, that is, in Goldstein's term, as *dedifferentiated.* The men *neglected* some chores, acted *inadvertently, carelessly,* and *less effectively* on others. Their "interests" had been "narrowed." They had become "indecisive," "restless," "unable to concentrate," and had "difficulty in developing thoughts." In their "irritability," they seem again to have come closer to acting by impulse and without attention to detail. They had displayed reduced behavioral information transfer. The determination of most of their behavior had clearly remained abstract; they had processed information proactively. Yet the abstract patterns or plans they had followed had become simpler, less well articulated. They had become *dedifferentiated.*

The impairing effect of high drive upon differentiated behavior can be shown by a simple test. If a pigeon is trained to peck at an illuminated circle slightly more than ½ inch in diameter for food reward, and later tested with that stimulus and others of varying sizes, he will normally peck at some of the others though most frequently at the one on which he was trained. Responses to stimuli that resemble the training stimulus are said to be due to "stimulus generalization." Less differentiation is evident in behavior that shows more stimulus generalization. When hungrier animals are tested in this way, their actions reveal relatively more generalization and less discrimination. This effect is thoroughly confirmed with other sources of drive (Kimble, 1968).

The propositions that emotion reduces personal differentiation (Barker *et al.,* 1943) and that drive reduces the range of cue utilization (Easterbrook, 1959) have been known in psychology for some time. They seem to predict these facts. Both hypotheses assume that the less thorough the learning that underlies differentiated behavior, the more readily will emotion or drive reduce differentiation. On this assumption, high drive would cause dedifferentiation most readily in naive animals and would also prevent their learning new discriminations easily.

These hypotheses are, therefore, compatible with Maslow's view that the learning required for self-actualization is inhibited by living with unsatisfied basic drives. The relation between differentiation and freedom of choice among situational influences was pointed out in Chapter 3. It can now be asserted that, with the specified qualifications about prior learning, high levels of drive reduce freedom of choice in behavior. Not only do they evidently impair behavioral differentiation; they also cause an organism's resources to be directed in particular ways, generally toward relief of its driven state. By corollary, of course, reductions of drive level should increase freedom of choice.

The Relation of Drive to Automatism

Psychological discussions of drive reduction seem to imply precisely the opposite. They refer to the effect of drive reduction on the development of *habits*. It is thoroughly established that driven animals quickly learn to repeat actions associated with drive reduction, which is accordingly also known as "positive reinforcement" of these acts (Hull, 1943; Spence, 1958). This learning is called "conditioning," and the learned action is called an *instrumental conditioned response* (CR). It is also sometimes called a "conditioned reflex." So, it is implied that drive-reducing actions occur automatically or mechanically whenever appropriate stimuli arise in the environment. Drive reduction has consequently come to be regarded, implicitly, as promoting the stimulus domination of behavior.

Three sets of facts have to be appreciated to evaluate this supposition. The first two are fairly obvious matters of logic. One is that drive reduction can occur only from an elevated drive level. Thus some effects attributed to drive reduction may be due to the initial state of the organism. (That some simple CRs are known as "escape mechanisms" suggests as much.) Another is that control relations between animals and environments are reciprocal. The two interact (Ashby, 1960); so, it is just as true to say that incidents of drive reduction promote the animal's control of his environment as it is to assert the converse. Third, experimental studies clearly show that it is high levels of drive, rather than incidents of drive reduction, that lead to the development of automatism in behavior.

Some of these experiments have been performed on human beings, but in the present context the most pertinent of them is one that was performed with hungry rats (Bruner, Matter, & Papanek, 1955). The determinants of rat behavior are interesting because they are supposed to be simpler than those of human behavior.

One group of animals had been deprived of food for 36 hours and another for 12 when they were individually introduced to a training maze. Their task was to find the way from entry to feeding box through four walls, each with one open and one closed door, painted either white or black. They had previously learned to pick doors of the correct color and had done so with perfect accuracy 10 times in succession. In this maze, only the positions of the correct doors had been changed. Here they were set out in a simple alternation pattern, with open doors on the left, the right, the left and the right (or vice versa). That is, position cues were now introduced, correlated with the old—and still useful—color cues. After 20 trials on this maze, all animals were put individually into yet another maze with all eight doors painted gray but with the alternation pattern retained. The important observation refers to the comparative ease with which this task was performed.

The hungrier animals took almost as many trials to learn the gray maze as did control animals who had never run an alternation pattern. Those who were less hungry, however, showed significant *positive transfer* of their earlier experience to the later task. They had learned something of the alternation pattern while following the color cues. Those who had been starved an extra day did not. This experiment confirmed the results of an earlier study, in which water deprivation was the source of the primary drive. The increase in drive had reduced what the authors and earlier investigators called ''the breadth of learning'' (Tolman, 1948) or ''the range of the perceptive–reactive field'' (Masserman, 1943). Alternatively, the increase in drive can be said to have interfered with development of the differentiation that the earlier experience had created in the better-fed animals.

The very hungry and the slightly hungry rats had been rewarded with equal quantities of food for running the correlated cues maze. Of course, relative to their needs, the hungrier animals had *smaller* rewards, so their drive levels were presumably reduced *less*. Yet these were the very animals who had run the first maze like the automatons that CR theory imagines. Their later disadvantage must have been due to the higher drive level at which they were operating. It could not have arisen from greater drive reduction, because they had experienced the same or less of that. And the comparative liberation of the others must have been due, by contrast, to their smaller need or perhaps their proportionally larger rewards. Drive had created the automatism. It did not develop in those that were driven less desperately.

In the jargon of CR psychology, the mechanism of an automatism is a strong ''habit.'' The greater the strength of any habit, the more reliably or automatically the specified action occurs when the specified stimulus is presented (Hull, 1943). Notice that this criterion implies, obversely, that actions due to strong habits are relatively uninfluenced by variations in other aspects of the situation—like the alternation of open doors in this experiment. It follows that habitual actions must often be inappropriate to the situations in which they occur.

SUBJECTIVITY AND OBJECTIVITY IN BEHAVIOR

A considerable variety of automatisms is known in psychology, designated by such terms as *fixated* actions, *stereotypies,* and *addictions.* Some of them create spectacularly inappropriate sorts of behavior. One team of researchers has shown how strong habits can produce oddities of action by people who have been called crazy (schizophrenic) that may be sufficient to justify the term (Chapman, Chapman, & Miller, 1964). They showed for instance that, if "appointment to take a girl out" is the strongest habitual association of the word *date,* such persons often deny that "a date is a piece of fruit from a palm tree." To get such an odd answer, these researchers showed, you need only stimulate a strong habit with a double meaning word in a context that requires another response. The person will then fail to use those contextual cues, just as habit theory implies. Similar failures can also account for the inability to produce figurative rather than literal interpretations of proverbs, which has been inappropriately described as "concrete behavior" (e.g., Lewinsohn & Riggs, 1962; Downing, Shubrook, & Ebert, 1966; Gorham, 1956, 1963). What is characteristic of these instances of automated action is that they are determined by singular features in, or aspects of, a situation (i.e., "stimuli").

The concepts of differentiation and dedifferentiation can now be used to make two important general propositions that might seem mutually contradictory if stated in other terms. One is that driven actions, those that seem most clearly to be caused by singular events in the environment, are the very ones that appear to be most *subjectively determined.* The dedifferentiation, which reduces freedom of choice and the capacity for proactive information processing, results from the elevated drive or emotion. Second, and conversely, actions that are most appropriate or ideally fitted to a situation, because they take account of more aspects of it, can be described as *objectively determined.* Paradoxically, such abstract, differentiated, skillful, ideal-matching behavior requires greater amounts of prior learning and of extemporaneous organization than "subjectively" determined behavior. Human actions control environmental events most clearly when they are objectively appropriate, and they are most clearly controlled by environmental events when they arise in the "subjective" conditions of high drive or emotion.

Prolonged hunger increased the number of objectively inappropriate elements of behavior by the Minnesota volunteers. One spectacular instance is the gluttony they displayed on their celebratory weekend, 2 weeks after they had finally returned to their normal diets of about 3500 calorific units per day. They gorged themselves at rates of 6000–7000 units per day, apparently having become addicted to food. Another instance is their persistence in licking their plates! These actions may have been appropriate when they were eating only 1570 units per day, but were no longer so. Notice, incidentally, that the plate-licking habit seems to have developed during the 274 days of small daily reductions of considerable drive, while no comparable habit had been formed in the 306 *months* (the average age of the volunteers) of normal hunger and larger daily meals. According to CR theory, however, another factor besides primary hunger and strong habits was probably involved in producing these examples of apparently mechanical behavior.

ACQUIRED DRIVES AND FREEDOM OF CHOICE

Drive induction is a term that refers to another type of elementary learning or conditioning. When an individual undergoes an emotionally arousing experience, events in or aspects of the environment that were remarkable at that time can attain the power to recreate, later, a state resembling the original experience. So for instance, a place where one has been frightened may later evoke fear. Such reactions are, of course, conditional on the prior experience, and are called *classical CRs* because they were the object of the first research into learned automatic behavior (by the Russian physiologist I. P. Pavlov).

When the original experience involved high drive, the state evoked by a conditional stimulus (CS) on later presentation is referred to as an *induced* or *secondary drive*. Animals in such a state are impelled to act for its reduction just as if they were operating under primary drive. This proposition has been well validated, initially by Neal Miller (1951) with fear in rats. Many aspects of the Minnesota meal situation were regularly associated with hunger, so they would be expected to develop drive-inducing properties.

In secondary drive theory, even the sight or taste of food could become a source of induced hunger for men who had endured prolonged periods of semi-starvation. Eating and plate licking would, of course, constitute pertinent drive-reducing actions. The ill-restrained eating and the inappropriate plate licking that occurred on the celebratory weekend may thus be explained as consequences of secondary "hunger" induced by the sight or taste of food.

Anxiety as a Secondary Drive State

The term *anxiety* is commonly applied to secondary drive states. It is often thought that anxiety is a fearful state that is unjustified by present objective circumstances, and of course secondary drive states have a similar peculiarity. Primary hunger can be satisfied fairly readily by eating, but the secondary drive due to hunger should produce overeating. That the Minnesota volunteers may have become susceptible to irrational secondary drive states, resembling anxiety, is in fact suggested by some of the reports of their behavior:

> The subjects exhibited a possessive attitude toward their food. At the table, some hovered closely over their trays with their arms placed so as to protect their ration [Franklin *et al.*, 1948, p. 31].

> The men dreaded waiting in line while their meals were measured and weighed, each man defensively guarding his place in line [Franklin *et al.*, 1948, p. 31].

Several subjects insisted that they had grown unusually anxious to save money for a "rainy day" and attributed this to the insecurity they felt in the experimental situation [Franklin *et al.*, 1948, p. 35].

The word *insecurity* alludes to a condition of central importance to any discussion of freedom of will. It signifies recognition of threat that one *may become helpless* to command something of vital importance to oneself. Presumably this condition arises from experiences in which one has in fact been operating under the biological imperative of a primary drive. In the semistarvation situation, the means to satisfy hunger were not under the subjects' control—except by methods they would not use—and their need had reduced their ability for intentional control of events (Table 4.2). Such experiences would justify a perception of susceptibility to external control of one's rewards or one of reduced freedom of choice in one's actions.

One strong theory, supported by considerable interlinked experimental evidence, interprets symptoms of anxiety as habits acquired under high emotional reactivity or drive (Spence, 1960). "Emotional reactivity" in turn is conceived as a sensitivity, which increases the strength of emotional reaction to "aversive" stimuli. In this view, people who are called anxious display their symptoms because they have a large number of strong emotional CRs, traceable to high emotional reactivity, whatever its cause. The associated theory of behavior then contends that such people will produce *habitual* responses in any pertinent situation more rapidly, more reliably, and with greater force than others who are less anxious.

Evidence in support of the theory of *emotionally based drive* comes from experiments that assessed simple CRs, like defensive blinking of the eye after a flash of light or response to single conditional stimuli (CSs) with which no other actions had been associated (Kimble, 1968). In view of such evidence, the theory seems to be acceptable for understanding differences in the strength of simple defensive reactions at least. Pertinent studies with more complex tasks do not support the theory's predictions, but that fact can be assigned to a weakness in the associated theory of complex behavior—that theory has also failed to give an adequate account of complex behavior under the influence of drive from other sources, like hunger. In any case, the evidence from studies of simple reactions shows that, after training, people who reveal more symptoms of anxiety are more impelled to execute those simple actions than others who manifest less anxiety.

Comparability of Anxiety and Other Sources of Drive

On the other hand, people who display more anxiety learn mazes less readily than others who are less susceptible to it, according to evidence reported by Spence (1960), author of the theory of emotionally based drive, and by others (e.g., McNamara & Fisch, 1964; Parsons, Maslow, Morris, & Denny, 1964;

Murphy, 1964; Freedman, 1966). Emotionally based drive reduces the number of task relevant cues people use simultaneously, as represented in maze tracing proficiency. There seem to be no reports whatever of contrary evidence, and men who are merely more highly motivated to perform well actually do less well in tracing visual mazes (Eysenck & Willett, 1962, 1966). Manipulations to produce emotional reactions also reduce the so-called immediate memory span, which is another defining measure of the number of relevant cues in simultaneous use (Easterbrook, 1959; Hodges & Spielberger, 1969; Bacon, 1974)—although the evidence on the effect of "trait anxiety" (susceptibility to symptoms of anxiety) is equivocal (Phillips, Martin, & Meyers, 1972). The language development of emotional children is comparably retarded, perhaps from the same cause (Carmichael, 1946).

In different general terms, such evidence indicates that something like drive is associated with symptoms of anxiety and reduces the length of action sequences articulated to perfectly match specified standards. To put it yet another way, anxiety reduces the rate of information transfer, which is the total amount of relevant information the behavioral system deals with in a unit of time (Woodward, 1953). Like hunger, it thus causes a reduction of the differentiation displayed in behavior.

Dedifferentiation under the influence of emotionally based drive has also been demonstrated with simpler tests for stimulus generalization (e.g., Gaines, Mednick, & Higgins, 1963). In one instance, the investigator used four related tests—including Witkin's Embedded Figures Test, which is a standard measure of differentiation—in a study of people with various levels of susceptibility to anxiety symptoms. He showed that threatening instructions slowed discovery or recognition of target figures by the more susceptible or emotionally reactive. The threats reduced differentiation. So did a motivating manipulation. By contrast, the same treatments facilitated task performance by people who were less prone to symptoms of anxiety (Longnecker, 1962). This may have occurred by its diverting them from involvement with cues irrelevant to the task, that is by "focusing attention" onto the task. Referring to many experiments performed in his laboratory, another investigator has indeed claimed that, in general, both of these kinds of manipulation cause a constriction in "the space–time distribution of attention" (Solley, 1969). Presumably the "constriction" process goes too far in those cases in which dedifferentiation occurs; there, it inhibits the use of some task cues as well as nontask cues. In any case, it is evident that manipulations which should produce emotional reactions cause dedifferentiation in the behavior of more susceptible persons.

The subjectivity associated with high drive is ascribed to anxiety in a review by Phillips, Martin, and Meyers, which says that "reduced responsiveness to the environment" is one immediate consequence of anxiety (1972, p. 417). This generalization may be somewhat misstated, but evidence to support it is not hard to find. One good demonstration comes from a study of learning under stress by people who differed remarkably in susceptibility to anxiety (trait anxiety) as measured by questionnaire. The investigators designed a task that required the learning of a series of movements under one of three conditions, "blindly," with a relevant cue, or despite an irrelevant cue. Groups differing in trait anxiety were observed under each of these conditions. What happened was that less susceptible persons performed better with a relevant cue and worse with an irrelevant one, evidently having used those cues. By the same criterion, the presumably more anxious persons evidently failed to use the added cues (Zaffy & Bruning, 1966). Other experiments agree; the number of (objective) *task cues* in the environment to which one responds is reduced by anxiety. The anxiety, meanwhile, amounts to involvement with one's (subjective) emotional state and associated events.

The same arguments about freedom of choice can be made in reference to emotionally based drive as apply to drive states due to needs like hunger. Increase in drive reduces freedom of choice in two ways. It *impels* habitual actions previously relevant to its reduction. And it reduces the number of cues an individual employs at any moment in time. Since it simultaneously *reduces discrimination,* the evidence of its dedifferentiating power is complete. A smaller number of alternative constructions of his environment is accessible to the individual who is driven by emotion. So the probability of problem solution is reduced, and this in turn may be due to the impelling effect of drive on habitual response tendencies, that is, to what has been called the "mechanization" of behavior (see pp. 60 and 82). The emotional person's behavior is more impulsive, subject to control by a narrower range of information from his prior experience. It is more nearly reactive, less fully proactive.

The Snowball Effect

According to the principles of classical conditioning, emotional reactions like those in emotionally based drive ought to become linked with previously neutral stimuli. This would give those stimuli the power to produce conditional emotional reactions or secondary drive later. Moreover, the number of similar stimuli with this capability should also increase with time because higher drive produces greater stimulus generalization. Susceptibility to emotionally based drive ought therefore to "snowball." Indeed, such accumulation is sometimes observed (Spence, 1960). Apparently its frequency is kept low by an emotion-attenuating mechanism known as *habituation,* which all theories recognize. Nevertheless, conditioning theory suggests the snowball proposition. The more frequently a person experiences *intense* emotion, with its associated effects on behavior, the more frequently he is likely to do so in the future. Low efficacy may be self-propagating.

REMOVAL OF EMOTIONAL REACTIONS

Once acquired, secondary drive states and associated reactions can be very difficult to eliminate. A common approach to the task uses the strategy of increasing the individual's "resistance" to emotional reaction by showing that the stressful unconditioned stimulus does not necessarily follow the conditional stimulus that has come to elicit the reaction, that is, by preventing reinforcement of the CR. The most useful resistance-creating procedures are the short-term process known as "habituation" (or sometimes "negative adaptation") and its long-term counterpart, *extinction*. The first of these is the diminution in strength of response due to repetition of an eliciting stimulus on any one occasion. It occurs with all but very intense reactions. The second is the diminution in strength of a conditional response that occurs when the relevant CS is presented without reinforcement on a number of different occasions. Extinction is often a very long and tedious process. It may even be impossible in some cases, depending on the speed with which events developed in the learning situation (Solomon & Wynne, 1953, 1954). However, its attainment is considerably facilitated by the production of a strong response that is physiologically or neurologically incompatible with the emotional reaction.

The terms *counterconditioning* and *reciprocal inhibition* have been used to designate processes by which secondary states of aversive drive come to be inhibited by incompatible reactions. The classical investigation, reported by Mary Jones (1924a, 1924b), focused on the terror evoked by the sight of a rabbit in a boy named Peter, who was not quite 3. Peter's distress when shown the rabbit at a distance of 12 feet was (reciprocally) inhibited when he became engaged in some pleasant activity, such as playing with a person he liked, or eating candy. By keeping him pleasantly occupied and bringing the rabbit closer day by day, the experimenter changed the boy's reaction to it, so that, ultimately, Peter could fondle the animal and allow it to nibble at his fingers. Possibly it had become a CS to a pleasurable reaction, which was incompatible with the fear reaction it had evoked earlier. Thus enjoyment of "good" interactions with his environment, together with the processes of conditioning, had freed Peter from his conditional drive state and had increased his freedom of action toward the animal. In both cause and effect, his *efficacy* had been increased.

Many new cases of this counterconditioning of anxiety have been described since the original Jones report. Some of these accounts are due to Joseph Wolpe, who coined the term *reciprocal inhibition* and used it as part of the title for a book on "psychotherapy" in 1958. To inhibit symptoms of anxiety, Wolpe particularly recommended cultivation of assertive behavior, "the outward expression of friendly, affectionate, and other nonanxious feelings [p. 114]" and of "sexual situations in which pleasurable feelings are felt exclusively or very predominantly [pp. 130–131]." An earlier advocate of the use of CR theory for treatment of anxiety had designated such assertive activities as "expressive"

(Salter, 1949). Both terms refer to activities of greater efficacy than anxiety reactions. And the facts they refer to complement other evidence on the relation of efficacy to anxiety. They show how such assertive activities can inhibit anxiety, rather than merely arising in its absence (because it normally inhibits them).

Assertive or consummatory—that is, gratifying—actions as a class reduce drives. Where possible, as in the case of primary hunger in fortunate economies, the biologically relevant activity is "naturally" the preferable one. However, when that is not possible for any reason, engagement in another pleasant activity will serve to attenuate these distressing conditions. In the latter case, too, the temporary relief such distractions bring can be made relatively permanent if—as in the case of Peter and the rabbit—the stimuli for the induced drive are simultaneously present but repeatedly unreinforced. Accordingly, a person who is *chronically* driven ought to be found to have enjoyed few need-reducing activities of any kind. This deduction may have been confirmed by the report that those anxious patients who *do not* recover "spontaneously," that is, without psychiatric intervention, are more often ill-educated, unemployed, and unmarried than those who do. A history of frustration could develop either because a person's environment had been hostile and unresponsive to his actions or because of multiple deficits in his knowledge or skill. Either factor would lead to a general state of helplessness.

ANXIETY AS HELPLESSNESS

Seymour Epstein's contributions to the psychology of anxiety developed out of his own experimental work and his reviews of other theories on the topic. He has defined anxiety as "undirected arousal following the perception of danger [1972, p. 305]." Some general sources of "danger" have been described by Epstein. One of them, which he calls *primary overstimulation,* is generally regarded as an instance of emotionally based drive. It occurs when any high intensity energy source operates on an organism's sensory system so as to provoke "frantic feelings . . . corresponding to the statement 'Stop it, I can't stand any more' [p. 303]," that is, to a pained state of helplessness. Notice that this condition arises, by definition, only when the individual has in fact been unable to do anything about it. So it resembles, for experienced individuals, the effect of primary sources of drive on naive individuals.

Besides the elemental vulnerability that may affect either naive or experienced individuals, Epstein postulated two further sources of anxiety that are supposed to operate unconditionally on experienced animals especially. One of these is *cognitive incongruity.* This occurs when an individual's expectations are not fulfilled by events or when he meets a situation in which he notices novel or inconsistent features. Feelings of confusion, disorganization, disorientation, and helplessness are said to be implicated in the reaction to cognitive incongruity.

Helplessness is the central cognitive aspect of reaction to the third source of anxiety, *response unavailability*. This awkwardly named and distressing condition arises whenever an individual is unable to complete execution of response tendencies that have been aroused in him, due, for instance, to ignorance of what to do, to fear of the anticipated consequences of a prepared act, or to the presence of insurmountable obstacles. "Freedom of movement" in Rotter's (1954; Rotter *et al.*, 1972) theory and the "sense of competence" in Stotland and Canon's (1972) operate in precisely the opposite way and are assumed to prevent anxiety.

Thus, what is proposed, with these two terms, is that a state of helplessness constitutes the danger and provokes the energy arousal of anxiety. *Helplessness amounts, of course, to a recognition of external control* (see also Hiroto, 1974).

The undirected arousal of anxiety can be readily displayed by various measures of the functions of the autonomic nervous system. The exact pattern of arousal varies from person to person, but increases in heart rate and in the ease with which the skin conducts electricity occur very commonly (Malmo, 1966; Lynn, 1966). Muscles generally also become tense, as if ready for action, and this sometimes occurs in the smooth muscles of the autonomic nervous system as well as in the striped muscles with which "voluntary" actions are executed (Jacobson, 1929). Various "psychosomatic" disorders can develop as a result of this involvement of vital energy-exchanging organs in anxiety reactions (Beck, 1972).

Clearly Epstein's "primary overstimulation" is Spence's "aversive, stressful stimulation," and his "undirected arousal" is Spence's "emotionally based drive," as it is supposed to function in naive or helpless minds. In addition, other writers on behavior theory had earlier demonstrated sources of drive that are essentially equivalent to the two other sources of anxiety postulated by Epstein (Amsel, 1959; Berlyne, 1960). Although written in mentalistic terms, Epstein's theory thus embodies knowledge from a very large number of experiments on behavior. Notably it also assumes the conditioning of secondary drive. Due to learning, Epstein points out "the range of potential sources of arousal is increased, while the primary impact from old familiar stimuli is reduced. That is, the predominant source of stimulation shifts from raw energy inputs to that from cues associated with expectancies, that is, to meaning [1972, pp. 306–307]." Expectancies are, of course, the mentalistic counterparts of (the perceptual components in) conditional responses.

An Evaluation of Epstein's Theory

This much of Epstein's theory is compatible with the experimental evidence. Two qualifications must be noted, however. One refers to the conception of anxiety as an unorganized condition of arousal and the other to time relations in anxiety-creating situations.

All instances of undirected energy arousal following perception of danger are episodes of anxiety, in Epstein's view. When frightened animals take organized action they are merely frightened, not anxious. It is well established, however, that people who are known to be anxious in specified sorts of situations, do in fact produce organized behavior in those situations. For instance, test-anxious persons, who frequently report such thoughts as "I am stupid" during a test, nevertheless execute their tasks, although less effectively than when they think they are not being "tested" (Sarason, 1972; Wine, 1971). To apply Epstein's theory to such data one must either deny that those people were anxious or postulate that they merely suffered *moments of anxiety* and not a continuous state.

The second necessary condition for regarding the basics of Epstein's theory as compatible with experimental evidence concerns the temporal relations it imagines between events in (moments of) anxiety. In strict interpretation, its definition requires that, in every case, either the arousal or a failure in its direction is a consequence of perception of danger, due to perception of one of the three basic sources of danger or of a sign of one. On this point the evidence is ambiguous. The true time relations may go exactly the opposite way. In a broader context, this general issue has remained in doubt for years because pertinent experiments are extremely difficult. It is not known whether the arousal of emotion generally follows or generally precedes recognition of its referent. However, it seems that either *can* precede determination of the precise form of emotion (Schacter, 1966). Spence may be correct in assuming that the arousal ("emotional") reaction is primary, Epstein may be correct in assuming the reverse, or both may be correct.

In Epstein's theory, "anxious" persons have expectations that render them susceptible to perceptions of helplessness in the face of environmental conditions. According to the experimental evidence, moreover, such people act driven, as if their freedom of choice had been reduced. Their actions are more often impulsive and less consistently discriminating and appropriate to objective conditions than the actions of "less anxious" people. They resemble the actions of animals operating under high drive. These people act in fact less competent and more nearly helpless in the face of environmental events. Hence, for them, perceptions of helplessness would often be justified.

THE EFFICACY CONSTRUCT

Anxiety theories resemble theories about deprivation drives in focusing upon the behavioral effects of uncontrolled environmental conditions, past and present. Efficacy, by contrast, focuses upon the satisfaction of personal needs, past and present, and the expectations of future satisfaction that such experience should produce. The efficacy concept takes seriously the fact that people who report their fate to be outside their control are commonly anxious (Joe, 1971) and that denials of personal responsibility for particular outcomes follow failure more often than success (Rotter, 1966; Wolosin *et al.*, 1973). Such reports are not considered to be ego-defensive, produced to protect their authors from anxiety.

The concept of "ego defense mechanism" was introduced into psychology by Sigmund Freud (1950) to account for some kinds of behavior he found in people with low "ego strength" (Freud's equivalent of strength of will). Such persons would, for example, speak and act as if unaware of pressing needs that they seemed to have but be frightened to express (repression). Alternatively, they might mention those needs in a *denial* of relevant wishes. Or they might attribute to another an attitude toward themselves that they held toward that other (projection). Such tactics were thought to *attenuate* the fear of expressing relevant wishes and also to prevent need-reducing activities. When found with evidence of anxiety and of unsatisfied basic (*id*) needs, they have been treated in many texts on "adjustment" as (inefficient) "escape mechanisms" or "adjustive techniques." And they have been regarded both as signs of low ego strength and as explanation of the associated *high* drive and low efficacy! Thinking in terms of defense mechanisms, the association between anxiety and reports that one's reinforcements are externally controlled might be given a similarly circuitous interpretation. One could say that the anxious people who deny personal responsibility for their fortunes are defending themselves against fear of recognizing their inadequacy. To postulate that such self-deprecating mechanisms are used for ego defense or enhancement is to create an explanatory morass. In this context, particularly, it is more productive to treat claims of external control quite simply as true and as revealing the direct cause of the associated anxiety.

The opposition of efficacy to drive differs in several ways from Freud's opposition of ego strength to anxiety and id frustration. It focuses directly on relations with the environment. Efficacy is independent of intelligence, which is considered as potential for adjustment. Hypothetically influencing the effectiveness with which intelligence can be exercised to attain future satisfactions, efficacy is an aggregate of experience with the situational factors that determine past and present satisfactions. These include the ease with which one's environment can be controlled for personal rewards, and the associated expectancies. They also include the effects of other sorts of good fortune, such as inheritance of a nurturing environment, of valuable material resources, or of valuable physical attributes like beauty.

People whose behavior in particular situations is commonly marked by efficacy are accordingly expected to differ from those who, in such situations, are frequently driven or anxious in ways corresponding to the following italicized attributes. They will be *confident* (rather than *apprehensive*), for their needs have commonly been, and are therefore expected to be, *satisfied* (rather than *frustrated*). As both a consequence and a contributing cause of these conditions, they will also be more *assertive, self-expressive* (less *timid* and *inhibited*). They will display more abstract or planful behavior, in acting *emotionally stable* (not *irritable, easily upset*) and in the shaping of their actions to match personal ideals that has been designated *will control* or *self-sentiment control* (rather than acting *casually* or *expediently*). They will, in other words, have the characteristics Cattell and associates (1964, 1967) ascribe to "good adjustment" as plotted on the horizontal axis of Figure 2.2—the nonintellective component in freedom of will.

In the words of Immanuel Kant, "The will is a faculty to choose *that only* which reason, independent on inclination, recognizes as practically necessary, i.e., as good [1785/1910, p. 343]." States of high drive create strong "inclinations" to action and to "subjectivity" in the determination of action. They reduce the driven individual's capacity for choice by reducing the differentiation he can display in action and by preempting his adaptive resources. Freedom from such states accordingly confers more than "the illusion that one can exercise personal choice," which Lefcourt (1966) finds associated with reduced stress. It confers the possibility of will control and of self-actualization.

The Minnesota semistarvation experiment clearly demonstrates the reality of *self-actualization,* as construed by Goldstein and by Maslow. Presumably some sort of (abstract) personal ideals were involved in producing the remarkable demonstration of self-control achieved by 32 of the original 36 volunteers for that study. Yet the same experiment demonstrated the operation of pressures that operate against self-actualization. These and related facts are generally consistent with Maslow's claim that satisfaction of elementary personal needs, that is efficacy, is essential to its attainment. A self-actualizing individual personifies freedom of choice, the efficacy component of free will. Evidence for this basic freedom, from research into self-actualizing endeavors, is the next topic for consideration.

SUMMARY

Selected human adults have demonstrated the ability to deprive themselves voluntarily of half their normal intake of food for 6 months. Although they displayed remarkable "strength of will" in doing so, their hunger nevertheless produced its theoretically recognized effects on other aspects of their behavior.

Hunger is one of a variety of need states that arouse animals and normally stimulate need-related activities, while inhibiting others. Such "primary drive" states express a physiological imperative that threats to life be removed. They restrict freedom of choice.

"Self-actualization" was postulated by Goldstein as the ultimate expression of a free will, the result of a person's having voluntarily influenced the course of his own life. The suggestion that satisfaction of basic biological needs is necessary to self-actualization is due to Abraham Maslow. Although the human semistarvation experiment demonstrated remarkably prolonged courses of intentional action, it also showed that hunger inhibits some self-actualizing activities and reduces "self-control."

The supposition that stimulus domination of behavior is promoted by rewarding an individual with need-reducing supplies is fallacious. It is elevated drive, not drive reduction, that reduces freedom of choice. It does so by reducing the number of discriminations a person makes in dealing with his environment, and the number he can deal with at one time. Accordingly it impels simplified, habitual actions that are often inappropriate to environmental circumstances, and it therefore reduces the "objectivity" of action. These generalizations also support the assumption of the implicit theory of responsibility—that freedom of choice is reduced by coercive environmental conditions.

A type of habit is involved in the induction of secondary drive states, some of which have been described as anxiety. People who display more symptoms of anxiety behave like people under high drive. Their freedom of choice is correspondingly limited, and their behavior is correspondingly simplified, dedifferentiated, and liable to government by habit.

States of induced drive are not so readily relieved as are biological needs. Their existence involves the anticipation of primary need states that do not exist, derived from prior experiences in which those states developed despite the individual's actions. They can be treated by creating resistance to their induction. This technique is slow, except in the presence of another affective state incompatible with the unwanted secondary drive. Assertive, affectional, and consummatory activities thus serve to inhibit anxiety and to increase resistance to anxiety-inducing stimuli. They promote "efficacy," both directly and indirectly.

Involving anticipation of unsatisfied needs and being reducible by pursuit or enjoyment of other rewards, anxiety has been conceived as a state of undirected energy arousal associated with perception of helplessness. The ineffectuality it promotes tends to perpetuate this state.

Both the anxiety and the deprivation forms of drive theory focus on the energy arousal and helplessness that develop in an individual who lacks the means to reduce some undesirable condition or need. "Efficacy" is the positive characteristic that contrasts with and opposes the negative states that have been called "drive." This concept focuses upon the confidence and freedom of choice that arise with past, present, and anticipated satisfaction of personal needs.

Imagination and Venturing

As conceived by Goldstein, the "capacity for freedom" of self-actualizing persons is the "capacity to deal with . . . the possible" or the imaginary. Brain damage reduces it. So do need states that create high drive, according to theory and evidence just reviewed. Not only do driven individuals act less well differentiated but they become preoccupied with current conditions of pressing importance. Satisfaction of their needs releases preempted resources. Need satisfaction seems also to permit development of the intelligence or capacity component of the "attitude toward the possible" and of proactive information processing.

The concept of "efficacy" can be understood as a dispositional or environment-interpreting component in free will and responsibility. For instance, as shown in Figure 2.2, people who are characterized by *efficacy* tend to be "imaginative." This would be appropriate to both the proactive strategy of information processing and the similar "attitude toward the possible." They also tend to be venturesome, "will controlled," and relatively free of perceived threat. The purpose of the present chapter is to review additional evidence on the dispositional component of free will discovered through research into imaginative and venturing behavior.

Studies of the disposition to proactive information processing could begin in various ways. Instead of asking people whether they are responsible for their actions and looking for associated personality characteristics, an investigator might seek out and examine people who differ in initiative or enterprise. Or he might try to discover how people imaginatively interpret standard person–environment situations: What degree of freedom of action they attribute to persons, and what degree of mutability they attribute to situations. One important line of research has followed both of the latter approaches.

Consider the four brief stories that follow. Each of them was written within 4 minutes after their authors had looked for 20 seconds at a picture of four men sitting and lounging informally in a furnished room. The writers had been asked to tell (a) what is happening in the picture; (b) what led up to it; (c) what the characters are thinking and feeling; and (d) what they will do. Since the picture did not provide this information, it had to come by interpretation. All of the stories are, in this sense, fantasies. The meanings the authors ascribe to the picture are imaginary, or what Goldstein called "propositional" in the sense of "This is the sort of story the picture could illustrate." Presumably the stories indicate something about the interpretive aspects of their author's minds. Writers of stories like B have been found to display more initiative and enterprise and greater efforts to control their environments than those of stories like A.

A

Here is an informal discussion between 4 teachers about some modern day topic. Something like politics or something to that effect.

One of the four men said something which started the discussion. All four men had something to say on the subject so it developed into a full discussion about topic.

Each man is thinking something different, but some of their ideas are similar. They want to discuss the subject fully, but no swaying of their opinions is wanted.

Nothing will happen except they will have a good discussion and it will end for some other time.

B

People look like business men. One has stumbled on an idea and is telling the rest about it. They seem enthused.

These four men have worked together, and had been searching for a particular idea. Their success may depend on outcome.

The fellow is trying to convince the others about it. He wants them to invest their money in it. He has to capture their enthusiasm.

He probably will succeed. The others seem eager enough, and want something good.

C

These men are business associates who are planning a hunting trip. They are discussing the time of departure. They will go north to hunt birds.

They have met and become friends by working together as executives for a large industrial firm. This association forms their only friendships.

They are thinking how they will enjoy the trip, but they are also (some of them) somewhat concerned if they can get away because of business conflicts.

They will go on the trip. One or at most two won't make it because of business responsibilities.

D

A group of men who have known each other for a long time are discussing politics.

They have known each other for a long time and feel free to express their opinions.

Three men are thinking about the views of the fourth man. They want to decide how they should vote or convince others to vote the same as they will.

They will finish the discussion and no one may change his opinion.

[Smith & Feld, 1958, pp. 787 and 794]

Stories can be analyzed both for content and for style, and both kinds of analyses are valuable. The important research to be considered first has relied upon content analysis alone. This is the work of David McClelland and John Atkinson and their many associates and colleagues (e.g., McClelland, Atkinson, Clark, & Lowell, 1953; Atkinson, 1958; McClelland, 1961; McClelland & Winter, 1969). McClelland and Atkinson attend to two aspects of the content of a story: What kind of action is imagined and what course it takes.

FANTASIES OF PROACTIVITY

The action a character takes or contemplates taking in an interpretive story has some stipulated beginning or ending that may indicate a need or a goal. Following Freud's assumption about the primary process in mental events, that a felt need immediately gives rise to an image of a need-fulfilling object or action (Freud, 1938), needs and goals are supposed to represent the same underlying concern. The first decision required in the McClelland–Atkinson method of analysis is accordingly whether a story reveals such signs of a particular concern, for example, for food, for escape from fear, for independent achievement, for affiliation, or for power. If it does, it is said to show that sort of goal "imagery." The pertinent need or goal is, of course, attributable to the author whose mind developed the interpretation of the picture. Its presence therefore earns a score of one, as a partial measure of that need. Thus Story B displays both "achievement" and "power" imagery, but Story A contains no evidence of any such concerns.

A goal is the object of an intention. According to Roget's classification of the terms *goal* and *intention,* this first decision reflects whether or not the story attributes the *conceptual* aspect of *prospective volition* to one of its characters (Roget, 1939).

The course of action a person imagines in a depicted situation is also examined in the McClelland–Atkinson analysis. Is the inferred need explicitly mentioned in the story? Does it lead to action *intended* to reduce it? Are attainment and (or) failure to attain the goal explicitly *anticipated?* Are attendant feelings of satisfaction and (or) disappointment similarly *imagined?* Is there reference to conditions in self and (or) world that might *possibly* prevent goal attainment? to encouragement from others that might *possibly* promote it? Is an account of *purposive action* the central theme of the story?

These potential features of an interpretation refer to aspects of what McClelland has called "the adjustive behavioral sequence," in the belief they describe kinds of events that characterize most purposive actions (see McClelland, Atkinson, Clark, & Lowell, 1953). According to Roget, they all refer either to *individual volition* or to *prospective affections.* The number that occur in different

interpretive fantasies is the greatest source of differences in scores among stories
that suggest a given "need." It is the greatest source of variation in measures of
that "need." References to "individual volition" and "prospective affections" are exemplified in Story B, which has four (plus one, because it has two
basic "images"), and Stories C and D which have three each. Story A has none.
While the others display imagination of intentional action in several ways, A has
disavowed any goal, and the action it depicts is reactive on all sides.

It is important to note that, to earn the highest possible score for a given need,
a story must refer not only to hope of need reduction and to conditions that might
promote it, but also to conditions that might prove frustrating and to the unpleasant reactions they could cause in one. The authors of such stories presumably
need a realistic or "balanced" appreciation of the possible outcomes of purposive actions. They must display what Freud referred to as "secondary process"
thinking, which differs from the primary in being more objective.

In the McClelland–Atkinson system, a story that contains many references to
different aspects of prospective volition earns a high score. It is then interpreted
as evidence of a strong motive on the part of its author. Such scores have been
shown to rise as need presumably rose under conditions that promote hunger
(Atkinson & McClelland, 1958), fear (Walker & Atkinson, 1958), or concern for
independent achievement (McClelland, Clark, Roby, & Atkinson, 1958), for
power over others (Veroff, 1958), or for social affiliation (Shipley & Veroff,
1958; Atkinson, Heyns, & Veroff, 1958). Clearly, the attribution of particular
kinds of intention to fictional characters is promoted by increases in associated
needs on the part of the interpreters. However, it is not clear that the scores are
simply measures of those needs, as McClelland and Atkinson imply.

Similarities among Various "Need" Scores

In the achievement, power, and affiliation cases at least, the McClelland–
Atkinson scores for different "needs" have two features in common. The first is
that, beyond the unit accorded for relevant imaginary intention, each is a strict
function of the number of different references it contains to selected aspects of
prospective thinking ("volition" or "affection").

The second similarity between stories that earn high scores for different
"needs" is that, in all cases, what is imagined as the goal "image" is an
approximate match between an altered form of present conditions and an imaginary version of a "perfect type" of similar situation (Heckhausen, 1967), that is,
an *ideal*. Manipulations to arouse different "needs" presumably activate these
different ideals. The original terminology unfortunately obscures the bases for
this assertion. For instance, although McClelland and associates wrote of
achievement imagery as evidence of concern about "competition with some

standard of excellence [McClelland, Atkinson, Clark, & Lowell, 1958, p. 181]," the details of their scoring manual show that "competition" includes matching performance to some high standard. In the power case, the relevant ideal is control of the means of influencing a person; for affiliation, it is friendship.

Stories with high scores on "needs" for achievement, power, and affiliation, respectively, resemble one another in depicting imaginary instances of prospective volition under the influence of an ideal. They differ in the ideals concerned: proficiency, power, and affiliation. However, low scores can be due either to the absence of references to the sort of goal a picture normally suggests or to impoverished representation of the details of "the adjustive behavioral sequence."

Differences between High- and Low-Scoring Stories

The characters of high-scoring stories show more initiative than those of low-scoring stories. They more often imagine satisfactory forms of the situations in which they find themselves and more often set about creating them. They more often encounter difficulties and anticipate failure and frustration, as well as success and satisfaction. They more often process information proactively. By contrast, the characters in low-scoring stories more often accept their situations, sometimes even without thought of more suitable alternatives. Although they may sometimes wish circumstances to be different, they seldom form or enact an intent to alter them. Nor do they often explicitly anticipate either the difficulties or the support they might encounter if they did so, nor the success or failure they might achieve. They do not think *proactively;* they *react,* apparently as pawns of circumstances. The activities of the two sorts of fictitious characters differ, thus, in acceptance of the given and in attitude toward the possible. Moreover, since one sort sometimes succeeds and the other never can, they differ in that aspect of *efficacy.* And so, it seems, do their authors.

In each of the cases of achievement, power, and affiliation, the authors of high-scoring stories are evidently more disposed to take appropriate constructive action and more likely to attain appropriate results than are the authors of low-scoring stories. Presumably their needs are less often frustrated. In the achievement case, at least, they also produce fewer "anxiety" responses on questionnaires (Raphelson, 1958; Heckhausen, 1968).[1] Theoretically they differ in "efficacy" from those who produce low-scoring fantasies.

[1] Heckhausen (1968) also cites evidence that people with high fantasy achievement scores produce superior performances on learning tasks, notably with mazes (p. 135), are better able to handle "foreseeable calculable risks in driving which might lead to traffic offenses and accidents" (p. 43; see also p. 59), and are more highly "differentiated" on Witkin's measures (p. 136).

PROACTIVE MINDS

Writers of stories ought to behave like their fictional characters in other ways as well. Their conceptions of what should be, and their knowledge of the processes and conditions necessary for bringing it about, are available for use in both fantasy and fact. So, the differences in information-processing strategy they attribute to their imaginary characters ought to appear in differences in their own actions. Two quite different sorts of additional evidence support this interpretation of the facts, at least for the case of men who differ in fantasy achievement scores.

The proactive strategy of information processing depends upon recognition of sequences in time. So, individuals who vary in readiness to employ it in their daily lives ought to vary in the way they experience time. In fact, studies of preferences in poetic metaphors for time show this to be true, both among American and among German subjects. In those studies, large numbers of judgments were collected and analyzed with objective mathematical techniques. According to a summary statement by Heckhausen, who had repeated in Germany the original investigations of Knapp and Garbutt (1965), the results showed that "Highly motivated [persons] find their time experience best expressed in images indicating fast directed movement, such as a space ship in flight, whereas less motivated [persons] express it in static images, such as 'a quiet motionless ocean' [Heckhausen, 1967, p. 44]." In addition, Green and Knapp (1959) reported that the present seemed to extend further into the past and the future for the authors of high-scoring than for the authors of low-scoring stories. Time appears remarkable to the former for its relation to ongoing, directional activity; and to them the present appears appropriately protracted.

The second notable set of facts concerns time differences in the mobilization of energy resources. Raphelson (1958) monitored the ease with which electricity flows over the skin of the hands—the palmar skin conductance (PSC)—of 25 young men during a task alleged to be like a test used by the air force to measure intellectual and motor abilities. The PSC is known to be highly sensitive to variations in energy arousal due to emotion or effort. The records were divided into four phases. During the first, the men had not yet been instructed about the alleged test and merely manipulated a lever. The next phase occupied the first 2 minutes after they had been given their instructions. During the third phase, the men worked (for 10 minutes) at the frustrating task of trying to keep an erratically moving spot on a target. And, in the final phase, they were fiddling aimlessly with the lever again while waiting to be dismissed. Theoretically, variations in PSC level among these four periods could reveal when maximal energy mobilization had occurred.

Raphelson's subjects differed in fantasy achievement scores and in anxiety, measured by questionnaire. The majority (16) of them had scored high on one of these measures and low on the other or vice versa. That is, they differed in *efficacy*.

The more efficacious men produced higher PSC levels in the preinstructional period. Average levels of both groups then rose after they were told what to do. During the "test" period, however, the average PSC of the high-efficacy men *fell* below its prior level, while that of the low-efficacy men continued to *rise* to a new high. Finally, after the "test," the PSC of both groups fell to the lowest observed levels. The same differences in change were also found between groups selected solely for high and low fantasy achievement scores. The latter results are depicted in Figure 5.1.

As Figure 5.1 shows, the peak metabolic activity of men with high fantasy achievement scores (and also of efficacious men) had been anticipatory or prospective, that is, *proactive*. The peak for men who had scored low in fantasy achievement (or efficacy) had been relatively *reactive*. Alternatively, one might say, as Raphelson did, that the changes in PSC signified motivation in the former and emotion, possibly due to frustration, in the latter.

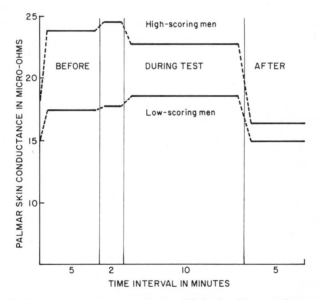

Figure 5.1. The time course of energy arousal by men differing in achievement fantasy. The vertical divisions mark different periods of observation: 5 minutes at the apparatus before task instructions, 2 minutes after, 10 minutes during task performance, and 5 minutes after. The solid lines are observed averages; the broken lines are interpolated. Similar but more divergent results were obtained from samples differing in efficacy, that is, in both achievement and anxiety scores. [Adapted from A. C. Raphelson, The relationships among imaginative, direct verbal, and physiological measures of anxiety in an achievement situation. *Journal of Abnormal and Social Psychology*, 1957, *54*, 13–18. Copyright 1957 by the American Psychological Association. Reprinted by permission.].

Raphelson's work, along with that of Knapp and associates and of Heckhausen, supports the interpretation that the authors of high-scoring achievement
fantasies characteristically do employ the *proactive* strategy of information processing that they describe in their interpretive fantasies. Those who write low-
scoring interpretations of pictures that suggest achievement themes seem by
contrast to deal *reactively* with events in their environments and may be liable to
frustrative emotion as well. Presumably both sorts of stories reveal their authors'
conceptions of what they believe to be normal information transfer relations
between person and environment.

It has already been demonstrated (de Charms *et al.*, 1965) that the persons who
most often judge story characters to be free and responsible are the same persons
who report themselves to be more responsible on Rotter's questionnaire. An
earlier series of investigations had shown a comparable relation between personal
attitudes and fantasy productions. It focused on prejudiced persons, who differed
from unprejudiced individuals in claiming that the world is managed by coercion
and obedience. Their interpretive stories more often described imaginary characters as motivated by the demands and regulations of authority, and afflicted by
unpredictable misfortune (Aron, 1950). The products of human imagination
seem to reflect their authors' views of normal person–environment relations.
Presumably they reveal, in the process, something of the content of minds that
attain or do not attain freedom of will.

THINKING UNDER THREAT

Effects of Arousal on Achievement Fantasies

One aspect of the interpretation test situation that clearly affects the proactive
content of imagination has been construed as mediated by energy arousal. Fisch
and Heckhausen (Heckhausen, 1968) obtained interpretive stories from German
students who were anticipating a comprehensive examination that would influence their life careers. One group was tested 1 year before its examination,
another 3 weeks before, and the third on examination day. The four stimulus
pictures depicted situations that resembled examination settings to varying degrees. The total imaginary proactivity by story characters was higher on examination day than on the earlier days. So was physiological arousal in their authors,
measured by the galvanic skin response (GSR), which is like the PSC of Raphelson's study (although normally less influenced by muscular activity). But the
story content was paradoxically influenced by the cues of the four pictures.

A year before examination, the number of scorable references to achievement
increased steadily and remarkably as a function of the similarity of the picture to
the examination setting. The GSR measures confirmed this evidence of the
arousal potential of the pictures. On examination day, however, and possibly 3

weeks earlier, interpretations of the most examination-like picture contained *fewer* references to the scorable features of imaginary intentional action than those written about the moderately suggestive picture. This result applied equally to contents suggesting hope of success and to those suggesting fear of failure (although, in both tests—examination day and 3 weeks prior to it—contents suggesting hope of success outnumbered those suggesting fear of failure). Up to a point, the more closely a depicted situation resembled a real one of importance to its interpreter, the more imaginary references to different aspects of intentional behavior did it elicit. Beyond that point, such references declined, although physiological activation continued to rise. What was thus observed, accordingly, was an optimum level of arousal for the production of achievement fantasies (or an optimum degree of cue similarity). This fact has considerable theoretical importance.

Effects of Arousal on Perceptual Proficiency

Earlier indications of the relation Fisch and Heckhausen discovered had been interpreted as indicating the elimination from imagination of threatening material, which Freud called repression (Clark, Teevan, & Ricciuti, 1958; see also Atkinson, 1958, pp. 14, 117–125, 130–131, 572–585, and 611–615). Fear of failure was believed to inhibit thoughts about the risk of failure, and so to reduce scores.[2] It may be contrary to this hypothesis that both hopeful and fearful images occurred less frequently in examination day stories about the most examination-like pictures. The principal alternative hypothesis postulates a nonselective reduction of mental content under supraoptimal arousal, due to reduction of the channel capacity of the brain (Easterbrook, 1959). This hypothesis suggests that the arousal factor may be one cause of the negative relation between anxiety and fantasy achievement scores and of that between anxiety and perceived internal control. On certain assumptions, it also implies an optimal level of arousal for maximal imaginary efficacy.

Two experiments that seemed at first to support the repression hypothesis were reported by Moulton, Raphelson, Kristofferson, & Atkinson (1958). Fantasy achievement scores were calculated for stories told about achievement pictures by two groups of young men, without special arousing instructions. Measures were then taken of the minimum time that various words had to be shown before being recognized (recognition duration thresholds). This was done under either a neutral condition, which involved no special treatment, or an "aroused" condition. Arousal was produced by two methods; first, by instructing the men that they would be given a test that was important to the research and that measured ability to work hard and efficiently; second, by setting them to work at solving

[2]Both fear of failure (i.e., status concern or anxiety) and repression figured prominently in the theoretical explanation of prejudice offered by the authors of *The Authoritarian Personality* (Adorno, Frenkel-Brunswick, Levinson, & Sanford, 1950).

anagrams, for a time that was too brief to allow much progress, before taking the recognition threshold measures. Speed of recognition was then assessed for each of four failure words, four success words, and five neutral words. Some individuals were unable to recognize the neutral words, and these men were eliminated from the study.

Men with high fantasy motivation scores proved to be more proficient in recognizing both success and failure words, though only under the aroused conditions. The difference was particularly great for failure words. Moreover, men with low fantasy achievement scores were less proficient at recognizing failure words in the aroused than in the neutral condition. The evidence seemed complete and was interpreted as indicating a "perceptual defense" process in low-scoring men. That is, the arousing treatment was assumed to have stimulated fear of failure of such intensity as to cause them to avoid thoughts of it by avoiding recognition of failure-related words.

The repression interpretation of this evidence is not fully acceptable. The arousal manipulation had reduced the perceptual proficiency of both groups. This effect was not highly reliable, but it is quite impressive because two of every five subjects in the aroused condition had been rejected from the first experiment for failure to recognize the neutral words, whereas only one of every eight in the neutral condition had failed that way. Indeed, on certain assumptions, all of the reliable findings of this study can be attributed to impairment of proficiency by arousal. These assumptions are that (as some of the data show or suggest) the men with low fantasy achievement scores were perceptually less proficient and also more susceptible to loss of proficiency under the arousing treatment. However explained, the evidence of this study is consistent with that due to Fisch and Heckhausen. In perception, as in fantasy, information transfer is reduced when arousal becomes too great.

Effects of Arousal on Mental Rigidity

A third important experiment on arousal, performed by A. S. Luchins (1942), demonstrates the same process at work on a unique measure of mental freedom. Luchins presented people with a series of problems of the same general form. For example: Given three empty jars, one of which will hold exactly 3 ounces, one 21 ounces, and one 127 ounces, show how you can measure out exactly 100 ounces of water. The method is circuitous. One has to use all three jars, subtracting 21 ounces and then twice subtracting 3 ounces from the 127-ounce jar. After working a few problems like this, one is presented with, for instance, 15-, 39-, and 3-ounce jars and asked to measure 18 ounces. Some people proceed in the same complex way, not noticing that 15 and 3 give 18, although they would have done so easily if they had not already worked through the earlier problems of the series. Luchins called this phenomenon "rigidity" and the process by which it was reached "mechanization." It illustrates the effect of habit in narrowing attention to mental content, and it becomes more common when people are more highly aroused (Maltzman, Fox, & Morrisett, 1953; see also Easterbrook, 1959). Also, of course, it represents a lapse from proactive into reactive information processing.

The Luchins problems were given by R. W. Brown (1953) to men varying in fantasy achievement scores. He had also obtained their scores on a questionnaire that detects prejudiced, "authoritarian" personalities—those who tend to be aggressive toward and suspicious of others, and to be dogmatic and rigid. These scores were negatively related to fantasy achievement scores; that is, little intention fantasy was evident in stories by dogmatic persons.

Individuals with low fantasy achievement scores made more mechanical responses on the rigidity test than those with higher scores. They did so, however, only when under influence of the threatening treatment generally used to arouse achievement motivation. Under neutral conditions, such persons displayed no more rigidity than the contrasting subjects. Here again, arousal caused a loss of information transfer in subjects who are described as relatively low in achievement motivation. This loss showed itself, as comparable losses on visible maze tests do, as a lapse into the reactive strategy of information processing, a surrender of the government of action to the dictates of routine.

Motivation and Imagination

The level of emotional or motivational arousal a situation elicits seems to influence the number of different aspects of prospective volition that are evident in interpretations of still pictures. The number seems to reach its maximum at some moderate level of arousal. Similar phenomena have been observed with other measures of effectiveness. An optimum level of energy arousal is a condition of maximal performance of many tasks, apparently including interpretive fantasy tests.

Fears and anxieties do of course inhibit imaginative activities, apparently excepting those involved in the emotional reaction. This is evident, for example, in facility at the imaginative elaboration of "suggestions" given by a "hypnotist." According to Barber (1970), people who most readily "think with and vividly imagine the suggested effects" are relatively free of anxieties. Moreover some of the customary procedures of hypnotists seem to operate on "willingness" to imagine the suggested effects by creating "positive motivations" and reducing fears, apprehensions, or anxiety, as relaxation does for example (Barber & de Moor, 1972). Creative people have also been characterized as unafraid to elaborate imaginatively upon unusual thoughts of their own, and their creativity has been ascribed in part to this facility (Barron, 1966). In fact, such persons are also generally reported to be free of anxieties, besides being highly intelligent.

Incidentally, two quite different books (Barron, 1963; Kubie, 1961) have developed the theme, to be considered in a later chapter, that creativity and neurosis are opposed to one another (and both treat creativity as promoting mental and behavioral freedom).

All of these facts and considerations mean that what is measured by the McClelland–Atkinson system for scoring interpretive fantasies is not simple motivational arousal or need, but something more complex. To make high scores, one must be adequately aroused—neither too complacent nor too concerned or anxious—and one must have an ingrained, intimate knowledge of the kinds of thought that are involved in formulating and executing intentions.

How is this sort of intimate knowledge developed? Some detailed discussions on this topic will be undertaken in later chapters, but general answers to it are not hard to find. To develop intimate knowledge of the kinds of thought involved in formulating and executing intentions, one needs relevant experience. This simple statement has many implications. Not only must a person recognize the possibility of bringing about desirable changes in the world; he must have the power to do so. Not only must he have relevant knowledge and intelligence; he must also have social permission, and, in many cases, tools and other material means. Two lines of research have provided information to illuminate some of these points: One concerns the development of expectancies of internal control; the other is a long and adventurous series of investigations into achievement motivation.

EXPECTANCY AND EFFICACY

One group of studies concerning familiarity with purposive enterprises is due to Julian Rotter and associates (Rotter, Chance, & Phares, 1972). These investigators were interested in the determinants of generalized expectancies about the adjustability of the world to a person's needs. Expectations are extensions of thought to the future, that is, prospective thoughts, or "images"; expectancy is a *state* of expectation—specific when referred to a given situation and generalized when referred to a variety of situations. Rotter and associates have sometimes discussed such anticipatory states in terms of a perceived internal or external locus of control over rewarding or punishing events ("reinforcements"). They commonly assess generalized expectancies with the questionnaire that was previously described as appraising responsibility. But these beliefs are also evident in the contents of imagination.

A strong generalized expectancy of *external* control appears in interpretive fantasies, according to Dies, as "the relative absence of self-initiated, responsible action or personal mastery" and in portrayal of the central character as "almost powerless in the face of favorable and/or unfavorable events or as unable to overcome life's dilemmas [1968, p. 488]." It is evident in imagining persons who are pawns of circumstance. By contrast, a strong belief in *internal* control is evident when "central figures are depicted as highly competent and in control, or at least responsible for, whatever happens to them [1968, p. 488]." These, of course, are, respectively, the reactive and proactive relations between persons and situations that were also evident in the low- and high-scoring stories of the McClelland–Atkinson system. The scores Dies obtained from such story content agreed with questionnaire scores for 80% of the individuals he tested.

People who differ in generalized expectancies about locus of control differ also in the imagined efficacy of their fictitious characters. And according to studies reviewed by Rotter (1966) and by Joe (1971) they also differ in the prospective volition their own activities reflect in various situations. "Internals" behave like people with high fantasy scores in the McClelland–Atkinson system. They, more often than "externals," demonstrate initiative toward control of their environments, both directly and in seeking information for the purpose. In academic situations, when selected with an appropriately worded questionnaire (Crandall, Katkovsky, & Crandall, 1965), "internals" spend more time in intellectual activities, are more interested in academic pursuits, and do better on their tests. In other situations they show comparably more foresight, and some evidence indicates that they are more able to control their impulses—for instance in breaking smoking habits and in practicing birth control. These results are supported by personality questionnaire findings as well, a fact that lends credence to some other evidence arrived at by such methods alone.

Personality tests show "internals" to be less anxious, particularly about failure, and less disabled by anxiety than "externals." They also appear more assertive, better able to produce constructive reactions to frustration, less dogmatic, and less aggressive toward and less suspicious of others. Incidentally, they appear to be more interested in social approval as well. Such statements seem to refer to the *efficacy* dimension in Figure 2.2, and some of them confirm findings reported there. They are, of course, consistent with the theoretical propositions in Chapter 4 about anxiety as opposed to efficacy.

The personality differences between "internals" and "externals" can be regarded as evidence, respectively, of proactive and reactive relations between them and their environments.

In general form, Rotter's hypothetical explanation of the generalized expectancy of internal control is consistent with the notion that it develops from experiences of the kind that also produce efficacy. More specifically, it is supposed to develop from experience in a considerable variety of situations where an individual saw his rewards and punishments as contingent upon his actions. The contrasting belief in external control is supposed to arise from experience in environments where such events were understood to have occurred erratically, as a result of chance or the arbitrary decisions of powerful others. Moreover, these generalized expectancies hypothetically determine perceptions of new situations and, accordingly, what one learns to do in those and later circumstances. Of course, perceptions of contingency between action and consequence are greatly influenced by the reality of such contingency.

Rotter's theory suggests causal sequences that may readily become circular. For instance, external control may be inferred if one's actions in past environments were apparently ineffective in producing reward—due either to the nature of the environment, as Rotter suggests, or to faulty perception, or to inappropriate kinds of action. Subsequent action, shaped reactively as if important events were unresponsive to it, could then become skillful and achieve efficacy only by chance. Presumably the generalized expectancy of external control would then be strengthened, and frustration, apprehension, and low confidence would also develop.

This latter formulation is a hypothesis that Rotter might not endorse.[3] It makes the degree of a person's responsibility and his freedom of will a consequence of the correspondence between his actions and those that would in fact produce preferred outcomes. It makes freedom a function of efficacy, which may be regarded as proportional to the degree of such correspondence in all situations recently encountered. Circumstances in which rewards were distributed according to irrelevant personal characteristics, like beauty or family name, rather than responding to particular types of action, would of course produce perceptions of external control in those who lacked the necessary attributes.

DETERMINANTS OF PROSPECTIVE THOUGHT

Rotter's hypothesis emphasizes the structure and perception of environments as major determinants of generalized expectancies of control. Different perceptions of the action–reinforcement relationship certainly produced appropriate changes in the behavior of the people who took part in relevant experiments,

---

[3]Rotter (1966) stressed the perception of contingency between actions and consequences, treating skill only as a consequence, not as a determinant, of the perceived contingency. And he claimed that locus of control questionnaire scores are independent of intelligence. However, Rotter, Chance, and Phares (1972), commenting on the effect of symbolic rewards and punishments on learning in retardates, mention "the ability to acquire appropriate behaviors [and] faulty interpretations [p. 35]." Also, in the same volume (pp. 500–509), Cromwell discusses the utility of some theoretical assumptions to account for (a) the influence of developmental level on the relation between reinforcement and behavior change; and (b) a significant correlation between mental age and perceived locus of control.

even when the actual relationship was held constant. The most convincing of the relevant experiments used what psychologists call "partial reinforcement." That is, correct actions were rewarded and incorrect actions punished only some of the time, perhaps once in every two trials on the average. Real life experiences are probably like that. These experiments also used tasks at which a person could not readily recognize his proficiency, except through the rewards or punishments he received. This feature is built into experiments on learning by adults, in an attempt to simulate the learning conditions of naive persons. It is a necessary condition for a demonstration with human adults of the effects of rewards and punishments that are easily shown with young children and lower animals.

In such situations, then, individuals who had been led to believe their rewards and punishments were dependent upon skill behaved quite differently from those who had been led to believe them due to chance. In bets on the next trial, they expressed greater gains of confidence (anticipation of proficiency) after a success marked by reward, and greater losses of confidence after a failure. Later, when all rewards were cut off, they quit appropriately sooner than those who understood reinforcements to be under chance control. One important influence on perception of contingency between action and consequence, in the absence of special instructions on the topic, was the percentage of rewards received in a series of trials. If it was either notably higher or lower than chance, subjects behaved as they had when told that reinforcements depended on skill. It has already been noted that success, as manifest in frequent reward, induces perceptions of responsibility or internal control (see p. 38). Another important factor was whether the sequence of rewards appeared to have a pattern. A third, of course, was generalized expectancy, assessed by questionnaire. All of these findings are consistent with Rotter's hypothesis.

It is well established that certain aspects of picture interpretation influence the content of imagination. Some pictures evoke particular sorts of imagery from most persons (Haber & Alpert, 1958; Birney, 1958). Recent experience of failure, together with an introduction suggesting that the stories to be written could reveal desirable attributes in the author, increases the imagination of prospective volition by figures in the pictures (Heckhausen, 1967). There is a tendency, thus, for particular situations and contexts to create imaginary references to details of relevant purposive action. However, with adults there is no clear evidence—such as that for perceived locus of control—that situational characteristics directly influence the sort of proactivity depicted in the content of interpretive fantasies. Some indications can be found in studies, to be reviewed in a later chapter, concerning the effect of parental behavior on fantasy achievement scores by boys. Although they seem to operate principally over the long term to shape a child's disposition, parental actions that promote a boy's independent success at a task are associated with his later producing more imaginary references to prospective volition.

KNOWLEDGE OF PURPOSIVE TALES

Further theory and evidence about the determinants of both fantasy achievement scores and initiative has been produced by McClelland's cross-cultural research (McClelland, 1961; McClelland & Winter, 1969). In the initial study of that series (McClelland & Freedman, 1952), carefully selected samples of folktales from a small number of American Indian cultures were scored for fantasy achievement. These scores were found to be associated with differences in child training among those cultures. A later study used improved methods on 43 preliterate cultures and found high fantasy achievement scores were more frequent in cultures in which individual entrepreneurs were more important and agricultural and religious occupations were less important (McClelland, 1961). Some related theory and information is reviewed in Chapter 10.

An even more ambitious study, on 40 literate cultures, scored samples of the stories in elementary school reading texts and compared differences in these scores with differences in other characteristics of those cultures (McClelland, 1961). Countries with dictatorial governments had texts with high scores for power imagery and low scores for affiliation imagery. Larger affiliation fantasy scores were associated with higher birthrates and by inference with child care, too. And differences in fantasy achievement scores were associated with differences in an index of relative economic growth in subsequent years. Not only was this so, but the children's stories from the economies that grew at a faster rate than their capital assets could be expected to promote differed from those that grew more slowly. They more often described intentional or "instrumental" activities and contained more references to obstacles in self and world. Thus the stories described more purposive action and were more objective or reality oriented. McClelland called them "'means' oriented rather than 'goal' oriented."

Finally, similar appraisals of the relation between economic activity and the achievement content of literature were made for England at 50-year intervals, from 1500 to 1900, and for the United States at 20-year intervals, from 1800 to 1950. In both cases, again, changes in economic activity were positively and closely associated with variations in the achievement scores of the literature in preceding periods.

McClelland took all this evidence as showing a causal relation in which the cause was displayed in the achievement scores of the stories. He suggested that story content revealed the tastes and thought processes of the culture. Another possible interpretation is that stories which appeal to their readers might serve as models for courses of action (Bandura & Walters, 1963) and shape thought processes. Perhaps for this reason, when McClelland later set out to teach people to think and act as achieving persons do, he chose instruction in the writing of achievement stories as one means of doing so.

TRAINING IN PURPOSIVE BEHAVIOR

Some recent research by McClelland and associates has concerned the economic effects of teaching achievement thinking to aspiring businessmen in Mexico, Spain, the United States, and India; it is reported by McClelland and Winter (1969). The students in both the experimental classes and the control groups had volunteered for the training. So hope of economic self-improvement did not initially differentiate the trainees from the comparison groups. McClelland construed the objectives of training as twofold: the setting up in the students' minds of appropriate "affectively toned associative networks" (McClelland, 1965) and increasing their salience relative to other associative clusters.

The instructional program used a many-pronged approach to these ends, with specific manipulations of four types. The first of these was theoretically the most important to the plan, though not demonstrably most important in effect. It involved teaching the trainees by demonstration and exercises both how to write stories that earn high scores for achievement motivation and how to act in choice situations like men who write such stories. Second, each trainee was led to reconsider in detail the relation of his values and goals to the achieving style of life. Third, he was required to set himself specific goals, with detailed work plans, and to keep a record of his progress. Finally, he was made part of a group of like-minded persons. In the longer courses, a total of about 100 hours' work over a period of 10 days was devoted to instruction and exercises.

Not surprisingly, this training regime produced remarkable increases in the achievement imagery of interpretive stories written by trainees. It also increased economic enterprise, as reflected in working hours and new businesses started. However, it had the latter effect only on men who controlled businesses or family decisions, not on the other trainees. The increase was evident by comparison with both their own prior performances and the subsequent performances of untrained (control) volunteers in similar circumstances. For a particular class of person, thus, instruction in thinking and acting in a classroom setting as do the authors of stories that score high in achievement motivation evidently facilitated purposive enterprise.

Clearly, there is some causal relation between knowledge of the general plot of high-scoring achievement fantasies on the one hand and economic enterprise on the other. Evidently such knowledge is a necessary condition for such enterprise. But it is clearly not a sufficient one.

Additional Qualifications for Enterprise

The report provides two clues to the missing condition(s). As family decision makers, the trainees who were activated to new enterprise presumably had social support, rather than social resistance, in translating fantasy intentions into action. Moreover, they were presumably efficacious persons because they already had command of some necessary resources. Their control of business or family decisions no doubt reflected, and increased, their freedom of action. Had the training been restricted to people like them, as exposure to early English and American literature may have been restricted to people "of means," all of its recipients might have shown increased enterprise.

Trainees who changed their economic activity after the course differed in another way from those who did not. The interpretive stories they wrote showed a different style.

One aspect of style is obvious in the exemplary tales on page 74. The events of Story A are poorly analyzed: Someone said something on the topic—the word "something" actually occurs five times in it, never in the other three stories. This writer has avoided specification. He has also avoided describing how his characters resolve the situation. The author of Story C has left the situation unresolved, too, and his description of it is almost as global as that of Story A. The term "problem avoidance" was used by Pizer (1969) to describe this sort of style. Problem solving, by contrast, can be found in conditional clauses that attempt to clarify logical sequences in a story. Explanatory statements can be seen in all four of the stories. B uses the modern technique of short sentences, rather than conditional clauses, and sequential relations are not precise in either A or C. But Story A seems to stipulate only one sequential relation, B five, and C and D two each. The stories differ, then, in the frequency and precision of their analytic statements.

Pizer examined interpretive fantasies by changers and nonchangers among the McClelland–Winter trainees for differences in style. He found four further differences among stories—differences that he associated with differences in "problem solving" by their authors—and he used all five to form a new scoring system that served to differentiate them. The first of these was the use of specific descriptions of the depicted environment, rather than global allusions to "the world" or "society." This may be another sign of analytic precision. So may the second, the specification of goals in terms of doing rather than being. Relative precision of terminology constituted the third characteristic: When referring to graphic art, the phrase "to be an artist" commonly means "to paint," although it has other meanings as well; so the latter is a more precise statement. The last two differences seem at face value to be matters of content, rather than form. Changers tended (*a*) to ascribe resources such as competence and ability to the heroes of their stories, indicating realism or objectivity; and (*b*) to describe originating rather than compliant activities. These sorts of statements are associated with perceived internal control, as Dies showed. However, since all the stories Pizer analyzed had achievement imagery, such statements may also be regarded as explanations of the fantasized achievement and, therefore, as matters of form.

Although the usual scoring system does not seek them out, sequential analysis and explanation are usually found in association with high fantasy achievement scores. For instance, the numbers of sequence explanatory statements in Stories A, B, C, and D are perfectly concomitant with the highest fantasy scores for these stories (see p. 76). Their separate appearance in Pizer's research may be attributable to the special training in writing of achievement themes that had been given to all the authors, as reported by McClelland and Winter. That training had evidently failed to dispose the nonchangers toward the analytic and explanatory thoughts the changers displayed (presumably like the usual writers of high scoring stories).

Environmental Determinants of Enterprise

The McClelland–Winter course evidently did not provide all the training needed to make its students think as achieving persons think. However, that it gave relevant experience to some persons is a major achievement. The attempt, after all, was to alter in 100 hours of experience some ways of behaving that had been shaped over thousands of days. The next task for social development research, therefore, is to discover how that brief experience should be supplemented so that it might activate all candidates. According to the two clues provided by the report, enquiries should now concentrate on the knowledge and dispositions associated with differences in precision of analytic thought and with being decision makers for businesses or families.

Leadership in business or family attests efficacy and assumption of responsibility. Presumably it also promotes generalized expectancies of internal control. "Problem solving" as opposed to "problem avoidance" also attests efficacy and the assumption of personal control. According to Dies, story features associated with strong belief in internal control are presented with "greater clarity," whereas "few attempts to solve problems realistically are shown . . . in stories associated with a strong belief in external control [Dies, 1968, p. 488]." The McClelland–Winter trainees who displayed increased enterprise after the course seem to have stood relatively high in freedom and its efficacy component to begin with. On both counts, too, they may well have placed higher than nonchangers on the educated intelligence dimension. This is often the case with leaders (Mann, 1959). It is implied by the relative precision of changers in causal analysis and explanation (which Bernstein regards as a consequence of being reared to use the elaborated code—see pp. 45–47, this volume). Apparently, the task of activating people like the nonchangers, of making them resemble the changers, will involve altering some quite enduring attributes and conditions that affect intelligence and efficacy. Among these may be relationships, dispositions, and resources acquired over years of social experience. Some evidence on how such factors can influence freedom of will must now be considered.

SUMMARY

Initiative can be predicted from products of imagination identified by David McClelland, John Atkinson, and their colleagues in developing fantasy measures of motivation. Following motivating manipulations, interpretive stories are written about stimulus pictures. Motivation appears in fantasy representations of heroes in pursuit of pertinent goals. Given this basic score, the probability of initiative increases with every imaginary reference to an additional one of the various conceptual aspects of prospective volition that were identified in that research—anticipation of success and/or failure, of satisfaction and/or disappointment, of possible blocks in self or world, and of possible support from others.

The characters of stories that score high on fantasy measures of motivation imagine better conditions, appropriate methods of producing them, and possible sources of interference or assistance in doing so. They often set out to achieve their imaginary goals, behaving proactively. By contrast, the characters of low-scoring stories react to events. In both cases, the authors of the interpretive stories act like the heroes of their imaginary tales. Those in the one group often develop intentions and attain what they will; the others, intending nothing, attain nothing independently.

People who more consistently report their fortunes as being under personal control write interpretive fantasies that differ in a similar way from those by fatalists. Their characters are competent, controlling, and responsible, rather than anxious, powerless pawns of circumstance. In this research, too, story authors tend to behave like the heroes of their fantasies. These different sorts of behavior seem to develop from differences in efficacy, due to experience of environments differing in responsiveness to individual actions.

Authors of high-scoring achievement fantasies differ from their low-scoring counterparts in additional ways. They seem to understand time in terms of movement, rather than rest, and the present as extending further into the past and the future. They are less anxious. They mobilize more of their energy resources in preparation for a task than in reaction to it.

There is evidence that a person's energy arousal may be too high for the production of high-scoring fantasies of (freely willed) intentional behavior. In addition, experiments have shown that authors of low-scoring stories are particularly susceptible to losses of proficiency in perceptual and in problem-solving tasks when thus aroused. Fantasy achievement scores do not measure simple motivational arousal or need.

Cultural and temporal fashions in fiction are associated with variations in economic enterprise. Presumably folktales transmit ways of thinking that are useful in formulating and executing intentional projects.

Training in this sort of thinking seems to promote self-controlled purposive enterprise by men of means in backward economies. However the fantasies of such persons displayed more analytic and explanatory differentiation than those by similarly treated men for whom that training was ineffective. In addition, their circumstances revealed a history of greater effectiveness and power.

III

INDIVIDUAL AUTONOMY
IN A SOCIAL CONTEXT

Obedience

The men whose economic activities were changed by McClelland's achievement training program had evidently been used to wielding power. Moreover their achievement fantasies revealed detailed knowledge, or analytic thought, about how successes were to be attained. Their heroes were represented as competent and as engaging in original, rather than compliant, activities. The contrasting group, whose economic activities did not subsequently change, had contrasting characteristics. They were accustomed to others having more power than themselves, and their fantasy characters tended to act conforming and compliant. Similar interpretive stories have been reported to be produced by men with generalized expectancies of external control. It appears, accordingly, that tendencies to compliant thinking and action inhibit the freedom of will that initiative and enterprise demonstrate. It is the object of this chapter to describe some evidence and theory on these tendencies.

APPEARANCES AS CRITERIA FOR ACTION

An experimental test of two types of conformity was introduced to psychology by Solomon Asch (1956). A number of people sitting together are requested to take turns making vocal reports or judgments about visible figures—for instance, to say which in a set of three lines on a wall display is the same length as a target line. The discriminations are easy; virtually no one makes a mistake when tested alone. For several trials every individual judgment is correct. Then, on a "test trial," other "testees" who are confederates of the experimenter each in turn give the same incorrect answer, and the real testee, coming last, is faced with a quandary. What does he do?

In fact, about one out of every three testees will go along with a group of three or more who are in unanimous agreement, although the exact ratio depends on the shapes of the figures and other factors. Moreover, the response a testee makes on that first test trial seems to set the pattern for his responses in subsequent tests in the same situation. Yielders continue to yield, and resisters generally continue to resist.

Asch described yielding to a unanimous incorrect majority as "conformity," and resistance as "independence." The terms of these characterizations can be misleading, however. It is true that essentially everyone makes correct judgments when tested individually. And it is also true that yielding increases as a function of the number of unanimous persons, up to three, uttering the erroneous earlier judgment. What can be misleading is use of the term *conformity,* without qualification, to label these events.

When individuals are tested for willingness to act contrary to customary values—for instance, by purposely causing unnecessary damage—few will do so. They will, however, quite frequently join in with a group that is engaged in the forbidden actions (Zimbardo, 1969). When tested for readiness to help another in distress, solitary persons commonly act as good Samaritans, but people in groups "pass by on the other side," so to speak. The probability that one person will intervene to help another falls as a direct function of the number of unhelpful bystanders in whose company he learns of the need (Latané & Darley, 1970). In each of these cases, going along with the group becomes more common as the size of the group increases. It is quite clear in these instances, however, that we can only speak of such behavior as "conformity" at the price of regarding ethical behavior as nonconformity. What is at issue is the *standard* to which behavior conforms or does not conform.

Two kinds of "conformity" can be discerned in the Asch experiments, which differ only in the criteria they meet. The yielder's response defers to two possibilities: first, that his own judgment may be wrong, second, that the others may be playing some kind of game as a group. The yielder's response is thus self-consciously biased toward the *appearance* of either being as good a judge as the others or of being a member of the same group as they. The resister's response is not influenced by these possibilities. If he recognizes them, he does not believe the first, and, on the second, is less concerned about appearing like others than about truth or objectivity—that is, about responsibly producing a match between what he says or does and what is true of, or appropriate to, the object of his statement or action.

The importance of this contrast in criteria to the present discussion is clear. One who shapes his behavior for its appearance is not only treating others as supervisors, obediently, he is also either disregarding the effects of his actions or assuming that the others have the effects under control. In either case, he is abdicating his own responsibility for them, his own control over them. In another context, it has been suggested that responsibility is *diffused* in groups (Wallach,

Kogan, & Bem, 1964). This is a reasonable proposition, but only to the degree that individuals in groups cease to be concerned with the effects of their actions. They might continue to act responsibly either if they persuaded the group to do the correct thing or if they changed their ideals.

When tested in the Asch conformity situation and allowed to bet on each response, responsible "internals" were found in one study to yield less frequently than fatalistic "externals" (Crowne & Liverant, 1963). Rotter (1966) interpreted this result and those of three further experiments as showing that "internals" resist subtle attempts to influence them. That is what they must do if they are to remain responsible.

The terms *resister* and *yielder,* like Rotter's terms, imply that some enduring personal dispositions are involved in producing the responses Asch observed. They imply, accordingly, that similar behaviors would be displayed in other situations where like choices were offered. This is what some of the evidence indicates in fact (Blake, Helson, & Mouton, 1957; Krech, Crutchfield, & Ballachey, 1962; Rosner, 1957); and it is, of course, supported by the evidence that perceived locus of control is related to yielding behavior.

However not all instances of following others can be described as conforming to group pressure, nor yet as a surrender of responsibility. Situational influences and particular types of ability are clearly involved. Willis (1965), for instance, has demonstrated yielding by university students who had been led to understand they were relatively unskilled at an assigned task. An earlier comparable report (Samelson, 1958) included the additional observation that the confidence manipulation had its principal effect on men with low fantasy achievement scores, and that it caused very little change in the behavior of their high-scoring and consistent counterparts. That people display alternate leading and following behavior, presumably influenced by similar variations of confidence, is evident in studies of consumer behavior (Katz, 1957) and of group problem solving (Bales, 1958). These may be instances of "informational social influence" (Deutsch & Gerard, 1955), in which followers were shaping their actions responsibly by making use of information provided by carefully selected others.

All of these considerations clearly limit the utility of the propositions that people vary in how "conformity prone" they are and that this postulated disposition therefore constitutes a "dimension" of personality (Krech *et al.,* 1962, p. 522). However, it is important to avoid throwing out a valuable baby with some terminological bath water. So, the essence of that proposition will be considered under another name.

THE COMPLIANT DISPOSITION

Erich Fromm (1941) suggested that surrender to supervisory others of control over one's actions is done to escape from emotional distress. In support of this hypothesis, one team of investigators has shown that the confrontation of a testee by an incorrect unanimous majority caused physiological arousal, and that yielding reduced it (Bogdonoff, Klein, Estes, Shaw, & Back, 1961). By appearing the same as others, yielders gained a short-term advantage, removing some stress that resisters continued to endure.

Another short-term advantage can be gained by yielding. It is implied in the Jones and Davis (1965) theory about the inference of dispositions that one avoids displaying one's personality to others by behaving like everyone else. In confirmation of other evidence supporting this view, judgments collected by de Charms *et al.* (1965) showed that people who shape their actions to match the requirements of supervisors are generally not held accountable by the judges for the effects of those actions. Moreover, such exoneration comes particularly readily from people whose answers to Rotter's questionnaire deny responsibility for their own fates. Since such persons are themselves likely to yield (Crowne & Liverant, 1963), it appears that they expect, in yielding, to avoid being known by their deeds. Conceivably, their "escape" involves a change in expectation about accountability for their actions as well as the recorded change in stress or emotion.

People who deny responsibility for their own fates on Rotter's questionnaire display some other inclinations on other personality tests that relate to behavior in stress situations. Joe (1971) has reviewed the relevant investigations. "Externals" appear to be more anxious than responsible persons, particularly about failure; they seem to be more disabled by anxiety, less insightful and self-assertive, less able to produce constructive reactions to frustration, and more rigid and dogmatic. Consistent with the conception that they feel relatively powerless (Seeman, 1972), they also appear to be more suspicious of others, less trusting of others and less trustworthy, and more inclined to take hostile actions against others and less interested in earning their approval. At face value, these latter assertions appear incongruous with indications that such persons should defer to the judgments of others. However, they are confirmed in direct investigations of the differences between yielders and resisters.

Samples of individuals who had shown themselves in several situations to be consistent yielders or resisters were examined by tests and through observations made by skilled judges and collected over a period of 3 days without knowledge of test results (Krech *et al.*, 1962). Yielders made lower scores on intelligence tests and lower scores for verbal fluency. They showed themselves less insightful and less able to cope under stress; they displayed more anxiety and revealed pronounced feelings of inadequacy and inferiority. Their moral judgments were rigid and dogmatic. Although preoccupied with other people, they displayed considerable evidence of disturbed social relations, including suspicion and distrust, and low proficiency in judging others. The personality test results were supported and supplemented by the observers' judgments.

Self-reliance, independence of judgment, self-expression, and a high evaluation of personal autonomy were attributed to resisters. By contrast, submissiveness, deference to the opinions of others, liability to guilt, and a tendency to unnecessary inhibition of self-expression were seen in yielders, who were also judged prone to confusion and disorganization under stressful stimulation. People who surrender objectivity and shape the form of their actions to match the example or command of others display traits that are diametrically opposed to those associated with efficacy, free will, and responsibility.

It is accordingly almost redundant to note that yielders display little originality in their thinking and little interest in originality. Moreover, when people are sorted into groups according to proficiency on batteries of tests for creativity and later tested in the Asch or similar situations, those who produce more commonplace answers have been shown repeatedly to yield. Original thinkers, by contrast, report the facts as they see them, with objectivity (Barron, 1966).

Fromm described powerlessness, anxiety, and disturbed social relations as precursors of escape into subservience. Besides being correct in his conception that escape is involved, he seems also to have correctly identified elements of the social–emotional condition of those who take the short-term benefits it produces. Thereby he advanced our understanding of the basis of "the compliant disposition."

SOCIAL INFLUENCES ON FREEDOM OF CHOICE

Whether a person's life experiences create anxiety or efficacy, leaving him driven subjectively or free to manage his environment objectively, is not solely a result of physical and physiological accidents. On the contrary, social influences on personality development are ubiquitous. Nurturance in infancy depends solely upon actions by other people. In childhood and youth, others ensure more or less thoroughly that each of us is protected from, and taught to cope with, the hazards of life. We avoid many physical sources of punishment, and so of anxiety, as a result of cultural support. Accordingly many of us—notably the firstborn of families—seek the company of others when we are frightened or uneasy (Schacter, 1959).

Yet all of us have some anxieties of social origin. We compare ourselves with one another, as we have learned to do, and may be upset when we are found wanting. We discipline one another, and one person's emotional expression may be another's punishment. The fact of the matter is that *a large number, maybe a large proportion, of our anxieties develop from distressed social relationships*. Some refer to failures by boys and men to match social standards for masculine behavior (sex role anxiety), others to difficulties encountered at school, like school anxiety (Phillips, Martin, & Meyers, 1972) or test anxiety (Mandler &

Sarason, 1952; Sarason, 1972; Janisse & Palys, 1976). The arousal manipulations of studies into achievement motivation may have a similar basis. People become distressed about public speaking (audience anxiety or stage fright—see Argyle, 1967), about talking to policemen, clergymen, and other "authority figures" (Phillips *et al.*, 1972). In one large study of adolescents, susceptibility to anxiety was found to be linked with liability to guilt feelings, self-criticism, feelings of inadequacy in and hostility toward school, and feelings of frustration and of generalized hostility toward others (Phillips, Hindsman, & McGuire, 1960). All of these concomitants of anxiety are recognized as social in origin, and so presumably is the anxiety.

Ways in which others distress us are easy to specify. People assault one another and create physical pain, as some parents do to their children. They scream orders or shout threats or insults, causing overstimulation while they implant uncomplimentary suggestions about one. They point out errors, sometimes in an angry manner. Or they simply frustrate one's wishes for affection and fellowship. Each of these kinds of actions can lead to development of anxiety, according to the theories of Epstein, of Rotter, and of Stotland and Canon.

An important factor in the conditioning of anxiety may be more obvious in the social context than in reference to the physical environment, though no more true. The way others treat us depends commonly (though not invariably) upon what we do and how we treat them. The number of assaultive or insulting punishments we receive, like the number of our social rewards, is partly a consequence of our skill in managing the social environment. Of course that skill depends fundamentally upon the predictability of "the environment," which includes actions by others. It depends upon the "objectivity" with which their behavior toward us is determined. If their actions arise "subjectively," in ways that look abritrary or capricious, they will seem impossible for us to control. If they are in fact instigated by our actions but do not occur soon afterward, we may not appreciate the connection and may consequently fail to modify our own actions. All of these factors, operating independently of our intelligence; theoretically determine the probability that we will be able to influence the social environment in its delivery of reinforcements to us and the likelihood that we will accordingly report ourselves to have ("internal") control over them (Rotter, 1966).

In many cases, no doubt, influences beyond a learner's control determine the social actions that reward or punish him. The case of the ugly girl needs no comment. No more does that of the boy whose voice breaks late or whose reach is too short. Some social exchanges are also influenced by such facts as whether a child's father collects garbage, unemployment checks, or capital gains. In the face of insoluble problems, animals and people learn not to strive. With minimal "freedom of movement" or a weak "sense of competence," they develop "conditioned helplessness" or become "discouraged" and "depressed" (Seligman, 1973).

Evidently, thus, the promotion of efficacy and freedom of choice has to be a social and cultural project. Parental knowledge and efficacy both influence the experiences of children. It makes a difference to the youngster whether mother is healthy and happy, jealous and angry, or poor and desperate. Does she reward or punish him according to her moods or his actions? Does she know how to shape his actions in ways that ultimately increase her peace of mind and improve their relationship? Theoretically, the smaller the number of unsatisfied needs and causes for anxiety affecting a child's parents and playmates, the smaller will be the number of occasions on which he will find their actions unpredictable or unmanageable—and the lower the probability that he will become anxious or discouraged. There are circumstances, moreover, in which the development of behavioral control over events by a child is deliberately inhibited by adults.

Societies differ in who is expected to control what, and in how one is expected to achieve control in his realm. In some cultures, each person is expected to control his own actions and their effects at all times (Lee, 1965). In others, however, a special category of person is charged with control over the behavior of other persons, at least until they have reached a certain age. Our own society charges parents (and people like teachers who fill parental roles) with control over the behavior of their children. They are held accountable for it, as for the actions of their dogs and horses (but not their "feral" beasts, like cats). In turn, they may delegate control over the effects of those actions to their charges, retaining only the power to influence them by the use of rewards, punishments, and guidance. Or they may not. Some attempt, instead, to exercise direct control over the actions of their charges by mechanizing them and driving them like cars or like horses of broken spirit. Cultures and subcultures differ, that is, in the freedom of choice their ideologies permit their junior members, and in the importance they place on *obedience*.

Cultures that value obedience are coercive, characterized by contests of will and the outcomes of such contests. These incidents may develop before the fact—for instance, when one person confronts another at the beginning of a prepared intentional or planned action, like the domineering father who demands to know where his son is going. Or they may occur afterward, punitively. Of the two, the latter is probably preferable for the development of behavioral control by the child. Whenever and however they arise, though, all such confrontations involve a demand by a powerful person that another submit to his will. And by corollary they all involve a "subject" who is relatively helpless to pursue his own desires in the face of the dictator's power.

REINFORCEMENT OF OBEDIENCE AND COMMANDS

A disciplinarian need not always use his power punitively in order to enforce his will on another. He may work by a principle of least force, deploying his major weapons only when necessary to reinforce his demands. Perhaps he uses no physical force at all, but merely reveals his readiness to use some other sort of power. The impersonal corporation does this when it enforces mechanical rule following by the threat to discharge the nonyielding employee. In any case, the dictator's object is to enforce compliance by a relatively helpless subject to a pattern of action that he has decided upon and the subject has not. His aim is to achieve control over the subject, to establish "discipline." It is to cause the subject to act in an approved or dutiful manner, even if, indeed perhaps especially when, he must take that action unwillingly.

The exact means by which one person brings about compliance or obedience by another vary widely. So, one useful theoretical possibility cannot be assumed generally applicable. It is that compliant persons have been conditioned by the primary drive of pain, so that cues from authority figures have come to induce secondary drive, which in turn facilitates drive-reducing obedience. All of this may be true in some cases, of course, and may underlie some instances of compulsive compliance. It could account for the arousal observed at the moment of challenge in the Asch conformity test situation, and the fact that yielding reduced it. However, there is absolutely no evidence to justify the supposition that all obedience has such antecedents.

What can be assumed is that, on each occasion of successful coercion, the subject perceives the dictator's power and his own relative helplessness. If arousal accompanies this perception, then anxiety exists, according to Epstein's theory, and compulsive obedience can develop as escape from it. However, helplessness in itself seems to be a sufficient condition for another type of obedience.

Developmentally speaking, helplessness is given. At an early age, accordingly, every child displays what may be called *primarily compliant* behavior. He does what he is told, with no coercion. It apparently occurs at a stage in cognitive growth when the child is capable of using a sufficient number of verbal cues at once. Then his comprehension of action words automatically results in overt production of the designated actions, that is, in "ideomotor action" (Allport, 1954). Even adults reveal "covert" automatic responses of this kind in the faint electrical activity of relevant muscles when they imagine themselves climbing a rope (Jacobson, 1929). Primary compliance normally disappears in older children, perhaps after they have learned to attend to important cues other than those of the command—as a very old theory suggests.[1] It is certainly not displayed by subjects who are simultaneously occupied with other actions or thoughts when the instruction is given. These, however, are the very occasions when the earliest coercive pressures are likely to be brought to bear.

---

[1]The theory that hypnotic suggestibility involves "reduction of determining tendencies" (see Allport, 1954, pp. 25–28).

Consider the first occasions on which a developing child has failed to display primarily compliant behavior after repeated command. Some interference is usually postulated to account for the failure of a reliable action, and the generic term for it is *inhibition*. That repetition of the instruction failed to produce the suggested action means that the inhibitory process was protracted. By definition, proactive information processing is protracted, while reactive information processing by contrast is "distractible." Since one well-known cause of protracted inhibition is involvement with a competing project, the suddenly noncompliant child may be suspected of having been engaged in the proactive processing of information from some other source than the command.

Is it possible? Primarily compliant behavior looks automatic and responsive. Can a child who was thus compliant one moment be capable of proactive information processing the next? The answer seems to be yes.

Instructions are nothing less than vocally communicated plans for a sequentially integrated set of actions. In following them, one is in fact engaged in the protracted, sequentially selective, and integrative use of all information necessary to their execution. Like the taxi driver whose customer tells him where to go, the child who brings a coffee cup when asked must steer his way to the object and back without accident. The only aspect of voluntary behavior that is not fully displayed in following such instructions is that of setting up the sequence of actions in response to a need of one's own. To add this aspect to the complex may require little or no further intellectual development. The same language experiences that underlie ability to execute vocal commands promote the ability to produce sentences for instructions to oneself or others. Indeed it may be quite common for a child to *give* simple vocal commands even before he is ever asked to execute one. And young speakers are often observed "thinking aloud" their plans for action (e.g., Piaget, 1948). Probably those who can execute vocal commands can think up their own. Supposing this is so, then the difference between a child who complies immediately and one who does not *may be* simply a matter of the timing of instructions. When an individual is "concentrating" on a project of his own he will not "notice," but will seem to "ignore," irrelevant stimulation.

Young people are capable of following another's commands cooperatively, as they do in games, and behavioral differences between cooperative compliance and primary compliance are difficult to delineate. Whether the suddenly noncompliant child had earlier followed instructions from choice, cooperatively, or by "ideomotor action" mechanically does not matter at that moment. What matters is how the adult behaves.

Given an adult who expects immediate compliance and a child whose information-processing capacities are fully engaged with a project of his own, the stage is set for a conflict of wills. If the adult is impatient to see his commands carried out, he may resort to coercion. Perhaps he is more likely to do so if he believes that children must be taught to obey. The least he will then do is to seek the young subject's "attention." This means, of course, interrupting the ongoing voluntary behavior. To this end he may raise his voice, clap his hands, or possibly even slap the child. He may create high-intensity stimulation, or an expectation of it, in order to interrupt the ongoing action. And this will amount—both in method and in effect—to the creation of circumstances that Epstein and others construe as sources of anxiety. What might happen next will then depend upon the intensity of the anxiety reaction. If the child's project had great importance to him or if the adult's attention-getting actions were harsh, a strong emotional reaction and intense feelings of helplessness could develop in the child. Otherwise the disturbance could be mild.

Having gained the attention of his charge and created much or little anxiety, the adult will then repeat his command anew. Probably it will then dominate the child's mind and accordingly be executed—except if the emotional reaction has set up another competing process or has reduced the child's information-processing capacity below the level required for comprehension of the instructions. If the child is emotional and cannot comply, the dictator's attack may be renewed and further distress will ensue. Instructions may then have to be simplified for the driven child in order to produce compliance.

When compliance finally occurs, two important results follow. First, the adult is rewarded for his coercive action, so that the probability he will behave that way again will be increased. And second, the child is rewarded for his compliance, at least by the cessation of attacks, thereby increasing the probability of his future compliance. Indeed, if the child's distress has been severe, the tendency to compliance in the presence of anxiety may become so strong as to be *compulsive* and may later generalize to other social situations. In that event, not only would an early instance of voluntary, freely willed endeavor have been suppressed, rather than being nurtured, it would have been supplanted by submissiveness, a disposition to yield to the will of others.

INHIBITORY EFFECTS OF PUNISHMENT

The sequence of events in which voluntary behavior is interrupted and replaced by anxiety may lead to development of another conditional reaction, if it is repeated sufficiently and the anxiety is impressive. The onset of voluntary behavior can theoretically become a conditional "stimulus" for its own inhibition. So, individuals whose early enterprises were often supplanted by anxiety reactions are more likely (relative to others who have experienced less anxiety or fewer interruptions) not to resume, or even to remember much about, interrupted tasks. Men with low fantasy achievement scores, known to be susceptible to anxiety, actually do behave this way in comparison with the less susceptible authors of high-scoring achievement fantasies (Moulton, 1958). And their interpretive stories refer to fewer thoughts of events related to long-term enterprise. When project interruption has been associated with anxiety sufficiently often, the development of autonomous, long-term projects is likely to be inhibited both in fact and in fancy. In that event, a person's "will" might be said to have been "broken"—which, it may be remembered, was the end for which John Wesley advocated severe punishment.[2]

In this way, authority figures can punish others by merely creating distressing interruptions of ongoing behavior. Unfortunately, such punishment is often more effective in suppressing desirable behavior than is its deliberate counterpart in suppressing undesirable behavior.

In order to achieve its objective of inhibiting tendencies to repeat unwanted actions, simple punishment should be administered at the beginning of, during, or very shortly after an offending act. The suppressive effect of punishment alone does not work more than a few seconds (or perhaps a few minutes) backward in time (Estes, 1944). Disciplinarians commonly punish wrongdoing much later, however. The effects of their actions then operate against repetition of any actions that the subject was engaged in, or starting, at that moment or shortly before. Punishment is likely, for instance, to inhibit confessions of guilt if they are demanded just before it is administered. And it can promote the development of anxiety, based on expectations of unpredicted punishment. Since delayed punishment does not inhibit the focal act but does create the conditions for later anxiety, it is suspected of causing "the neurotic paradox." This is the condition of many anxious people in our society in which they persist in actions for which they are repeatedly punished (Mowrer & Viek, 1948). None of this means that delayed punishment cannot aid in the shaping of obedient behavior. It only means that the mechanism by which it does so is more complex than it may seem.

That unpleasant reactions to punishment frequently become "conditioned to" salient aspects of the situation in which it occurs is now a familiar generalization. Salient aspects of the social punishment situation include the punishing person, or at least those characteristics he displays that are unique to his punitive role— perhaps an appearance of anger, his dictatorial manner, or the critical remarks he makes about the victim's behavior or personality. Sensitivity to "criticism" may begin here. If words referring to the offending action are salient, they, too, may be associated with the aversive reaction and become able to evoke a form of it later. When delayed punishment serves to inhibit the action it was intended to suppress, it presumably does so because anticipatory thoughts of that action have acquired unpleasant associations. *Semantic* conditioned emotional reactions

---

[2]When he reproduced in his journal, "For the benefit of those who are entrusted as she was, with the care of a numerous family," a long letter on this subject from his mother, Susannah, dated 24 July 1732. (Reprinted in Curnock, 1960, pp. 34–39.)

(those provoked by stimuli resembling the CS only in meaning) could later occur at the optimal time to suppress that action.

Unfortunately delayed punishment serves to establish other features of the disciplinarian, by the same conditioning mechanism, as CS for aversive emotional reactions. It makes the victim anxious in his presence and gives a threatening connotation to any ambiguous actions he takes or remarks he makes toward the victim, including instructions he gives him. Perhaps it creates not only evaluation anxiety but fear of failure to meet the disciplinarian's demands. Such effects could also be expected to generalize, so that similar "stimuli" presented by other people would later tend to create the same sort of secondary drive state, albeit less intensely. According to a review about the average person who is dominated by fear of failure, "If forced to choose between rational task performance and conformity to the group as the source of social evaluation, he will choose the latter [Birney, Burdick, & Teevan, 1969, p. 200]." Some of the apparent effectiveness of punishment in establishing obedient behavior is theoretically a result of its rendering commands by all authority figures neurodynamically dominant in the subject, due to their association with the anxiety evoked by such persons. Punished persons presumably obey commands in compulsive escape from the anxiety that arises with those commands. Thus punishment can generate, and escape from fear of it can reinforce, the commanding power of others. That power of course reduces the freedom of choice of subject persons in the face of such commands.

This is not to say that all instances of obedience are compulsive. People can obey one another cooperatively. Each sort of action presumably has two components, one of habit or expectation and another of drive or energy arousal. So, relatively unemotional, merely habitual, forms of obedience must be expected. The same is true of aggression.

PUNISHMENT, ANXIETY, AND AGGRESSION

Another well-documented effect of punishment is due to the example of aggression the disciplinarian's behavior provides. Not only does the punishment show that others may hurt one; it also teaches that one way in which people deal with one another is by causing injury or distress. And it teaches the value of power to do so. Mastery over others will later seem particularly important when attack threatens, and this will occur as often as aversive CRs are evoked by others. So, punishment tends to increase the frequency of aggression in a culture.

It happens, indeed, that many assaultive young men who were studied in reformatory settings had been frequently and severely attacked by their parents for aggressive or other hostile acts (Glueck & Glueck, 1960; McCord & McCord, 1956). In the old theory that merely said punishment suppresses the punished behavior (without noting the importance of timing), this fact was regarded as so remarkable that young men like these were thought to have a peculiar learning disability and were given a special name. "Constitutional psychopathic" personalities were supposed to be unable to learn from punitive experience. It is now clear, however, that they had learned, only too well, two unintended lessons of punishment. They had not learned submissiveness or obedience but had learned fear of other people and the value of assaultive power for reducing that fear. Driven to escape it by responding in kind to anticipated assault, some of them finally got their anxiety under control and achieved some freedom of choice in a subculture that distributed such freedom competitively, according to punitive power. And then they lost their freedom when society at large incarcerated them! Their skills no longer yielded freedom. They had in fact interfered with the development of behavior that would be appropriate in the larger culture, which is to say, their skills had *negative transfer* value.

Development of efficacy in the long term will be promoted when behavioral dispositions or skills shaped in one's primary group can be used without modification or loss of effectiveness in the larger culture. Ideally they should yield *positive transfer*.

The relation between distrust of and hostility toward other persons, as effects, and punishment by others, as cause, is particularly remarkable and well established in the "psychopath" case. Some basis for postulating similarly punitive or coercive experiences has also been provided by research into the antecedents of "yielders," of those who report their fates to be externally controlled, and of the "authoritarian personalities" to be described in what follows. Orders from, or disagreements with, others hypothetically create drive states in such persons that impel obedient or conforming actions, in accordance with old habits or dominant ideas.

A CULTURE OF MISTRUST

The investigations of the "authoritarian personality" reported by Adorno, Frenkel-Brunswick, Levinson, and Sanford (1950) began as studies into anti-Semitism. It soon became evident however that the anti-Semitic attitudes were merely part of a set of attitudes that expressed comparably dogmatic rejection of other minority groups and of mankind at large, and a paradoxical, *dogmatic acceptance of majority group ways and values*. There were, in addition, covert indications in prejudiced people of low self-esteem, anxiety, powerlessness, and disturbed social relations, including suspicion of and hostility toward others, that is, of low social efficacy. Such persons publicly professed disapproval of aggressive and sexual impulses. They alleged such impulses to be characteristic of minority groups, and, paradoxically, used these beliefs to justify advocating severely punitive aggression against the minorities. They further reported marked preferences for attending to practical matters, rather than to personal feelings, images, and sentiments. Finally, they described a strict, punitive, dogmatic, and autocratic regime in their childhood homes. Frenkel-Brunswick (1954) later reported on the home discipline of prejudiced children in similar terms.

Compliance was evident not only in the rigid ethnocentrism and dogmatic, conventional morality of authoritarian personalities but also in the biographical information they gave the investigators, in opinions they expressed, and in the interpretive stories they told about standard stimulus pictures. Their stories often depicted imaginary characters as motivated by the demands and regulations of authority (and afflicted by unpredictable misfortune—see p. 80, this volume). Their aggressive themes were also commonly focused on authority figures, whom antiheroes attacked and heroes defended. They accordingly reveal a compliant resolution of ambivalence in aggressive attitudes about such persons.

Adorno *et al.* developed a questionnaire, the "Facism (F) Scale" (1950, p. 224), for detecting the authoritarian personality, which they described as a measure of "implicit antidemocratic trends" (p. 222) or "implicit prefascist tendencies" (p. 224). Although some technical faults with the scale were later discovered, the major findings obtained with it have survived later scrutiny (Christie & Cook, 1958). Among these are the facts that authoritarian answers were given to the questionnaire most commonly by persons who had made low scores for formal intelligence, had relatively little education, and were badly off economically (Christie, 1954; Hyman & Sheatsley, 1954). These variables are often supposed to be causes of the authoritarian answers. However, it is quite possible that impaired educational achievement and reduced proficiency at intelligence tests both result from life amid unsolved problems as exemplified by poverty. It is a tenable hypothesis that, being reared in low-efficacy groups, in which aggressive use of power is common and variety of experience is impoverished, produces all the characteristics associated with the "authoritarian" personality (Kelman & Barclay, 1963).

Whatever their causes, differences in both of the major components of personal responsibility or free will that were displayed in Figure 2.2 are evident in a complementary manner in the studies of Adorno and associates. The so-called authoritarian personality is characterized by the anxiety, low self-esteem, and practicality that signify low efficacy and, accordingly, resembles "yielders" and "externals." He is also characterized by relatively low education and intelligence test scores and, accordingly, falls into that quadrant of Figure 2.2 that lies opposite the responsible "internals." Apparently he is neither well adjusted nor free, socially and economically, and his compliance to, and distrust of, others is a consequence of this—and ultimately perhaps contributes to a similar state in his associates.

Alternative Responses to Frustrating Conditions

When a learner fails to behave as his teacher wishes, he creates *frustration* in the teacher. This is the state of drive (Amsel, 1959) or anxiety (Epstein, 1972) that develops when motivated activity is blocked and that commonly gives rise to aggression. It is often overlooked that a situation in which motivated activity is blocked also constitutes a *problem* (Humphrey, 1948) and that high drive reduces the probability of effective actions of a creative, productive kind to deal with it. When frustrated and creative behaviors are classified as reactive and proactive information processing, respectively, it can be seen that aggression arises in the presence of an unresolved social problem and that its occurrence is a demonstration of failure. The failure it expresses in a disciplinary context is, of course, that of inculcating *self-discipline*.

The "authoritarian personalities," studied by Adorno and associates, advocated reactive use of punitive power to sanction the sort of behavior practiced by the ingroup. During interviews abstracted by these investigators, such personalities also spoke as if mutual surveillance were part of the general order of social affairs. Moreover, they claimed a degree of perfection in themselves and their families that suggests fear of revealing imperfections. It seems probable that they expected from others the distrust that they displayed toward others. They came, it appears, from groups in which mutual distrust prevailed—hypothetically as a result of unsolved problems in social relations.

An instructional relationship in which one person merely demands specified effects and punishes others for failure to produce them must be minimally efficacious. It assumes that the subject already knows or can find out what the ruler should be teaching him, as Dewey (1922) pointed out more than half a century ago. To be effective in shaping a learner's future behavior toward self-discipline and trustworthiness, punishment or reward must be administered objectively and proactively. Its use must be guided by an accurate understanding of what the junior person needs to learn in order to behave appropriately. From the learner's point of view, moreover, the instructor's use of power must be predictable, that is, trustworthy and subject to some rule of law, or it will engender anxiety. When these conditions are missing, punitive "discipline" is mere aggression and will not engender the necessary self-discipline in subordinates. The instructor may then consider continuous supervision of his subordinate to be necessary, with reactive "aggressive" punishment of misdemeanors. Subordinates, on the other hand, may come to believe that the only safe course of action is to follow the instructor's example.

Whether or not it be due to a history of coercive or punitive training by other people, there is a well-established relationship between trait anxiety and submissiveness, that is, readiness to shape one's actions to comply with or correspond to those of others. Not only do anxious yielders submit to authority figures and conform to incorrect group decisions but their adoptions of an experimenter's suggestions about an ambiguous display also tend to increase as anxiety becomes more intense (Walters, Marshall, & Shooter, 1960; McNulty & Walters, 1962). Anxious children are more readily trained by comments from others (Walters & Ray, 1960). Imitation appears to be promoted by emotional arousal (Bandura & Walters, 1963). As drive, an anxiety state ought to excite enactment of the dominant response tendencies; so, anxiety, regardless of its ultimate source, may create compliance. On the other hand, obedience training seems to be capable of creating both susceptibility to anxiety and a disposition to obey the dictates or follow the examples of others. Coercion and punishment are, after all, intended to promote "discipline."

SELF-DISCIPLINE AND OBJECTIVITY

A classical series of investigations illuminating the relation between autocratic influence techniques and aggression on the one hand and democratic techniques, efficacy, and self-discipline on the other has been reported by White and Lippitt (1960). In the typical investigation (originally reported by Lewin, Lippitt, & White, 1939), adults played various leadership roles as leaders of hobby-time boys' clubs over a small number of meetings. Their role behaviors were recorded, as were the effects of their actions on certain kinds of behavior by the boys. By comparison with what happened under democratic leadership, obedience to the dictates of autocratic leaders reduced the strength of personal motivation by individual boys and reduced the originality they displayed in their activities and the satisfactions they gained. It also reduced their solidarity with one another. A number of field experiments with adult industrial workers have yielded comparable results. In one instance, higher morale was achieved, labor turnover was reduced, and productivity was increased when democratic techniques were used to involve workers in the planning of administrative changes, rather than imposing them autocratically (e.g., Coch & French, 1948; Morse & Reimer, 1956; Miller, 1967).

The autocratic "regime" created a higher incidence of aggression among the boys whose behavior was reported by White and Lippitt. In his interpretation of the autocratic role, the typical adult started by giving orders. He would set single tasks for the boys, without indicating the relationship between tasks within a project. When a task was finished he would comment on its product or perhaps its producer, in global subjective terms, like "good" or "bad." His "leadership" not only failed to take account of the needs of individual boys; it also omitted specification of the objective features of good or bad work, so as to appear arbitrary, unpredictable, and perhaps unjust. These are conditions in which anxiety may develop.

By contrast, the typical adult in the democratic role would suggest two or more courses of action involving sequences of subordinate tasks and encourage the boys to make their own choices. In so doing he presumably stimulated his followers to recognize sequences of steps in a project. He also seems to have stimulated them to compare plans for action in terms of likely costs and effects, to make independent choices, and to accept personal responsibility for their decisions. When he later offered detailed evaluations of their products, pointing out (objectively) the good and bad features in detail and indicating their probable causes, he no doubt facilitated self-critical, objective, relational analysis of the sort required for effective proactive behavior. Not only did he thus design his own actions (responsibly) to permit expression of personal preferences by the boys and make his evaluative criteria explicit and learnable; he thereby also acted in ways needed to cultivate temporally integrated, self-disciplined behavior in his charges.

Two features characterize "self-disciplined" behavior, and both are necessary to it. First, the precise form of its action is independent of the immediate influence of other persons, although it is often responsive to input from them about its *effects*. Second, it is designed to attain effects that match personal standards or ideals (which are normally shaped by earlier social influences). When the first feature is reduced or absent, as in compliant actions, neither freedom of will nor any sort of responsibility is remarkable. When it alone is present and social control is entirely absent, there is "causal" without "normative" responsibility— the condition ascribed to wrongdoers. The autocratic role described by White and Lippitt inhibited expression or development of either characteristic (see Chapters 7, 8, and 11). Under the regime it established, "good" behavior had to be obedient and subjectively pleasing to the dictator. In the democratic regime, by contrast, "good" behavior was shaped from internal knowledge and matched explicit objective criteria. It was responsible and self-disciplined.

Further consideration of the conditions that promote development of self-discipline and responsible behavior, by contrast with those that promote irresponsibility and compliance, occupies the remainder of this book, but perhaps particularly the next three chapters.

SUMMARY

In experiments on perceptual judgment in groups, about one-third of all individuals faced with a unanimous incorrect judgment agreed with the false judgments of the majority. This sort of yielding to group influence has been described as conformity, but it may operate against adherence to enduring social norms or personal ideals. The actions concerned are shaped for appearance, rather than effect, and are accordingly irresponsible.

Responsible acceptance of social influence is also observable. It may represent an instance of cooperation through specialization.

Yielding to an incorrect majority has been shown to reduce physiological arousal. It probably also reduces social accountability for the effects of action.

People who more consistently report themselves in control of their fates are relatively unlikely to concur in an incorrect group judgment. The same applies to creative thinkers. On the other hand, the products of thinking by those who yield are commonplace. These persons show little interest in originality. In addition, they are commonly anxious and frustrated, liable to confusion and disorganization under stress, suspicious of and hostile toward others, and inhibited in self-expression.

A large number of our anxieties develop from distressed social relationships. These may result from situational influences as well as from our own actions and those of interacting others. The promotion of efficacy and freedom of choice must be a social and cultural project.

Cultures differ in the value they place on obedience. Training in obedience aims to inhibit the development of free will and of personal responsibility for the effect of one's actions. This is so because it aims to create a disposition to shape one's act in conformity with the will of a dictator.

Coercive methods for the sanction of obedience can theoretically engender the anxiety that is in fact associated with readiness to follow commands or examples. Some forms of coercion also constitute examples of the use of aggression for social influence.

Empirical studies of individual behavior have identified so-called authoritarian personalities. Such anxious, mistrusting, power-oriented, and obedient persons are commonly poorly educated and make low scores on intelligence tests. They display deficiencies in both of the primary components of free will. They appear to have developed in coercive cultures that reinforce demands for obedience with the aggressive use of power.

Social interactions in which one person commands particular actions by another and rewards or punishes the resulting deeds with global reactions have been construed as "autocratic," and they generate aggressive behavior. Conversely, those in which subordinates are instructed and guided in causal analysis while executing projects of their own design were called "democratic." While the one inculcates obedience and irresponsibility, the other generates self-discipline and freedom of will.

The Shaping
of Self-Discipline

As the preceding discussion shows, social "discipline," directed toward cultivation of obedience and perhaps "good" behavior in children, may serve to
create anxiety, distrust, and tendencies toward irresponsible compliance with the
implicit demands or explicit commands of others. Parental directions or commands
may interrupt progress in elementary forms of intentional behavior and create
distress instead. Rather than promoting the development of adult self-control, as
it is supposed to do, such discipline may actually impede it and impair later
adjustment as well. Quite clearly, it is possible for disciplinary training to proceed in ways that not only fail to attain its objective but also create unsatisfactory
social relationships.

On the other hand, the previous discussion implies that favorable social experiences might facilitate the growth of mental freedom in a child. Parental
actions can assist in cultivating the growing child's intelligence. If they are
responsive to the child's actions, rewarding him for meeting criteria appropriate
to his emerging skills, they may promote the development of a confident and
venturesome, that is, efficacious personality. They may begin the process of
cultivating the self-discipline and creativity that identify free will.

But what is the actual state of affairs? How well fitted are society's parents and
teachers to use their greater knowledge and power thus wisely in their interactions with children? There are, of course, no firm answers to these questions, nor
to many others that might be asked. However, psychological research has provided some tentative information that may be useful in developing partial answers. It has confirmed, for instance, what we might expect, that parental child-
rearing behaviors vary remarkably, and that some of them are better than others
for the cultivation of free will. And it has begun the experimental analysis of

115

these various behaviors, with the object of isolating the important from the unimportant differences among them.

FIELD STUDIES OF INDEPENDENCE
TRAINING METHODS

One interesting investigation of parental child-training behavior was influenced by the theory of Basil Bernstein (see pp. 45–47, this volume). It concerned the guidance some mothers provided their children in discovering relations between their actions and the outcomes of those actions. The investigators, Hess and Shipman (1965, 1967), observed "working-class" mothers interacting with their 4-year-old off-spring after they had given the mothers a copy of an intricate drawing and had told them that they and their children would be asked to draw it later on an "Etch-a-Sketch" screen. In the meantime, the mothers would be allowed a practice session to show the child how to use the toy. The object of the study was to see how each mother would approach her child in that difficult training task.

The toy resembles a television screen with two manipulable knobs. Turning one knob draws horizontal lines, turning the other draws vertical lines. Direction of line is determined by either a clockwise or counterclockwise turn of the knob. Curves can be drawn by twisting both knobs simultaneously, so that curves of different direction result from different combinations of knob turning. Each mother should have taught her child these basic manipulations with a view to facilitating his performance in the drawing task.

Very few of the mothers, however, showed any appreciation of what the children had to learn. One who did would begin by showing her child how the toy worked, by indicating the relation between the knob turning and the lines on the screen. She would show the child the different effects created by the two knobs and demonstrate the effects of using them jointly. She would also direct his attention to the pattern to be followed later. By such an approach she would be contributing to his own understanding of both the toy and the task, and thus to the probability that he could execute the task as required and reward them both. She would also be reducing her own work load in the later test session. However, few children received such treatment.

During the practice session, most of the mothers failed to indicate even that knob turning produced lines, let alone which knob produced which type of line. Instead, they demanded that the child turn the knob they indicated, without explaining why or even directing his attention to the effect of his action. Moreover, very few mothers showed the child the "target" picture he was to match. Instead, they directed his every move. These methods produced considerable frustration in both mother and child. Following such experience, the child would be lucky to leave this situation with even the simple knowledge that turning knobs produces lines. Certainly he would leave it with some relief because of his realization that what happened there was clearly beyond his control.

Developing Expectancies of Internal Control

This sort of realization is what Rotter and his co-workers have discussed as a perception of external control. Studies that have examined retrospective reports about the child-training techniques used by parents of "external" and "internal" college students report findings consistent with the contentions reported in Chapter 5. Greater consistency in discipline (Davis & Phares, 1969) and a higher degree of predictability of parental standards for behavior (MacDonald, 1971) were more uniformly recalled by internals than by externals. Such conditions would, as hypothesized, contribute to the child's opportunity to develop unambiguous conceptions of the act–outcome relations in his world.

An equally important finding in these studies deals with the emotional aspect of the child's relationships with his parents. Those who claimed responsibility for their own deeds reported having had a "nurturant" childhood environment, with affection and support of their independent endeavors from both parents. By contrast, rejection and hostile discipline on the one hand or high maternal protectiveness on the other were recalled by those who did not claim such responsibility. Among earlier studies supporting this interpretation of his results, MacDonald cited a factor analysis by Devereux, Bronfenbrenner, and Rodgers (1969), showing that his "nurturance" scores refer to supportive interactions whereas his "protectiveness" scores refer to interactions in which parents controlled children.

How are these reports to be understood? This question will later be pursued analytically, but two "global" generalizations relevant to the material of the previous chapter can be proposed right here. The first is that the "externals" seem to have lived in an "autocratic" social climate, in which the pressures of parental needs and emotions acted to the detriment of child education. The "internals" by contrast seem to have been more fortunate. The parental "support" they recalled suggests less pressure from parental needs and emotions, and that greater attention had been given to their needs. Perhaps this is attributable to greater affection for them by their parents, or possibly it is associated with higher parental efficacy. It could, however, be due to their parents having superior child-training skills.

In any case, and this introduces the second point, it seems probable that a parent who is "democratically" oriented to educating a child, rather than attempting to inculcate obedience, treats her child with *respect* and *trust*, according him something like *dignity*. Presumably she is able to govern her actions with an eye to both his present condition and his future potential. Thus, she might give the child information and the guidance of suggestions, where necessary, but she would also allow him the freedom to venture. She would neither give unnecessary orders to direct the child's actions, nor impose unusual ("overprotective") constraints on his exploratory endeavors. She would "support" rather than control him. In such a context, the child would understand an informative comment or action as supportive, whereas in an "autocratic" regime, the same initiative might be interpreted by the child as criticism, due to mistrust by the parent. The recollections of internals, more often than externals, suggest they had enjoyed such supportive relationships with their parents.

Somewhat comparable differences in the child-training attitudes of parents are suggested by observations made in a setting in which parents are observed teaching their children in what the literature calls an "achievement situation." In pertinent studies, the child and his parents are together while the child is required to complete some task prescribed by the investigators. However, it is the parents who are observed. Rosen and D'Andrade (1959) remarked on the differences in behavior between the parents of boys who had been rated high and low on "need for achievement." They reported that the typical mother of an achievement-oriented boy appeared to be more directly involved with her son's behavior, more ambitious in the standard she expected him to achieve, and more extreme in her approval of his progress than the typical mother of the other boys. The fathers of these achievement-oriented boys were described as positive, approving models.

These roles of parental involvement were reversed for the boys rated low on need for achievement. Here it was the fathers who were more concerned with their sons' activities while the mothers watched more passively. The pattern of emotions also differed. For this group, the typical father was described as hostile, punitive, and authoritarian in attitude toward the child, directing his every move and not allowing him to form any independent decisions. The mothers of these boys were cool and aloof. Further studies substantiate these observations, providing more specific information to fill in the general picture Rosen and D'Andrade portrayed. Thus, Crandall, Preston, & Rabson (1960) reported that direct positive maternal reactions to preschool children's achievement behaviors were related to the children's observed levels of achievement, although less direct reactions, such as general affection or the rewarding of independence, were not.

Studies of the relationship between birth order and achievement are concerned to find reasons for the greater historically observed achievements of firstborn children (Roe, 1953). Results show that mothers tend to oversee their firstborn's behavior more closely than that of their later born children, and to be more extreme in their affect toward the first child (Hilton, 1967). An environment of constant, informative, and pleasurable feedback for success, in a milieu of supportive involvement, provides the child with the opportunity of perceiving the relations between his actions and desirable outcomes.

In a review of some relevant research, Heinz Heckhausen (1967) has summarized a body of achievement motivation research that contains many conflicting findings. One investigation probed the effect, on the later enterprising behavior by children, of the age at which mothers began to encourage independent achievement. After an early beginning, (e.g., at age 2 years), the child did not develop strong achievement motivation. The same result was also observed in cases where this training was delayed (e.g., until 5 years of age). Heckhausen suggested a tenable resolution of the evidence. According to him, the child develops to a stage, at about 3½ years of age, wherein he perceives the relationship between cause and effect. If encouraged in task performance at this age of discovery, he will likely experience success in his independent actions and enjoy them. However, if he is unrealistically stimulated before he is capable of understanding the temporal sequence of events, the achievement situation may bring him aversive associations. Moreover, if he is not learning at this time that it is his own actions that produce desired effects, he must be learning instead that those effects derive from an external source. Thus, direct encouragement of achievement is only effective when the child is capable of comprehending the relations between task acts and task outcomes (see Chapter 5).

Yet another group of investigations was concerned with the determinants of abstract and self-controlled, as opposed to "concrete" and "situation bound," behaviors in children. A review of evidence from this theoretical perspective (Harvey & Felknor, 1970; see also Cross, 1966, 1970) links situationally bound behaviors in children to rigid, autocratic, control-oriented attitudes in parents. More abstract conceptual systems, which accomplish greater degrees of self-control, are found in the children of more open-minded and informative parents. The theoretical contributions of Basil Bernstein deal with the same relationships in a somewhat different manner.

ANALYTICAL STUDIES OF CONTROL
OVER THE ENVIRONMENT

Various aspects of parental behavior that influence the development of autonomy in children have attracted the notice of reviewers of literature. One group of theorists has been interested in the importance of perceptual or cognitive processes parents may influence, such as the comprehension of the cause–effect relations to which Heckhausen drew attention. Another, looking at the development of autonomy as a matter of instrumental learning or operant conditioning, has been particularly interested in the effects of various kinds and patterns of rewards and punishments, or reinforcements, by parents. Still a third group has been attracted by indications that learning children are influenced by the *examples* or "models" that parents provide. Subsequent experimental and theoretical attempts to develop more precise knowledge of the childhood determinants of behavioral independence have accordingly adopted different points of view.

Some developmental psychologists consider the most interesting aspect of "socialization" to be the development of *impulse control* in children. While this is far from being a unanimous approach to these problems, it is a convenient one to use in discussions of "self-discipline"—that is, of a person's ability to control society's responses to his actions by controlling those actions.

Two kinds of "impulse" are important, in the views of such influential theorists as Pavlov and Hull as well as of modern psychophysiologists. One has to do with the excitation of action, the other with its inhibition. Anyone who sets out to learn a skill must discover not only what to do but also what not to do.

One pertinent investigation, conducted with more and less impulsive kindergarten children, focused upon the control of habitual muscular actions by verbal instruction. In one condition, inhibition was to be achieved covertly, and here of course the more impulsive children were the less successful. In another condition, the inhibition was to be produced by vocal self-instruction—the children were required to remind themselves aloud how they were to act. The differences in impulse control then virtually disappeared. Perhaps the more impulsive children normally did *not,* while the less impulsive normally did, use covert linguistic cues in controlling their own actions. There was, however, an interesting difference between the two groups when instructing themselves aloud on one task that required faster or slower tapping. The more impulsive children said "faster" and tapped faster, as required. However, in contrast to the less impulsive, they tended to tap every time they spoke, or vice versa. The speech of the others was not so synchronized with their actions and seemed to be controlling the rate, rather than the onset, of movements—that is, to be guiding, rather than cueing the actions (Meichenbaum & Goodman, 1969).

One feature of "impulsive" action is its dependence on situational "stimuli" as opposed to previously acquired knowledge (aroused by task "cues"). The actions of an impulsive person, like those of Goldstein's brain-damaged patients, are "situationally bound." If he reports correctly on the matter, such a person must refer to external influences as causes of his actions. An experiment that focused on this aspect of the phenomenon was conducted with Grade 5 children (Achenbach, 1969). Some of them had been rated as impulsive, and they had been found to make relatively low scores on standard tests of information and intelligence. In working the experimental problems, these children were found to place greater reliance on situational information that did other, less impulsive children. The investigator described their behavior as a failure to use knowledge previously available to them, and attributed this failure to a lack of rewarded experience in the use of internalized information.

An experiment relevant to this hypothesis was conducted with intellectually retarded children. Because such persons experience a greater number of failures than successes, the investigator (Cromwell, 1972) assumed they perceive events as being outside their control. In testing this supposition, he produced enlightening evidence. He exposed his retardates to three different reward contingencies in a simple training situation. In one condition, the negatively toned, failure was punished. The child was told "That was wrong. You did it wrong." In the positively toned condition, success was rewarded. The child was told, with feeling, "You were right. Good!" In the third, the neutral condition, no feedback was given. A control group of normal, "internal" children had responded equally to all three conditions. The retarded children did not perform very well in the first and third conditions, but they developed admirably in the second. When their actions were immediately followed by desirable events, they began to attend more closely to the task and so behaved like the normal child at an operation in which he believes he can control what happens. Increases in efficacy had evidently brought about expectancies of internal control at the same time as they helped the child to acquire skillful actions.

That variations in efficacy influence a child's willingness to rely on internalized knowledge is suggested by the results of a study concerning another aspect of "impulsiveness." The impulsive person presumably takes the rewards a situation presents—accepting reinforcements reactively—rather than striving for rewards he might gain by skill. In this respect he presumably prefers "the given" to "the possible." This investigation accordingly focused on determinants of preference for free, noncontingent rewards over larger rewards that might be earned (Mischel & Staub, 1965). It showed that experiences involving failure reduced preference for the contingent, "possible" reward.

The influence, on what psychologists write, of differences in theoretical perspective can be illustrated in this context. One reviewer (Wright, 1971), for instance, has introduced the terms *self-esteem* and *self-respect* in discussing the results of two experiments like the one just described. In those experiments, resistance to the temptation of young people to take immediate rewards had been in one case lowered by prior insult or frustration and in the other case raised by prior flattery. Wright asserted that "You weaken a man's self-control in morally tempting situations by damaging his self-esteem, and you strengthen it by increasing his self-respect [Wright, 1971, p. 61]." This is perhaps equivalent to saying that self-control can be raised or lowered by experiences that enhance or reduce efficacy.

Developing Resistance to Temptation

Most developmental studies of impulse control in reward taking have been concerned, like those just mentioned, with how a child best learns *not* to do something he wishes to do. Indeed, the term *impulsive* is commonly understood to refer to actions that are thought to need inhibitory control. Socialization experiments are commonly interested in the development of inhibitory control over excitatory impulses. Following reinforcement theory (but in opposition to the foregoing) it has long been supposed that punishment should be especially useful for this purpose.

One experiment of the impulse inhibition type is concerned with "resistance to temptation" (or sometimes "deviation"). Typically, a child is shown a collection of toys, including a particularly attractive one, which he generally reaches for right away. When he does so, he is thereupon punished, perhaps with a loud noise. Then he is either told that he should not touch that toy again (given a rule), or he is told *why* he should not touch that toy (given an explanation). In a third condition he is not provided any direction at all to help him in understanding the punishment and preventing its subsequent occurrence. (Note the relation of these different techniques to the communications codes Bernstein described.) Later the child is left alone in the room with that and other toys for a 15-minute period, and hidden observers note if and when he deviates. The results of three such studies (Cheyne & Walters, 1969; Cheyne, Goyeche & Walters, 1969; and Parke, 1969) show that when a child is punished and is not given either a rule or an explanation, he frequently continues to make the undesirable response, evidently not having understood the lesson. If he is given a rule, he shows more resistance to temptation, unless the intensity of the punishing stimulus was very high. Then, according to physiological measures, there is too much arousal for the child to recall the rule and it does not help him to resist deviation. By contrast with these two methods, the greater cognitive structuring provided by an explanation for the punishment produces remarkably more resistance. Even after high-intensity punishment, provision of an explanation increases resistance to temptation.

These studies may be understandable in terms of an influential theory of neurosis (Mowrer, 1953) that emphasizes the value of response alternatives in facilitating impulse inhibition and postulates their lack among neurotics (see p. 68, this volume). Both when a child is punished and not told specifically why, and when he is given a rule after an intensely punishing stimulus, he acts as if he had no alternative response. Perhaps his recognition of behavioral alternatives is inhibited by the effects of punishment. Physiological measures collected during these experiments clearly indicate that the weak resistance to temptation that did develop under the first two conditions was accompanied by a state of arousal, presumably due to conditioned fear or anxiety. No such evidence of distress accompanied the superior inhibition that the explanation promoted. An appropriate conceptual structuring of the temptation situation—perhaps associated with a greater liking for the experimenter—induces greater resistance to deviation than does either unexplained punishment or punishment after being given a rule.

Although they all refer to the development of "impulse control," the analytical studies just reviewed vary remarkably. Some are concerned with the learner's discovery of what to do to gain rewards from his environment. Others refer to his learning what he must not do in order to avoid punishments. Each of them focused on learning problems at a typical source of "error" in "impulse control." Yet, taken together, they all refer to the conditions that facilitate the development of skills for maximizing rewards while minimizing punishments. These are the skills to which Freud referred with his concepts of "ego strength" and "integration" (of *id* and *superego* needs); "neurosis" was supposed to develop in their absence.

As the findings of such studies reveal, the development of impulse control is more complicated than simple reinforcement theories imagine. Abstract processes seem to be involved, for instance, in self-instruction, in directing attention to relevant information, and in applying prior knowledge to new circumstances. Presumably these processes also underlie the development of informed intelligence and of efficacy.

REINFORCEMENT AND SOCIAL LEARNING

The studies of resistance to temptation have another notable feature. In these cases, and in some others, the learners have access to immediate environmental reinforcers, and many of them ultimately learn to take rewards only when their actions match specified standards, which they also learn. That is, these investigations refer to the development of knowledge about the ideal conditions for reward taking, and thereby of the value of actions that fulfill those ideals. Accordingly, they introduce the important topic of self-reinforcement.

Appreciation of the literature on self-reinforcement will be facilitated by knowledge of a particularly useful theory on the development of self-discipline due to Albert Bandura (1965, 1969a, 1969b). This theory has two additional advantages. It deals with the relationship of cognitive processes to reinforcement processes, and it accounts for their apparent influence on self-discipline, in addition to that of parental example. That is, it accounts for the complexity of findings in the studies reviewed.

Bandura assumes that, during every instance of instrumental or "operant" learning, a cognitive "transcript" or "plan" of the sequence of important events is created. Of course, each of the foregoing studies refers to instrumental learning. These events would include the perceived circumstances of the action—including the motivational state, the action itself, and finally its outcome or outcomes. They are assumed to be cognitively encoded and stored together, perhaps as a chain. The total number of different sequences a person has stored is said to comprise his behavioral repertoire. When recalled under the influence of appropriate stimulus conditions (the need for reward being one of these), each sequence is supposed to constitute an expectation for replication of the events and outcomes it summarizes. When its recall is stimulated, the sequence expectation then serves as a standard for future action. If the person acts as this standard prescribes to produce a particular outcome, and if that outcome indeed follows, the importance of the sequence transcript in the behavioral repertoire is assumed to increase. However, if a lesser reward ensues, the priority of the sequence is assumed to be weakened. Thus, the maintenance of learned behaviors is assumed to depend upon reinforcement, just as their initial acquisition is assumed to depend upon it.

When explaining the conditioning of an involuntary reflex, it is sufficient to consider the underlying action of a reinforcer in terms of its arousal-related properties alone, for instance its ability to reduce or to increase drive, as described in Chapter 4. However if reinforcement is also to establish cognitively encoded sequences for instrumental use, it must have further attributes.

The process of reinforcement is still something of a theoretical mystery, but the current state of knowledge about it has resulted in considerable agreement that reinforcement has not one property, but two. Locke, Carteledge, and Koeppel (1968) named them *incentive* and *informational feedback*. One gains feedback about one's actions on the basis of their outcomes. So, the occurrence of a reward *informs* the person about the fitness of his action. The magnitude of the reward then operates on the *incentive* for repeating the action, by showing how valuable it will be to do so when future conditions permit. Notice how these two aspects of reinforcement resemble the two dimensions of Figure 2.2. Both the fact of the outcome and its arousal-related properties are supposed to be encoded as outcomes of antecedent actions in the sequence transcript or plan.

These same mechanisms operate with negative feedback too. If a response produces a noxious event (punishment or frustration), a negative valence is supposed to become attached to that sequence transcript. However, fear, or the expectation of adverse consequences (e.g., pain), is a much more arousing one than the anticipation of pleasure, and has extra implications for learning that were discussed in Chapter 4.

The learner's dependence on reinforcement by environmental events is clear and direct in the development of conditioned responses. However, as even naive observers of human learning would note, only a small proportion of our learning occurs through direct training. A great deal occurs as a result of observation and imitation. Bandura (1965) argues, however, that such observational learning is merely a slight variation of instrumental learning. The difference is simply that the expectancy sequences are formed by watching somebody else's direct experience with the environment, rather than one's own. Reinforcement is also involved, but it operates vicariously.

Vicarious Reinforcement

Vicarious reinforcement is similar to direct reinforcement but it is derived from watching another person receive direct reward. How can watching such an event be reinforcing for an observer? The answer is that it cannot be, at least directly. However, watching the outcome seems to *evoke* in the onlooker a *rewarding memory* of his own experience with similar outcomes. This at least seems a reasonable interpretation of evidence that the pleasurable bodily reactions conditioned to a particular reward are evoked in people who see others given that reward (Craig & Weinstein, 1965). (A similar hypothetical explanation of sympathy is quite old—see Humphrey, 1922–1923.) So, theoretically, observationally learned instrumental sequences can be established and maintained by vicarious reinforcement. And many studies attest to the validity of this theory (Rosenbaum & Bruning, 1966; Berger & Johansson, 1968; Bandura, 1969a, 1969b). An obvious qualification, however, is that if the observer does not perceive a particular outcome as reinforcing, because it is not so encoded in his experience, he will not derive any vicarious satisfaction and thus not learn. His previous experience thus establishes the limits, at any moment in his life, on what sorts of observations he will benefit from.

Observational learning with vicarious reinforcement marks the beginning of a new sort of behavioral independence. For those with suitable earlier experience, the opportunity for learning about desirable outcomes is no longer limited to situations in which their own actions or reactions are externally reinforced. To an influential degree, both the information and incentive components of feedback to others may be available also to an interested observer, and guide independent learning.

It is the thesis of this chapter that, in freely willed behavior, the actor is relatively independent of environmental events not only for information but also for incentives. His abilities to be so are assumed to emerge from earlier experiences that cultivate the informed intelligence and the efficacy which Figure 2.2 showed to be associated with claims of responsibility and freedom. This viewpoint accordingly implies that a child can become independent of environmental reinforcement as a source of incentive, in addition to being independent from the environment as a source of information.

SELF-DISCIPLINED LEARNING

Having learned by observation some forms of action that produce specified results, and having experienced vicarious satisfaction or distress by seeing others receive familiar kinds of reward or punishment, the child is prepared for yet another stage in his developing autonomy. He can try out his observationally acquired knowledge and see how it works. Can he operate a lasso or lariat as the cowboy did on TV? Is this correct? If it seems so, he will feel some vestige of the vicarious pleasure he experienced when he saw the other rewarded for his action, and this result will reinforce his own enactment of the learned plan. If not, he may try a different form of action, until perhaps he is satisfied. Whatever the degree of his success, when he behaves this way he has entered a new stage in the development of autonomy. He is becoming motivationally independent.

Self-corrected practice has much in common with problem solving. Both involve making up a new pattern of action from elements within one's repertoire, guided in one case by an observationally learned plan and in the other by a notion that one can be developed. Both are presumably sustained by hope of success, because of rewards earned earlier. Both depend upon the ability to detect and reject inappropriate actions and to retain and improve upon the approximately correct. In terms of incentives, thus, both depend upon the conditional, "self-administered" reactions by which one feels good (and "warm") when one's output is almost right, or bad when it is clearly wrong. External reward no longer defines success. Instead, the realization of success now stimulates a rewarding internal state of affairs. And, in terms of information, both depend upon recognition of similarities and differences between output and ideal. The most patently "free" instances of willed behavior are, of course, those in which a person "invents"—which is to say "teaches" himself—novel ways of acting.

Behavioral autonomy is promoted through independent practice of the techniques for managing the environment that have been acquired either directly or observationally—as cognitive transcripts of event sequences. Independent practice on the part of the developing child has been labeled "independence striving" or "imitation." It may appear unmotivated because there are no external incentives available. However, it is now known that reinforcement occurs internally. For this reason, such seemingly childlike activities are paradoxically mature. The child is in fact practicing self-control. He is providing his own informational feedback, on the basis of an internalized standard or pattern for action. Also, if he approves of his effort he will be "pleased with himself," providing his own incentive feedback. He will be experiencing "self-reinforcement." According to students of self-reinforcement, notably Bandura (1969b) and Kanfer (1970), the approval results from the learner's making a simple comparison between present actions and those summarized by the conceptual behavioral sequence he is testing. A release of pleasurable feelings ensues when the actual and ideal sequences match (and it may be celebrated by taking an available environmental reward as well).

It is apparent from this description that the incentive feedback of internal self-reinforcement is even more abstract than that of vicarious reinforcement. Unlike the incentives of vicarious reward, it is not the recognition of a physically rewarding stimulus that evokes the internally rewarding state but the recognition of a match between the actual and the ideal event sequences. "Success" now rewards, and "failure" now punishes. More than ever, the child recognizes cause and effect and is able to manipulate them at his own will, to his own pleasure.

SELF-REINFORCEMENT AND
BEHAVIORAL FLEXIBILITY

One important point about self-reinforcement becomes evident after a little thought. A person may be correct or he may be incorrect when he judges his actions to have been successful. His self-reinforcement may be determined "subjectively," in accordance with his inclinations. Or it may be determined "objectively," in accordance with accurate conceptions of what ought to be, on the one hand, and what has indeed occurred, on the other. Since objectivity in the determination of behavior promotes freedom of will, the question of how to increase the objectivity of self-reinforcement becomes an important one.

Indeed there may be grounds for doubt that self-reinforced behaviors, once established, can ever be shaped at all by external reinforcements. If a person can provide his own incentives, how likely is he to be moved by the incentive effects of externally controlled reinforcements?

An Experiment on Shaping Self-Reinforcement

An experiment by Kozma and Easterbrook (1974) refers to both of these questions. Its object was to study the shaping of self-reinforcement by training with externally controlled rewards. And it was assumed that differences in personal rates of subjectively determined self-reinforcement (SDSR) would have an important influence upon the results.

Little is known about rates of subjectively determined self-reinforcement. However, a considerable amount of information has been gathered on behaviors that may be related. For instance, referring to studies on readiness to take rewards from an available supply, one theorist (Kagan, 1966) found reason to postulate a dimension of differences among people ranging between the "impulsive" and the "reflective." Kagan has gone further and developed tests to measure a person's position on this assumed dimension. Presumably, "impulsives" would have high SDSR rates, while "reflectives" would have low rates. The related theoretical work is not satisfactory, however. First, on the evidence of a number of influential experiments, there appears to be no warrant for the assumption that impulsivity is independent of intelligence. It is also questionable to assume that the opposite of impulsivity is reflectivity. A number of investigations indicate that what opposes impulsivity is *discrimination* in the control of behavior. This is true, for instance, of the classical Pavlovian studies on experimental neurosis. It is true also of the more recent studies of impulsive agreement with questionnaire statements (Couch & Keniston, 1960). In these cases, both excitatory or "stimulus-accepting" ("yea-saying") impulses, on the one hand, and inhibitory or "stimulus-rejecting" ("nay-saying") impulses, on the other, are observed, but only in the absence of normally balanced discrimination.

Although response inhibition or stimulus rejection seems to be one alternative to "impulsive" activity (or "stimulus acceptance"), a more dependable alternative is appropriately discriminative action. Impulsivity–reflectivity scores were accordingly adjudged theoretically unsuitable measures for the study by Kozma and Easterbrook.

Instead, the required measures were taken within the experimental setting, as pretraining baseline scores. Each of the university students who participated in the experiment had four switches, numbered 1 to 4, for recording his (or her) choices in the learning problems that would be presented. The students each also had a button labeled "correct," for recording whether they thought they were right (or wrong), which activated a lamp that signaled "correct." In the baseline period, they were individually shown diagrams, each with four quadrants numbered 1 to 4 like the switches, and asked to record their guesses of which quadrant the experimenter had in mind, by moving the relevant switch. Each was told that, if he (or she) felt correct, he should also press the "correct" button. Since no information on this point had yet reached the student, the frequency with which guesses were designated correct in a number of trials must have been determined by something within the individual. Accordingly, it can be designated the rate of subjectively determined self-reinforcement.

Wide variations in SDSR rates were recorded. About one-third of the people observed hardly ever touched the "correct" button (their average SDSR rate was 13%). Another one-third touched it on almost every occasion (average SDSR rate 98%). These differences may be analogous to "nay-saying" and "yea-saying," respectively, or perhaps to reflectivity and impulsivity. The remaining persons averaged an SDSR rate of 63%.

Each of the three SDSR groups was then divided and trained to recognize, for 4, 6, or 8 quadrants out of the 10, which quadrant the experimenter did in fact have in mind. That is, they continued to guess, but with the experimenter controlling the "correct" light. So they all had some "situational reinforcement" after seeing each of the 10 slides again, and even more after further guesses. This process continued until one subgroup knew the correct answer for 4/10 of the problems, another subgroup for 6/10 of the problems, and the third for 8/10 of the problems. In each of the SDSR groups, accordingly, one-third knew 40%, one-third 60%, and one-third 80% of the correct answers. And, of course, the groups had, by this time, been situationally reinforced at those frequencies. They were then equipped for the final phase of the experiment, a test for objectivity in the determination of their self-reinforcing actions.

Levels of SDSR could be expected to influence the *incentive* value of objective reinforcement, and this may be what indeed occurred. Self-reinforcement rates after training depended both on initial SDSR rates and on rates of situational reinforcement (SR) during training. *On the average, no SDSR group increased its SR rate unless the rate of situational reinforcement had exceeded its SDSR rate.* This means that the SDSR behavior had more than passing significance—it was not merely a reaction to ignorance, but seems to have influenced the incentive effect of external reinforcement. Presumably the SDSR rates represented (or established) minimal levels of situational reinforcement that would be required before its incentive effects would be felt.

The second major observation from this study refers to its main point. How is a person's rate of SDSR related to his ability to use objective evidence (provided by reinforcement during training) for judging and reinforcing his own actions? The answer is that neither the high nor the low SDSR persons made good use of that information. Only the moderate SDSR group did so in at least two of the three training conditions. By altering both the rates and the accuracy of their SRs under these conditions, the people in this group showed they had responded to both the incentive and information components of the situational reinforcement. They had learned quite readily to reinforce their own behavior according to objective evidence. That they failed to do so in the third condition, when the rate of situational reinforcement fell below their SDSR levels, suggests that the incentive value of the situational reinforcement had some primary significance.

The low SDSRs reacted to the training principally by increasing their SR rates, thereby showing their sensitivity to the incentive component of that experience. However, it was only after they had learned how to produce situational reinforcement 80% of the time that they began to reinforce themselves accurately. The high SDSRs, by contrast, responded to neither the incentive nor the information component of the externally controlled reinforcement. To influence them, *qualitatively* superior reinforcements would presumably be needed.

An Interpretation of The Results

A more complete understanding of behavior in this experiment will have to await experimental analysis of the SDSR rates. However, a tentative interpretation may be suggested. It is based on the supposition that both the high and the low SDSR groups were biased toward a belief that outcomes in the task they faced would be determined by chance, whereas the moderate SDSR group was comparably biased toward the belief that one could ultimately learn to control the outcomes. The former assumption would, of course, be likely to induce impulsive, rather than skill-determined, behavior, and following Rotter's analysis, anyone who made it would be expected consequently to ignore much relevant information that would be used by those who made the latter assumption instead. The incentive effect of situational reinforcements would then operate—by comparison with the incentive effect of whatever SDSR rate each consequently adopted—to confirm or refute his or her original appreciation of the situation.

The differences between high and low SDSR rates may be ascribed to differences in strategy for dealing with presumedly unpredictable situations. One such strategy might focus on "winning" matches between the self-actuated "correct" display and a chance-determined correct response. Pursuing this aim, it would be sensible to push the "correct" button with every guess. One would then have called every correct guess "correct." Another strategy might focus on avoidance of losing by mismatches. By never claiming to have been correct, one could be sure about three times out of four of not having produced a mismatch. These different strategies, one perhaps dictated by hope of success and the other by fear of failure, would produce, respectively, the high and low SDSR rates that were observed.

Presumably a person's choice of strategy in a chance situation is partly determined by personal dispositions he brings to that situation. Conceivably, for instance, preexperimental histories of situational reinforcement had created persistent fear of failure in the low SDSR persons. This, together with an expectation of external control, could have interfered with appropriate use of their undoubted learning ability in this situation. This speculation is consistent with the fact that they began to produce objectively justified self-reinforcing responses only after 80% situational reinforcement, that is, when both the incentive and information aspects were presumably obvious.

However the detailed results of this experiment are ultimately explained, it made two unambiguous points. First, people can and do learn to recognize when their actions would justify self-reinforcement according to objective criteria. Second, their initial, subjectively determined self-reinforcing pattern influences the facility with which they learn to do so.

Motivational independence and objectivity are not incompatible with one another. But some strategies for the subjective determination of self-reinforcement are evidently more likely than others to create a state of incompatibility between them. Although the term would not be strictly accurate, the resulting behavior might be described as "undisciplined" motivational independence. By contrast, the development of objectively valid internal criteria for self-reinforcement, which this experiment has demonstrated, amounts to development of self-disciplined motivational independence.

The discovery of self-reinforcement processes and their influence on the effectiveness of situational reinforcement has clear implications for a psychology of free will. It means that human behavior need not be regarded by reinforcement-oriented learning theorists as directly responsive to the reinforcing contingencies of situations in which it occurs. Accordingly, the sort of independence that Goldstein and Maslow discussed as "self-actualization" can now be reconciled with the well-established facts of situational reinforcement. So can some other examples of apparently self-motivated behavior.

SELF-DISCIPLINE AND MORALITY

One form of objectively determined self-reinforcement has long been known, in the sense that it has been a familiar assumption, in folk psychology. "Pricks of conscience'' and ''flushes of pride'' seem to be affectively toned, internal reactions to private comparisons of one's behavior and its consequences with one's conceptions of ideal forms of action and effect. Pushing the ''correct'' button on appropriate occasions in experiments, and celebrating accomplishments in everyday life, are presumably overt reflections of internal, self-approving reactions of this kind. Perhaps it can be assumed that the covert, electrically detectable forms of self-reinforcement occur in the same conditions as such visible self-rewarding actions. If so, the foregoing information should apply to self-directed behavior in general and moral behavior in particular. So it offers promise of helping to understand how ''the conscience'' controls behavior.

Following Freud's analysis of the *superego* as a source of guilt and pride, psychologists have long been familiar, also, with the notion that internal affective reactions control behavior. However, they have focused attention on the negative kind of self-reinforcement, traceable ultimately to punishment. Presumably they followed the old assumption that morality in behavior necessarily involves suppression or sacrifice of individual desires. When such a negative reaction occurred before an action, as ''moral anxiety,'' it could inhibit the occurrence of undesirable actions. When it occurred afterward, as ''guilt,'' it was ineffective and associated with ''neurosis'' (Mowrer, 1953). If this source of control was bad for the individual, that was thought to be unfortunate but necessary; for the suppression of selfish actions was regarded as essential to harmony in social affairs. That such control was indeed bad for some individuals was evident to Freud. He ascribed ''neurosis'' to the influence of a tyrannical *superego* upon a weak *ego,* and the consequent frustration of *id* needs. Thus the idea of self-reinforcement is not new in psychology.

What is new is evidence like the foregoing and the realizations that (*a*) self-rewarding reactions also occur; (*b*) they can be shaped to follow objective criteria; (*c*) they then promote self-discipline; and (*d*) objectively determined positive self-reinforcements are indeed more effective than their negative counterparts for the cultivation of self-discipline, for instance in resisting temptation. Consideration of this new information has brought about a new appreciation of the determinants of moral behavior and a new conception of superego strength.

It is now clear that undesirable, impulsive, self-serving actions need not be suppressed by anxiety-creating punishment in order to cultivate morally acceptable behavior. They can be more readily inhibited by knowledge that—and by knowledge of how—more attractive rewards can be attained by more complex actions. An illustration of this process can be found in the ''games'' research, which is reviewed in Chapter 9. It is also becoming clear that punishment-dominated discipline does not operate merely to reduce the net incentive to forbidden actions. It reduces efficacy as well and consequently impedes recognition or learning of the more acceptable action patterns. Some of this evidence was noted in the previous chapter, and some was mentioned in reference to studies of driven personalities, like yielders, externals, and authoritarians. However, further pertinent facts have been collected in studies of moral and other evaluative judgments. A review of that evidence begins in the next chapter.

It is interesting, meanwhile, to notice that something very like the foregoing view of moral behavior was implicit in the nearly 200-year-old writings of Immanuel Kant on morality and freedom of will, that is, on what he called "the good will." Contrary to some interpretations of his work, Kant did *not* advocate that actions in the service of personal needs must be punitively suppressed for the social good. What he advocated was the determination of behavior by abstract, "rational" functioning. "The good will," for him, was self-governed and reasonable, not externally controlled and self-denying.

In his *Fundamental Principles of the Metaphysics of Morals,* Kant argued that "the will is nothing but practical reason." And, "Rational beings alone have the faculty of acting according *to the conception* of laws, that is, according to principle, i.e., have *a will* [1785/1910, p. 343]." Kant's "laws" were, of course, "laws of nature," the subject matter of metaphysics.

> If reason infallibly determines the will, then the actions of such a being which are recognized as objectively necessary are subjectively necessary also, i.e., the will is a faculty to choose *that only* which reason, independent on inclination, recognizes as practically necessary, i.e., as "good" [1785/1910, p. 343].

It is clear, of course, that any action based on a valid perception of its circumstances, a valid "*conception* of law," must be objectively determined—as objectively as, though more abstractly (and with more "reason") than, stimulated response. This insight departs from Kant. In his terms, though, differences in behavior between the free "good will" and the driven reaction can only result from differences in conceptions of law and differences in capacity "to choose *that only* which reason, independent on inclination, recognizes as practically necessary." Note in passing that, if the conception of law be the business of intelligence and the capacity to choose a matter of efficacy, then that is the implication of the new evidence on the shaping of self-discipline. It is also the thesis of this text.

SUMMARY

Parental behaviors that provided informative, affectional support of independent endeavor and predictable, consistent discipline are recalled by responsible, "internally controlled" college students. Their "external" counterparts tend to recollect relatively uninformative, dictatorial parental actions that inhibited, intimidated, or disparaged their initiatives and gave the impression of hostility or overprotectiveness and of arbitrary disciplinary standards. Comparable generalizations have been justified by observational study of parental actions toward autonomous and dependent boys, selected respectively for having written stories with high and low fantasy achievement scores.

In one of a number of pertinent experiments, children with relatively low informed intelligence scores learned unusually slowly when their errors were punished but progressed admirably when correct actions were praised instead.

Providing children with explanations for punitive adult reactions facilitates their development of inhibitory control over their assertive actions, according to several other experiments. Comparably, audible self-instruction evidently facilitates personal control over muscular actions by unusually impulsive children, and may eliminate their difficulties.

Success in the use of prior knowledge to gain rewards has been linked with two further aspects of self-control in children. It promotes readiness to use prior knowledge, rather than current stimuli, in a problem situation, and to sacrifice immediate "given" rewards in order to work for the larger "possible" rewards that skilled performance could earn.

Information like the foregoing can be interpreted in terms of either instrumental conditioning or imitative, observational "cognitive" learning. However, according to recent theoretical developments, all learning involves both observation and reinforcement of actions, and every instance of reinforcement has both an informative and an incentive component. What is learned, in either case, is a *plan of actions and effects* that may vary in importance to the individual as needs and incentives vary.

Plans of actions and effects can be acquired by observation of others, followed by independent practice. The reinforcement that conditioning theory requires is, in this case, internally controlled by memorial processes that have important "cognitive" components. The achievement of a match between actual and ideal act–effect sequences stimulates rewarding internal reactions that effect self-reinforcement.

Attainment of the ability for "self-reinforcement" marks a new stage in autonomy and self-discipline. But it also entails new possibilities for maladjustment. Self-reinforcement of objectively *inappropriate* actions and beliefs is possible. That it may then impede adjustment to environmental realities in some circumstances has been demonstrated.

"Conscience" and "superego" are familiar names for self-reinforcing processes. The new experimental knowledge about socialization emphasizes the importance of personal satisfactions and of cognitive comprehension of the environment. It contradicts the belief that actions in service of personal needs have to be suppressed by punishment for the social good. Moreover it indicates that that view may have been the source of neurotic maladjustment. "The good will," as Immanuel Kant wrote long ago, is the ability to act appropriately in accordance with reason, independent of impulse.

Motivational (and Moral) Constancy

THE RELATIONSHIP OF
MORAL JUDGMENTS TO ATTITUDES

Internal emotional reactions may be set off by external stimulus events, so as to be externally determined. Evidently however, they may also be set off by comparisons of one's own deeds with one's ideals or "values." Such comparisons are not only the bases of self-reinforcement reactions. They are also, by this function, the general type of mental process to which the *superego* belongs. No doubt, too, they closely resemble the evaluations of acts by others and the evaluations of proposed actions or policies for action that are often regarded as expressions of "attitudes." The mechanisms, cognitive and emotional, of objectively justified self-reinforcements, of self-referring moral judgments, and of verbally expressed attitudes are descriptively alike. Knowledge of each should accordingly complement knowledge of the other. Hypothetically, moreover, the same mechanism is involved in each case.

People's attitudes are supposed to summarize their beliefs about, and evaluations of, past events or things and, when activated, to influence interpretations of present events or things accordingly. That is, they are supposed to determine both the affective and the cognitive *meanings* of current experiences for each individual and thereby to influence his future actions. Thus one knows it is "good" to solve a problem, and feels good when one does so, even though the solution may produce no external reward. In these respects, attitudes are supposed to produce the independence of behavior from immediate situational motivation that results from self-reinforcement. Therefore, pending contrary evidence, it can be assumed that the mechanisms of self-reinforced behavior are identical to those of attitudinally mediated behavior.

It is important to understand that no one has ever seen or heard an attitude, though one often hears evaluative opinions and sees evaluative actions, like tearing up letters or petting dogs. Attitudes are "hypothetical constructs," inferred to account for the individuality of evaluative actions by different persons in similar circumstances, and for similarities of evaluative actions by the same persons in circumstances so different that habit theory cannot be easily employed to explain them. They are considered unique to the individual, and conceived as organized dispositions

> to behave in a consistent way to a given class of objects, *not as they are but as they are conceived to be*. It is by the consistency of response to a class of objects that an attitude is identified. The readiness state has a *directive effect upon feeling and action related to the object* [English & English, 1958, p. 50; emphasis added].

Note that "consistency" implies similarity, not identity, and that "objects" are any definable entities—persons, for instance, or policies or *actions*. Conceptual generalization is characteristic of both the output and input sides of behavior that is attributed to an attitude. Thus one may dislike bigoted people and be disposed to anger and antagonistic actions when one sees signs of bigotry. Or one may admire clever work and be disposed to pleasant and approving responses to all instances of it, including deeds of one's own, which would accordingly be self-rewarded. When the "objects" concerned are social actions, the corresponding evaluations would be moral judgments and the corresponding attitudes moral dispositions.

As conceived, attitudes make a person motivationally independent of the concrete course of events in any situation. They link cues in the situation to concepts in the mind and hence to internal emotional responses and appropriate external actions. Of course, they can be wrong, and lead to errors or unnecessary distress, or right, and thereby save time and trouble. Whatever their adjustive significance, though, attitudes theoretically produce behavior that is minimally influenced by immediate external circumstances and maximally influenced by conceptions and values that derive from the actor's prior experience.

RECOGNITION OF ATTITUDES

Not everyone has attitudes toward every definable entity. This point is fundamental to an accurate appreciation of the experimental literature on attitudes and attitude change. It has been made most convincingly by Milton Rosenberg (1968). Rosenberg was concerned about research in which mere utterance of an evaluative opinion or action had been taken as evidence of an attitude. A research worker who had merely found a method of manipulating such utterances might well claim to have found a way of changing attitudes and therefore behavioral dispositions. What he would in fact have altered, according to Rosenberg, might be a situationally determined, quasi-attitudinal evaluative act. A dependable test for the presence of an attitude seemed to be needed, in order to prevent the science from being misled by such spurious findings. Rosenberg found one in his own theory of attitudes.

Rosenberg understood attitudes to be "affectively toned associative networks," to use a phrase McClelland employed in a different context (see p. 89, this volume). Each one, he assumed, implicates a minimum of two entity concepts (commonly more) and at least one associated emotional reaction or "value." So a person could have an attitude toward a novel entity only if he had a belief about how it would affect a familiar and valued one. Thus an attitude is logically ("psychologically") deducible from a value and a belief.

In Rosenberg's view, accordingly, attitudes are not only defensible; their components are mutually consistent. It follows that to differentiate a true attitude, with its self-controlling potential, from a superficial, manipulable statement of valuation, an investigator need only discover whether the statement is defensible and consistent with other beliefs and values. Rosenberg (1968) put the proposition in the following words:

> Intra-attitudinal consistency will reduce the likelihood that judgments of the attitude object will be easily influenced by mood changes, situational variables, and persuasion attempts. Or, to delineate the complementary hypothesis, . . . where a stated affective judgment of an object is not embedded in a set of supporting, largely consistent cognitions, *that judgment, as originally given, is more a product of situational forces than the expression of a disposition characteristic of the person.* . . . a quasi-attitudinal response rather than an attitude [p. 83; emphasis added].

In the context of moral affairs, or that of objectively determined self-reinforcement, the same argument can be applied to judgments about the worth, acceptability, or value of any human action. Self-disciplined persons should display the consistency associated with dispositional control of evaluative behavior.

In support of this proposition, Rosenberg has provided experimental evidence. In one of several pertinent experiments, he asked Yale University students to state the degree of their approval or disapproval of proposed action to make Yale coeducational, and asked them to do so again 3 weeks later. They were asked to evaluate a *proposed action*. On the first occasion, they were also asked to appraise some "value" conditions and to indicate how these would be promoted or blocked by admitting coeds. The compatibility of these views with the first evaluations was then calculated for each man. Then the compatibility scores were compared with measures of change in ratings over the 3-week period. Men who showed no change were found to have had high compatibility scores; those who could be reliably shown to have changed their opinions had low compatibility scores. The degree of stability in approval–disapproval ratings—the degree to which they could be regarded as enduring dispositions—was a function of their compatibility with other evaluations. The greater the number of beliefs and evaluations consistent with a given evaluation, the more constant that evaluation proved to be over time.

In the general terms of this discussion, Rosenberg's evidence means that attitudinally determined evaluative behavior differs from its superficially similar, situationally controlled counterpart in being more resistant to "spontaneous" change. It should be capable of change, of course. Experiences that introduce discrepant, but credible, beliefs or values ought to be incorporated and to alter the dispositions of objective persons. Yet when people differ, as they do, in the ease with which their approving or disapproving actions or statements can be altered, those who change less readily must be regarded as displaying more attitudinal and less situational control over those actions or statements.

This reasoning provides a method for answering some important questions about freedom of will. In what circumstances will such constancy become manifest? Under what conditions do a person's evaluative actions indicate attitudinal or dispositional control (and motivational independence)? When, on the other hand, do they come under external control? Relevant information can be found in the experimental literature on attitude change.

THE CONDITIONS OF DISPOSITIONAL STABILITY

An important set of observations on the matter of attitude change arose from an experiment on persuasion that was conducted toward the end of World War II (Hovland, Lumsdaine, & Sheffield, 1949). It had seemed that the surrender of Germany might have an adverse effect on the Allied war effort. Thoughts of resuming peacetime pursuits might interfere with a soldier's performance of his military duties. The experiment was therefore designed to discover how better to convince the troops that a formidable enemy remained and that the war would *not* come to the early end most of them desired. How should the arguments be presented? Should the propagandists raise both sides of the debate and write a better argument in favor of the likelihood of a long war? Or should they merely give reasons for believing the war would continue for a long time? The answers were not as simple as the questions.

Neither sort of propaganda showed a clear overall advantage, but important differences became evident when prior opinions were taken into account. Those who had previously expected an early armistice were better persuaded by arguments in the two-sided or debate format. Apparently, one-sided arguments were relatively useless against those who held contrary views; two-sided arguments were required, although even they did not succeed in persuading many men. Yet the one-sided argument was effective with those who were already predicting a long struggle with Japan; it strengthened this belief for them. With these men, two-sided arguments were found to be relatively ineffective, perhaps having confused some of them. In general, it seems that to be effective the argument either had to confirm a person's earlier opinions or treat those opinions as plausible while implanting a contrary case. Hence, in most cases, the recipients' later opinions were not a simple consequence of the propaganda they had received. Apparently they depended crucially on earlier beliefs as well.

What was true of the average soldier was not true of the poorly educated men, however. With them, the one-sided argument was generally the more effective. Conceivably, they had not earlier had any real opinions to influence their reception of the propaganda, or had little basis for confidence in their opinions.

In this research, the object of persuasion had been to change beliefs rather than attitudes. However, the applicability of its findings on the relative persuasiveness of one- and two-sided arguments was fully confirmed almost 20 years later in an experiment on the evaluative judgments of Japanese students (McGinnies, 1966). Thus, with the exception of poorly educated people, one-sided propaganda generally "persuades" only the converted. Most people are not easily manipulated by propaganda. Some, nonetheless, can be influenced to change their judgments, when the persuader first acknowledges their prior beliefs and evaluations as reasonable and then goes on to provide good reasons for placing greater faith in the opposing position.

Protection against Persuasion

A particularly valuable sort of belief to use in studies of persuasion is one that is generally accepted within a culture. Such beliefs are seldom attacked or defended, so few people learn relevant arguments. McGuire (1962), who first drew attention to the vulnerability of such beliefs to "brainwashing," called them "cultural truisms." An example is the (evaluative) proposition, "Everyone *should* brush his teeth after every meal if at all possible." McGuire and associates set out to discover the best way to prepare a person who had never heard arguments against such beliefs to resist their influence.

In the first study, two sorts of protection were tried, one for each of two, from a total of four, truisms. In one, the target persons were supplied with arguments supporting the truism. The other strategy exposed them to easily refuted attacks on the truism and then either provided them with a rebuttal or encouraged them to think up their own counterarguments. This procedure was called "inoculation." For each person, two truisms had no special treatment; these were the control truisms. (The experiment was so designed that, when everybody's results were pooled, each truism fell into each category equally often.)

After the initial treatment (or no treatment), acceptance of the four truisms was assessed. Then, 2 days later, all persons were exposed to strong attacks on all four of them, and their evaluations of all the propositions were reassessed. For the control truisms, the changes were marked. Both categories of experimental truisms showed less change than they did. However, acceptance of the truisms for which inoculation had been provided changed least of all. Relevant information and supportive arguments provided some help in maintaining beliefs held earlier. But experience in refuting weak attacks on one's beliefs evidently created more effective resistance to strong attacks upon them. Developing an argument might be described as tracing a path through one's beliefs and values. In any case, by the Rosenberg criterion, experience in defending evaluative judgments converts them into attitudes, with dispositional significance, and increases the independence of their advocates.

Why this should be so is not clear. One investigator (Scott, 1957, 1959) has shown greater change of opinion by debaters who were rewarded (by group approval) after producing an argument contrary to their prior views, than occurred in others who were not so rewarded. This result suggests that external rewards can alter one's attitudes by conditioning new values. Evidence supporting the belief that CR training can have such effects has long been known (Razran, 1938, 1940). Social rewards, like group approval, clearly influence one's adoption of group views (Kiesler, 1969). On the other hand, the task of developing contrary arguments seems actually to change a person's understanding of relations between the attitude object and his values, that is, to change his beliefs (Janis & King, 1954; King & Janis, 1956). One presumably discovers relevant considerations he or she had previously disregarded. Hence, it seems that beliefs and evaluations can both be altered by experiences like those that increase resistance to counterpersuasion. Although it is not yet possible to be more precise about how it occurs, it is evident that success in organizing beliefs into arguments favoring an evaluative proposition increases a person's resistance to counterpersuasion and gives the proposition an attitudinal character. Moreover, this general result is compatible with Rosenberg's conception of attitudes.

COGNITIVE CONSISTENCY AND NEW INFORMATION

Rosenberg's is merely one of a variety of "cognitive consistency" theories of attitudes, which deal with the relationship between prior beliefs and the effectiveness of propaganda. Each of them accounts for the fact that the acceptability of incoming information depends upon the beliefs, expectations, and values that underlie one's current attitudes. Given that new information is received and understood, then, according to these theories, its effect will depend entirely on how the message seems to the recipient to mesh with his prior "knowledge." If it is incompatible, it may be disregarded as incredible. On the other hand, it may be treated as credible, perhaps because of its source. It is then that it leads to a change in attitudes—or at least in those components of attitudes with which the new information is inconsistent. Theoretically, that change will be one that increases the mutual compatibility of the various elements of one's knowledge. This sort of consistency or compatibility is thus important in attitude theory, and psychologists are now engaged in finding out more about it.

Rosenberg's theory of "affective–cognitive consistency" speaks of two sources of consistency and inconsistency, both construed in terms of relations between entity concepts. It assumes that

> persons, policies, or institutions that are favored are usually cognized as serving the attainment of desirable conditions and impeding the attainment of undesirable ones, as having attributes that are admired or cherished, as grouped with other attractive persons, policies, or institutions, and as standing separate from unattractive ones [1968, p. 74].

The first source is thus positive or negative causal relations ("serving ... and impeding"). The second is the associative or dissociative relations that are implied by evaluative groupings ("grouped with ... and ... standing separate from"). The functions of these different sorts of consistency or inconsistency are illustrated in a well conceived experiment that also shows the utility of Rosenberg's theory for predicting the credibility of communications (Abelson & Rosenberg, 1958).

Nearly 100 university students were asked to make some judgments about the credibility of information on a business problem, each acting as if he were the manager of a large department store. In that role, each no doubt understood he was to set a high *value* on maintaining the highest possible volume of sales in all departments, but he was so instructed anyway. Each was also instructed, with appropriate supporting statements, so as to create three *beliefs* that posed the basic problem: (*a*) Fenwick, the manager of the rug department, plans to mount a display of modern art (MA) in his department; (*b*) during his time as manager, Fenwick has raised the volume of rug department sales; and (*c*) displays of MA in department stores have been found to *reduce* the volume of sales. Thus each was taught to believe there was a threat to the smooth functioning of the enterprise he was supposed to be managing.

In the experimental manipulation, the students were split into three groups and further persuaded to adopt different evaluations of Fenwick and of MA. Group A was asked to act as if they liked both, Group B as if they disliked both, and Group C as if they liked Fenwick but not MA. So, each person finally had three evaluations of the attitude objects (sales, Fenwick, and MA) and three beliefs about relations among them. Moreover, some inconsistency had been contrived for each of them. For those in Group A, putting a positive value on all three objects, the built-in inconsistency was due to the belief that MA would reduce sales. For Group B, holding an unfavorable attitude to Fenwick and to MA, but favoring sales, the inconsistent belief was that Fenwick had been good for sales in the rug department. Finally, for Group C, which liked Fenwick but not MA, the inconsistency was that the good Fenwick intended to display the bad MA.

Then the acceptability of various messages was appraised. All students were asked to read communications supposed to have come from three store officials, saying different things about the case. They were asked to score each message to show how accurate they judged it to be, how much it pleased them, and how much it persuaded them. Communication A said MA displays actually increase sales; Communication B said Fenwick had actually failed to maintain the volume of sales in his department, and Communication C denied that Fenwick was intending to display MA. A person could, of course, accept any one, any two, or all three of the messages. However, each one had been specifically designed to reduce the inconsistency faced by one of the experimental groups, and the theory predicted that it would be preferred to the other two on all counts. In other words, the theory predicted that the credibility of the three messages would vary among the groups as a function of their different evaluations of Fenwick and of MA.

The predictions were strongly confirmed, and these results were reproduced in a second experiment. The "managers" who liked both Fenwick and MA preferred to believe that MA displays are good for sales. Those who disliked both found it more acceptable to learn that Fenwick had not in fact been a capable department manager. And those who liked Fenwick but not MA were happiest to learn that he was not intending the threatened display.

Thus people in managerial roles probably consider their private evaluations of relevant entities when judging the credibility of consistency-restoring information. Any one of the communications could have resolved the basic dilemma, but for each group, two of them would have left some residual inconsistency of the associative–dissociative kind. For instance, Group A managers (liking sales, Fenwick, and MA) could have accepted the message that assured them that the good Fenwick was not intending to threaten sales by displaying MA. They preferred, however, to believe that MA displays actually increase sales, presumably because the former would have left them believing that the good Fenwick was dissociated from the good MA.

CONSISTENCY AND DISCRIMINATION

Rosenberg's two sorts of cognitive consistency are evident in this experiment. The one, which consists in a preference for believing that good things go together, involves a failure of discrimination in all respects but value. It is nonanalytic. The other involves a causal–analytic consistency. Given the value of sales, the basic dilemma had been posed by the implied contradiction of one belief with the other two. Recall that Fenwick was supposed to *intend* a particular kind of *action*. This became a cause for concern because displays of modern art were supposed to be *capable* of reducing the volume of department store sales. The quandary had also been biased by the belief that Fenwick was a competent sales manager, *capable* of promoting sales. Thus three causal relations and the high value of sales had established the basic "inconsistency." However, they had also produced recognition of a *threat*—that an assumedly competent department manager was about to do something that could be bad for business. This causal inconsistency is similar to the source of anxiety that Epstein called "stimulus incongruity" (see pp. 67–69, this volume).

Notice now that this description of the store managers' concern has been focused on attributions of *activity* to Fenwick and of *potency* to both Fenwick and modern art displays. Indeed it was these "beliefs," together with the *value* placed on sales, that defined the basic problem. The ascription to an impending *activity* of *potency* to block attainment of a *valued* condition constituted a threat. The same analysis applies to Rosenberg's definition of an attitude, as exemplified by cognitively consistent evaluations of the proposal to admit girls to Yale. Unless a respondent ascribed to the impending *action* the *power* of affecting some *valued* condition, his evaluative statements about that action varied considerably with time and could not be regarded as revealing an "attitude." This formulation accordingly suggests that enduring evaluative dispositions have their bases in attributions of value, potency, and activity to various entities.

Some Elementary Qualitative Cognitions

That people in fact commonly understand things and events in terms of activity and potency, as well as value, was demonstrated in an extensive series of investigations (Osgood, Succi, & Tannenbaum, 1957). The researchers had asked people to describe entity concepts in terms of as many as 50 pairs of adjectives—grading the concepts as between extreme adjectives. Altogether, they had collected information on hundreds of entities. Examples of the adjective pairs they used are heavy–light, sharp–dull, and sacred–profane. Each person had recorded his descriptions of each entity by marking the place between the members of each pair where he thought it belonged. These responses were easily translated into numbers or scores.

The scores for each entity on each of the 50 adjectival rating scales were then analyzed statistically to specify the relations among them. Clearly, any two entities that had been given the same ratings on all scales must have the same meaning in terms of those scales. Finally the statistics expressing those relations were submitted to factor analysis, to identify the major distinctions underlying the descriptions. Although analysis of some samples yielded four or more dimensions of discrimination, it was concluded that three independent distinctions accounted for most of the variation in ratings. In the order of their importance, the three independent dimensions of differentiation were: *evaluation* (good–bad, pleasant–unpleasant, etc.), *potency* (strong–weak, hard–soft, etc.) and *activity* (active–passive, fast–slow, etc.). All of the average ratings of each entity could be reproduced without great error from ratings on these three dimensions.

It must be clear that "engines" for instance, are not fully defined by saying that they are strong, active, and moderately good. Nor has such a claim been made. Even so, a description of engines in those terms makes some sense by contrast to comparable descriptions of, say, slime or dust. Such descriptions are imprecise but meaningful. The type of meaning they convey has been designated "connotation" as distinct from the "denotation" of dictionary definition. The relations they summarize are more like analogies than identities, more suitable to poetry than to algebra. Nonetheless, it is conceivable that these distinctions represent important, even fundamental, decisions about what things or events in one's environment deserve most attention.

You can pound or prise with hard, strong, heavy things. Such *potent* things are durable and may be useful, not only because softer, weaker, lighter things give way before them, but because useful things are potent. They may also be dangerous, of course, if they are *active*. Movement creates change and possible danger, whereas passive entities can be ignored—as the background against which actions stand out. And of course whether a thing is good or bad is a basic motivational decision about it. Although the evidence reveals judgmental agreement on perhaps as few as three dimensions of differentiation, those judgments do appear likely to have fundamental adaptive significance at the causal–analytic level, like that claimed for evaluative attributions at the motivational level.

ANXIETY AND THE ACCEPTANCE OF NEW INFORMATION

In the experiment with Fenwick, modern art, and sales, perception of a threat to a valued condition set the stage for attention to incoming information. What proved to be the most credible subsequent message was the one containing information that removed this basic threat without at the same time forcing recognition of another one. Acceptance of the other messages would have posed threats to other evaluations, for example, of Fenwick or of MA, and it was theoretically for this reason that they were rejected as "incredible." Evidently new information is incredible if it conflicts with many established beliefs, and credible if it reduces threats—which, of course, exist in similar cases of incongruity.

Attitude change investigators have described another selective process that has effects like the credibility testing just described and has similar relations to anxiety. Known as "selective exposure," this is the process by which people avoid information that seems likely to be incompatible with their beliefs, values, and attitudes. When free to choose, individuals in one experiment elected to work with people of similar, rather than different, social backgrounds more frequently after their confidence about acceptability had been lowered than after it had been raised (Walster & Walster, 1963). In another case, additional pamphlets in support of political opponents were requested less often by people who had first received strong arguments that presumably threatened their convictions than by others who had received weak ones. Of course the reverse was true when the pamphlets supported the preferred party (Lowin, 1967). What Berlyne (1960) has referred to as "stimulus complexity" and "novelty," and Epstein (1972) called "stimulus incongruity," seems to promote information seeking less commonly after confidence has been lowered than after it has been raised. When confidence is low, it may create avoidance reactions instead—even among the relatively efficacious persons who were studied in these experiments.

Threat, however, can also stimulate acceptance of new information and thereby provoke changes in attitudes. The initial experiment in a series that ultimately demonstrated this fact (Janis & Feshbach, 1953) was directed to persuading high school students to adopt recommended procedures for tooth care, and it used one-sided arguments. Four groups of students served as recipients. Three of them watched illustrated lecture films about dental hygiene, while the fourth, a control group, watched a filmed lecture about the human eye. The three dental care films all mentioned the bad consequences of neglect, but they differed in emphasis. Film A featured spectacular and frightening illustrations, Film B gave less spectacular factual descriptions of dangerous consequences, and Film C made passing mention of pain from tooth decay and mouth infection. The films were intended to induce varying degrees of fear, as opposed to confidence, while passing on the same advice about tooth care. A week later all four groups were asked for detailed information about their tooth brushing practices, and the resulting information was examined for evidence of persuasion.

The mild fear group (those who had seen Film C) was most persuaded and the strong fear group (Film A) least, if at all. In a later test for resistance to counterpersuasion, students who had been exposed to the strong fear appeal showed less resistance than those in the weak fear group. The evidence seemed consistent. It seemed also to fit the pattern of the Fenwick and selective exposure cases. Propaganda messages designed to arouse slight fear were more effective than communications intended to provoke great fear. Nevertheless this conclusion had to be modified. Other experimenters reported exactly the opposite relation between threat and persuasion with adults (Leventhal, Singer, & Jones, 1965; Leventhal, 1967). Influenced by these findings, the original investigators took a new look at their results and reported important additional facts (Janis & Feshbach, 1954). The students who had been most readily persuaded by the minimally threatening film were individuals whom their teachers regarded as notably susceptible to anxiety. By contrast, the strong threat had in fact often persuaded the more confident students!

Subsequent research has led to the conclusion that the normal relation between the persuasiveness of a message and the fearsomeness of ignoring its recommendations can be summarized in a hump-backed curve (McGuire, 1966). Up to a point, the more frightening the consequences of ignoring the advice, the more persuasion is achieved; but beyond that point the relation is reversed. If one is particularly susceptible to anxiety, the optimum degree of threat may be very low, and this seems to have been the case with the students who served in the original experiment.

EFFICACY, ATTITUDINAL CONTROL, AND FREEDOM

Take a moment to consider the meaning of the foregoing statement, before looking at its apparent explanation. A persuasive argument that evokes fear of ignoring its advice makes people behave like the poorly educated soldiers in response to one-sided propaganda. Regardless of their earlier beliefs, they seem to be persuaded. Presumably the ethnocentric prejudices of ill-educated, anxious, authoritarian personalities had been acquired in this way. The aggression they advocated against outsiders and the fear-laden reasons they advanced for such actions suggest as much. With less fear, people behave like the better-educated soldiers. Their judgments and actions are not readily changed by the propaganda. Presumably they are based upon enduring personal beliefs and values, which act as attitudes are supposed to act.

Within the lower ranges of anxiety, then, stimuli that should increase anxiety have the effect of reducing internal, attitudinal control of the judgmental process and making it more responsive to external events. Within this range, it appears, increase in emotionality acts to reduce the effectiveness of previously acquired values and beliefs, and to increase the effectiveness of newly stimulated motives. The greater the anxiety, within this range, the greater is the gullibility. Conversely, the greater a person's confidence or the higher his efficacy, the more likely is he to act under attitudinal, rather than situational, control in making his judgments.

According to a well-reasoned and widely accepted critical evaluation of relevant research (McGuire, 1968), the effects of threatening propaganda depend (as they logically should depend) upon the interaction between the message and the recipient. They depend on how the threat influences attention to the message and how it affects understanding and learning of message content. Threats call attention to the source of the threat, even as they evoke drive. Comprehension of the advice the persuader offers for dealing with the threat he has pointed out should then reduce anxiety, because it shows how the threat can be removed (see Epstein's argument, pp. 67–69, this volume). And, of course, such drive reduction during attention to a persuasive argument may reinforce learning to do what is advised. By evoking more attention and the possibility of greater drive reduction, messages that are more threatening should produce more adoptions of the persuader's advice.

However, there is a counteracting influence. High levels of emotion apparently reduce comprehension of messages (possibly by distracting the recipient or possibly by reducing his capacity to understand). Then, it appears, reaction to the incentive content of the threat impairs registration of accompanying information. When this effect develops, learning and consequently persuasion tend to be reduced. This should occur sooner when recipients are more anxious and the threatening communications more complex. At higher levels of arousal, accordingly, the relation between anxiety and persuasibility should be reversed. Confident people should be persuasible, while frightened people should be incapable of learning. The results of a number of experiments fulfill this prediction (e.g., Gollob & Dittes, 1965; and see McGuire, 1968).

The foregoing set of propositions has central theoretical significance, because it supports the assumptions of the implicit theory of responsibility that underlie inference of dispositions (see Chapter 2). What it shows, briefly, is that attitudinal or *dispositional control of* (evaluative) *behavior is most clearly evident under the conditions in which personal responsibility is imputed and personal dispositions are inferred.* In a general sense, the inference of dispositional control in these circumstances is evidently justifiable—although, of course, the particular inference may or may not be accurate in any given case.

In the higher ranges of emotional arousal, increases in external threat *reduce* persuasibility, apparently because the resulting emotion interferes with comprehension of the persuasive argument. If this is the correct explanation, then the relation between rising emotion and the strength of self-controlling mechanisms would be consistent throughout the whole range: the greater the arousal, the weaker the cognitive control. Attitudinal control of evaluative behavior would be merely the first victim of a dedifferentiating process that ultimately impairs cognitive registration of reality.

The fault of comprehension that seems to reduce the persuasibility of severely threatened and anxious persons theoretically operates to select the information they understand. They remain capable of following only the simpler arguments on threatening topics (and more complex arguments only on nonthreatening topics). Accordingly, their solutions to complex problems on frightening issues must often become oversimplified—like those of anxious, ethnocentric, authoritarian personalities.

The Need for Attitudinal Validity

As the preceding statement implies, attitudinal independence, alone, cannot be a sufficient condition for the maintenance of mental freedom over the long term, even though it be a necessary one. The dispositions must be appropriate to reality as well. Their motivational and informational determinants—values and beliefs— must be *valid*. However, a set of valid beliefs can be developed and maintained only when threatening as well as benign information can be approached, under- stood, tested for credibility, and adopted if necessary. According to the evidence just reviewed, confidence or efficacy facilitates such appraisal and adoption. The conditions that promote objectivity in evaluative judgment are, thus, much like those that promote the judgmental constancy that attests dispositional control of value decisions.

Attitudinal stability may be liberating and responsible or it may be enslaving and irresponsible, depending upon the validity of the attitudes and how their stability is attained. Closed-mindedness is a special, subjective form of attitudi- nal constancy. Likewise, the distinction between the irresponsible and gullible form of persuasion and the relatively responsible form that involves adoption of superior information is also a matter of their determinants. Under normally low levels of threat, efficacy retards the one and promotes the other. This is just what it does, respectively, for the subjectively and objectively determined sorts of attitudinal stability as well.

The latter, incidentally, is essentially the form of argument made by Kubie in preparing to defend his proposition that the essential feature of "normal" as distinct from neurotic behavior "centers around the freedom and flexibility to learn through experience, and to adapt to changing external circumstances." As he expressed the point, "Whether or not a behavioral event is free to change depends not upon the quality of the act itself, but upon the nature of the constel- lation of forces that has produced it [Kubie, 1954, p. 183]."

CONCEPTUAL SYSTEMS AND
ATTITUDINAL STABILITY

Human evaluative actions are, of course, subject to social influence by various techniques. Two contrasting ways in which people can influence one another's values and beliefs are *persuasion* and *education,* according to a theory by Harold H. Kelley (1967). These different approaches are supposed to have different effects on "the freedom and flexibility to learn through experience, and to adapt to changing circumstances." Theoretically, too, the attitudes produced by these different techniques vary remarkably in the "constellation of forces" required to change them. A review of Kelley's theory accordingly promises to promote understanding of the determinants of constancy and change in evaluative behavior.

People differ in the number of opportunities they are accorded to influence others. Our evaluations of different persons affect the attention we give to them. Those evaluations provide the cognitive context in which social influences operate. Consideration of Kelley's theory can therefore be approached conveniently by starting with an example of social evaluative behavior.

The example to be considered is a set of evaluations and beliefs about other people that were held by a 14-year-old boy named John (Doe). It will be remembered that attitudinal stability is due, according to Rosenberg, to the embedding of an evaluative judgment in a set of supporting, largely consistent cognitions. The example will show how a variety of persons (as attitude "objects") are understood to be related to one another in terms of various concepts.

Figure 8.1 shows the principal distinctions John made in specifying the ways in which 22 acquaintances were alike and different. It also shows how he labeled those differential attributes. According to Kelly (1955), who introduced the method used to produce the figure, it shows how John *construed* the various social *roles* of his community. "Roles" are the parts people play in society. Their differences reveal the "structure" of society, in the same way, for instance, as the complementarity of a "boss" role and a "worker" role shows the hierarchical structure of industry.

The information in Figure 8.1 was collected on a "role construct repertory grid" and subjected to a special analysis. A person is first asked to list the names of people he knows who fit a set of descriptions for different "roles." These names are then set out as columns on a grid, and he is asked to think about three designated persons until he remembers a way in which two of them are alike and differ from the third. He is to put an X under the names of those two and write a few words in the margin to say how they are alike and how they differ from the third. Then he is to go back and indicate everyone else who is like those two in that respect. These operations can be performed repeatedly, beginning with different trios, but a person usually starts to repeat himself after 20 or so repetitions, so the standard task calls for only 22 sortings. John began to have difficulty after 11. He was then provided with three more "constructs," one at a time, and asked to mark two further rows to show who had those attributes. The plot in Figure 8.1 is therefore based on a grid of X's and blanks, showing how 14 different concepts were applied to 22 different people.

The method used to analyze John's grid resembles factor analysis. The object of its first step was to find the most frequent general pattern of X's and blanks. It would represent some unknown attribute common to many of those that were named. Nine named constructs were found to match a single pattern more closely than chance would account for. The analysis then looked among the remaining five constructs for a second common pattern, independent of the first. Three of

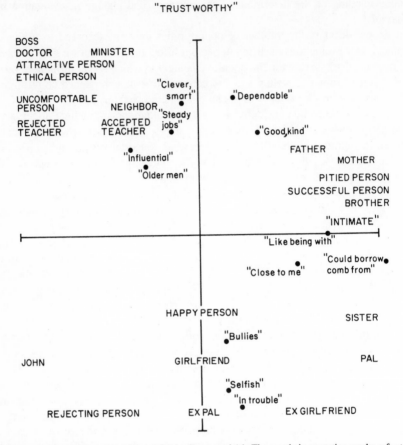

Figure 8.1. The role concept schema of John Doe, aged 14. The words in quotation marks refer to concepts John used to describe persons he knew who filled the roles designated by capital letters. Although the location of the various roles is approximate, the heavy dots beside the quoted words indicate their precise loadings on the two factors. The methods of data collection and analysis are described in the text. [Based on G. A. Kelly's (1955) method.]

them fitted it, as did one from the first nine. Third, these "general constructs" were set out as the axes for Figure 8.1 and each of the original attributions was plotted in the resulting space, according to the resemblance of its pattern to each of theirs. Finally, the persons John had described were scored in terms of the consistency with which the two general constructs had been ascribed to them, and they were plotted in a similar way.

The principal and most frequent distinction John made between people was an evaluative one. As the figure shows, this distinction has to do with being "good" (and "kind"), that is "dependable," as opposed to being "selfish," "in trouble," or "bullies." This seems to be a matter of trustworthiness and may reflect the fact that at the time he completed his grid, he was facing a court hearing on charges of having shot a man.

Two observations suggest that the principal distinction in Figure 8.1 also entails potency and esteem, or perhaps efficacy. First, dependable people are able to get others to do what they want. That is they are "influential," and they "have steady jobs." Second, all the high-status figures in the original list (two teachers, a doctor, a minister, an employer) are described as trustworthy. By contrast, John and his younger intimates not only lack jobs and influence, they are also deficient in the other characteristics of trustworthy people. Indeed, the plot implies that, in John's mind, being in trouble, selfish, and a bully are necessary concomitants of low potency or low efficacy.

The second distinction represents another sort of trustworthiness or "goodness." It differentiates people John liked to be with, people he was close to, or people he "could borrow a comb from" (his intimates) from others.

The display of Figure 8.1 can serve incidentally to introduce two observations about John's understanding of his social environment. These observations, in turn, raise interesting theoretical issues. One is that Figure 8.1 represents John himself as relatively low in value by comparison with other persons he knows. Some theorists consider low self-esteem, low self-satisfaction, or low self-regard to be criteria of maladjustment. This fact and these interpretations are therefore of considerable importance and will be discussed in a later chapter.

The second of the observations refers to the simplicity of John's role concept system. It represents people as differing along essentially three dimensions (a doublet construct having been omitted from the figure), whereas the average young adult uses five or six (Easterbrook, 1966). One possible interpretation is that the real social system John lived in was a simple one, containing relatively few different kinds of positions, and this may be true. Another is that some of its general descriptions are wrong as to implication—at least incomplete and perhaps untenable. It is surprising, for instance, to learn that people with "steady jobs" are regarded as "clever," "smart," and "dependable."

An accurate perception of reality has been regarded by many theorists as one mark, if not the criterion, of good personal adjustment (Jahoda, 1958). Although there are obvious difficulties to using this formulation, it seems to refer to the same phenomena that were discussed in earlier chapters as "objectivity" in the determination of behavior. Whether John's descriptions of reality are accurate or objective is no doubt open to question. It seems clear, however, that he is "maladjusted."

Thus, the two important observations about Figure 8.1 are that it may oversimplify, and perhaps distort, social reality; and that it represents John unfavorably by comparison with people of higher social esteem or status whom he knows. Both suggest maladjustment according to different criteria. There are, however, other possible relationships between these observations. For one, the appearance of cognitive simplicity and of low social potency might be common effects of the sort of influence techniques to which John had been exposed. The theory on the shaping of attributive judgments, due to H. H. Kelley (1967), suggests as much. It is directed specifically to the explanation of inconsistencies between personal experiences and expressed attitudes or beliefs.

CONCEPTUAL SYSTEMS AS PRODUCTS OF SOCIAL INFLUENCE

The principal difference of persuasion from education, according to Kelley's theory, lies in the criterion of truth to which each makes it major appeal. In education, the criterion is said to be *consistency* of personal experience with a given entity, both through time and between sensory modes. In persuasion, it is said to be *consensus,* which means agreement with those around one whom one trusts, to the neglect of inconsistent personal experiences if necessary.

Normally, according to Kelley, we all use both the consistency and consensus criteria in making attributions to entities in our environment, that is, in "the process of inferring or perceiving the dispositional properties of entities in the environment, . . . stable features of distal objects such as color, size, shape, intention, desire, sentiment, and ability [1967, p. 193]." Although designated "objects" and including characteristics of people, such "entities" may be the referents of such abstract concepts as "fair play," "justice," and so on. Theoretically, when a person's sensory impressions are distinctive in the presence of an entity, when his reactions to it are consistent, and when others agree with them, the entity will be confidently identified as the source of the reaction. Then a person will feel confident in its presence, make judgments quickly, and act with speed and vigor.

If all of the entities a person perceives in a situation are subjects of stable attributions, the theory says he will be capable of independent action in that situation. Otherwise, he will seek help from someone to whom he attributes both appropriate knowledge and trustworthiness—qualities that John found together in his lawyer who was the "attractive person" of Figure 8.1. It is when one seeks guidance from others that differential weight might be placed on the consistency and consensus criteria of attributional validity.

Assuming that the presumedly trustworthy expert does in fact provide guidance, the adaptability the learner achieves will depend upon what form the guidance takes. The expert might simply offer conclusions, evaluations, opinions, and directions, perhaps with illustrations of their application. This is a "practical" approach. If the learner follows this guidance, he will have done so out of respect and trust for the other. He will have used the advice because his expert produced it and not because it made sense to him in terms of the consistency of his experience with the object of guidance. The influence procedure would have been one of *persuasion* and its acceptance would refer to the *consensus* criterion. It would leave the learner only partly informed. When he met a new problem he would again have to consult an expert, would presumably be readily influenced by him, perhaps gullible, and would display little attributional stability of his own—except toward experts.

Psychologists know a good deal about the tendencies of people to use consensus as a canon for truth. For instance, large numbers of investigators have reported evidence in support of a number of similar theories, the root form of which spoke of "balance" and "imbalance" between cognitions (Heider, 1958). These theories hold that people who perceive themselves as belonging together (associatively) are distressed unless they can agree about a particular entity, whereas people who perceive themselves as belonging apart (dissociatively) are distressed unless they can disagree. Considerable evidence buttresses this proposition, although it supports particularly the first clause whereas the second is more questionable (Burnstein, 1969). As demonstrated in the Asch "conformity" situation, it is evident that people become distressed when their views of a thing differ from those of their associates, and that some of them adjust their views accordingly. Much, however, remains to be discovered about the determinants of preference for the *consensus* criterion of attributional validity.

The various techniques that might be used for *persuasion* and for appeals to the *consensus* criterion are not described in Kelley's theoretical paper. All of the behaviors by which leaders or advisers inculcate tendencies to "conformity" may be involved (see Chapter 6). Perhaps the advisers who practice persuasion do so by rewarding agreement, loyalty, obedience, and imitation, and by punishing or becoming distressed by divergent opinions or actions. Perhaps they display fears of their own while proferring advice and so, unintentionally, produce threatening propaganda (see pp. 145–147, this volume). Or maybe they merely fail to teach useful analytic and theoretical skills—because they do not know how or because their communication skills are inadequate, as Bernstein suggests, or because they are preoccupied ("do it because I say so"). There are no clear facts. Kelley's discussion, however, focuses upon educational deficits in their methods of influence.

The alternative strategy Kelley describes for the passing of information from expert to novice is the one he calls *education*. It is a nondirective, objective, and theoretical approach, conceived to be oriented to providing, "the means of obtaining consistency, both over time and modality" in new attributions. Kelley (1967) continues

> For example, B may demonstrate a new way of looking at or interacting with the entity which enables A to find consistency in his subsequent confrontations with it. What B provides may consist of new analytic methods, problem solving procedures, practice in the use of a given

modality in order to increase its consistency, new perspectives and frameworks for evaluating items, training in discrimination and judgment, the suggestion of crucial comparisons in order to sharpen discriminations and evaluations, a demonstration of the relevance of facts and information that A had not previously appreciated, or instruction in relevant verbal labels. These methods have in common the property that they may be used by A independently of B (once A has learned them) and they contribute directly to the fulfillment of the consistency criteria. . . . The content of this influence will be adopted and held by A because it affords him attributional stability, and not because of [any attribute of B] [p. 201].[1]

When a learner's lessons have commonly appealed to the consistency criterion of attributional validity and his use of them has produced consistent results, he will have achieved what Kelley calls a high information level. Provided that his attributions are well differentiated, he will also have attained what may be called *informational independence*. Thereafter, because his knowledge is analytic and theoretical, he will be able to deal with new situations on his own. The cognitive links between entities he knows about will often be logical relations, rather than associative groupings. So he will also have the means to attain confidence and motivational independence, and will have no more need for stimulation than for guidance from experts. Perhaps, indeed, his competence will then have surpassed that of his earlier instructors. They will then have shared fully the power their competence had conferred upon them.

The effect of inadequate instruction in methods for personal discovery of consistent attributions may well be, as Kelley portrays it, undue reliance on the consensus criterion of truth. What is true will then consist, much of the time, in what the experts say or do and what "everybody" says or does, notwithstanding contradictory personal experiences. The various entities that such deprived people know about would then be cognitively interlinked more by association (as in the case of the expert and his advice) or dissociation than by causal connection. Consequently, the people concerned would remain informationally dependent, presumably compliant, and readily persuasible in new situations, though perhaps closed-minded in familiar ones. Old societies composed of large members of such persons ought therefore to show considerable unanimity of opinion and belief. "Authoritarians," "yielders," and "externals," it will be recalled, have these characteristics and are often hampered by low formal education as well.

Attitudinal Rigidity Revisited

A simple set of beliefs, such as that depicted in Figure 8.1, seems to reflect what Kelley calls a low level of information. Several of them, no doubt, could

---

[1]Reprinted by permission of University of Nebraska Press from "Attribution Theory in Social Psychology," in David Levine (Ed.), *Nebraska Symposium on Motivation*. Copyright 1967 by University of Nebraska Press.

easily be proven invalid, and it is probable that John had experienced discrepant events. *If a person relies upon the consensus criterion of truth, he must often ignore contradictory experiences* (see pp. 97–99, this volume) *or construe them in such a way as to blind himself to the contradiction.* The discrimination required for the development of objectivity may be incompatible with reliance upon the consensus criterion of truth.

How might one blind oneself to a contradiction between new experiences and old beliefs? One reasonable suggestion, besides those implicit in the attitude change research, is that one's experiences are registered in terms consistent with those in which one's current beliefs are stored. The complementarity of perceptual and memorial categories is familiar to psychologists who study the relation between attention and memory (Haber, 1966, 1970). To particularize, as long as John continued to register as connoting "trustworthiness" all the various objective events he denoted by terms like "influential," "good and kind," "dependable," and "has a steady job," he would not appreciate any inconsistencies between them. That is, by use of inappropriate verbal labels (in Kelley's terms), he could continue to believe that those characterizations mean trustworthiness.

Complementarity in relationships between old knowledge and new learning provides a mechanism for resistance to change in what has been described as a *conceptual system* (Harvey, Hunt, & Schroder, 1961). Theoretically, it is as a consequence of this sort of systematic relationship between belief and perception that cognitive development proceeds, not by small steps, but by stages, as contended by a large number of *epigenic* theorists.[2] Before discrepant experiences can invalidate current beliefs, they must be *registered* appropriately. Cognitive development is accordingly assumed by many writers to depend upon the development of new differentiations or distinctions. It ought, accordingly, to be retarded by influences—like those involving anxieties in the Asch conformity test situation—that appeal to the consensus criterion of truth. And it ought to be promoted by influences that appeal to consistency of personal experience and promote independence in the appraisal of truth.

The conceptual system depicted in Figure 8.1 will become open to some new information, and accordingly more objective, once it has begun to perceive and to believe, for example, that some people with steady jobs are not dependable or trustworthy. Following Kelley's theory, influence by consistency-oriented advisers ought to facilitate such development. Being open to new information is not, however, the sole theoretical advantage of conceptual systems that develop under such influence. They should also be self-educating and self-correcting, after the

---

[2]Those who believe development occurs by qualitative rather than quantitative changes. The leading modern exponent of this view of mental development is Jean Piaget (see, for example, Piaget, 1952).

manner of the positivistic sciences, which are, of course, examples of consistency-oriented conceptual systems.

ATTITUDINALLY MEDIATED BEHAVIOR
AND THE SUPEREGO

On the basis of an argument introduced at the beginning of this chapter, the major generalizations stated in the foregoing discussion refer to the conditions of constancy and change in superego function. Of course, they also describe influences that alter the relative effectiveness of internally, as opposed to externally, initiated motivational processes. Accordingly, it can be argued that *superego strength varies directly with constancy in moral evaluation, that is, with the domination of decisions by previously acquired knowledge and ideals ("beliefs" and "values"), rather than by novel information and incentives found in the decision situation.*

Reinterpreted in accordance with these defining assumptions, the foregoing evidence supports two generalizations about superego strength. The first is that it *rises* as a positive function of the amount of prior knowledge a person uses in his evaluations. The pertinent evidence was provided by Rosenberg's experiments on attitudinal constancy. The second is based on the studies of persuasion with threat. It is that superego strength *falls* as a joint function of the severity of situationally induced threat and of the evaluator's susceptibility to anxiety. Briefly, then, superego strength seems to rise with efficacy and with the application of informed intelligence in decision making.

In this context, incidentally, a previously rejected proposition about behavioral control can be seen to contain a kernel of truth. The proposition stated, "To the extent that the person expects reward for his task he is unfree . . . the source of the reward is an external causal locus for his behavior [de Charms, 1968, p. 329]." The truth is that the "unfree" are remarkable for the dominance of current, external events over prior knowledge and motives in the determination of their behavior (and for whatever brings about this dominance). The "driven," it might be said, are remarkable for *lack* of that *freedom of choice* which appropriate internalized information and low levels of drive confer upon one. But it is not their expectation of reward, nor yet of external reward, which characterizes that reduced freedom. It is the domination of their behavior by a *singular* expectation of whatever kind, due perhaps to ignorance or to high levels of drive.

The remaining generalizations suggested by the foregoing review are more tentative and have to do with moral development and its arrest or fixation as moral rigidity. The sort of information that raises or reduces threats may normally promote the adaptation of the superego to new situations. In remarkably threat-sensitive persons, however, it can cause both a loss of attitudinal stability under minimal threat and a failure to adapt under high threat. This sometimes seems to occur because that information is ignored or rejected as incredible, and sometimes, theoretically, because the threat it creates renders its advice incomprehensible. Possibly the new information is sometimes also misconstrued as confirming the beliefs it contradicts, due to the inappropriate labeling of experience. In any case, the result amounts to *fixation* of superego development. The subsequent ignorance should then lead to ill-justified, over-simplified moral judgments of the kind that are called "dogmatic" in accounts of the value systems of anxious "yielders," "externals," and "authoritarian personalities."

Kelley's theoretical contributions are compatible with the foregoing generalizations. Moreover, hypothetically they integrate them. Motivational (and moral) constancy is a special case of attributional stability. And the confidence that comes with a high information level is due to *both* a large number of supporting cognitions *and* their proof in (efficacious) experience. Informational independence is conceived to be related to the same variables as are the twin concepts of free will and responsibility, that is, to informed intelligence and efficacy. Moreover, a high information level is supposed to facilitate the independent development of information from personal experience, rather than from the advice or example of others. Kelley's conception accordingly gives extra meaning to the differentiation of responsible from irresponsible adoption or rejection of information. In these terms, superego strength is a matter of informational independence.

The evaluative attributions of informationally dependent people, trained to rely upon the consensus criterion, should be readily modifiable by persuasion. Their dependence on the beliefs of persons they regard as trustworthy sources of information ought also to make them particularly likely to practice "selective exposure" by avoiding information from unfamiliar sources that apparently contradict their current beliefs. Their evaluative actions should therefore have a dogmatic quality that would mask a basic weakness of the "superego." Since they also lack confidence, theoretically they are readily persuasible by mildly threatening propaganda and unusually susceptible to the emotional disturbances that seem to impair learning. Their evaluative actions ought to be other-directed and readily manipulable by trusted others, that is basically irresponsible in both the causal and moral senses.

Finally, Kelley's theory and assumptions have pointed to a systematic relationship between the manner in which social systems shape the behavior of their junior members and the independence the juniors subsequently display. Social groups that practice persuasion, rather than education, are expected to produce informationally dependent individuals, who display little of the motivational constancy that is the mark of an independent mind. The two following chapters deal with theory and evidence on the effects of various social structures upon individual freedom and responsibility. Some of their contents refer to this hypothesis.

SUMMARY

In attitudinally determined actions, as in other instances of self-reinforced behavior, the individual's behavior is motivationally independent of the concrete course of events in his situation. In both cases, cues in the situation are linked with concepts in the mind and hence with internal, sentimental states and appropriate external actions.

People differ in the variability of their evaluative responses to various entities, and in the ease with which these evaluations can be manipulated. Constancy in evaluation is the defining evidence of an attitude. So, people differ in the degree to which their evaluative actions are attitudinally determined and motivationally independent. Those who display greater constancy cite a greater number of similarly valued entities they believe linked to the one being evaluated and a greater number of oppositely valued entities from which they believe it dissociated.

Evaluative actions by men who have achieved little formal education are easily manipulated by propaganda. Conversely, resistance to persuasive attacks on previously unquestioned value judgments can be increased by learning arguments in support of them, especially when the learner develops such arguments for himself. In addition, within the lower ranges of anxiety, adoption of the advice of another is promoted by exposure to mildly frightening portrayals of the consequences of disregarding it. Such persuasion occurs particularly readily among less confident persons. In general, situational control of evaluative reactions is advanced, and dispositional control is retarded, by circumstances that reduce informed intelligence and efficacy, and vice versa. *This proposition supports the assumptions of theories described in Chapter 2 about the circumstances in which behavior is dispositionally controlled.*

In the higher ranges of anxiety and with more severe threats, less persuasion is attained. The current explanation is that emotion then interferes with learning and that this is *pseudo-resistance* due to failure of the learning component of self-control. Throughout its range, thus, emotional distress seems to reduce the strength of influences favorable to the internal or dispositional control of behavior.

Avoidance of information that seems contradictory to one's beliefs is another sort of closed-mindedness that increases as anxiety rises and efficacy falls. Closed-mindedness can be distinguished from informed resistance to propaganda by what brings about each of them. The same is true of gullibility as opposed to the alteration of opinion by superior new information.

Attitudinally mediated behavior appears to develop from a network of beliefs about, and evaluations of, interlinked entity concepts, that is, from extensive "knowledge" of the environment. This is illustrated in the detailed account of an attitude change experiment, which also shows the importance of two general kinds of discrimination beyond the evaluative one that is central to the attitude. These discriminations are appraisals of entities in terms of activity and potency.

Another example is a set of attitudes toward people held by a "maladjusted" boy. It appears to be oversimplified and inconsistent with some probable experiences of its author. Inappropriate conceptions of reality have been proposed as the crucial evidence of maladjustment.

A theoretical explanation was introduced to account for discrepancies between an individual's private experiences and his attributions to entities around him. Such discrepancies are ascribed to undue reliance upon *consensus,* as opposed to *consistency* with personal experience, as the criterion of truth. This theory accordingly postulates two different types of relationships between the cognitions in which attitudes are embedded. The bias toward consensus as the criterion of truth is attributed to a person's having frequently been influenced by persuasion, rather than education, when he consulted advisers.

Education is assumed by this theory to promote informational independence. This involves individual credibility tests of perceived information for consistency with personal experience, and it culminates in confidence when such consistency is frequently discerned. Persuasion, by contrast, is supposed to promote informational dependence, lack of confidence in private interpretations of experience, and reliance upon consensus as the criterion of truth.

Considering attitudinal constancy as a special case of the attributional stability it ascribes to informational independence, this theory seems to integrate the foregoing evidence. In its terms, superego strength is a matter of informational independence. That, however, is a theoretical consequence of the influence techniques that are commonly employed in the social system in which a person is raised.

IV

THE SHARING
OF FREEDOM

The Creation
of Social Cooperation

Emotional control and abstract self-control should be evident in some of the different ways people develop for dealing with situations that are potentially emotion producing. Self-controlling, "free" persons should react to such circumstances with "self-discipline" and "will power." Their actions should be determined "rationally" and objectively to establish control over predictable events, "independent on inclination" (to quote Kant's term). "Driven" persons, by contrast, should behave emotionally, reacting on inclination as stimulated by events. Such differences in behavior exist in fact, as demonstrated in previous chapters. It is the purpose of this chapter to describe some evidence that shows in greater detail how this occurs, and to do so in a way that raises further crucial points about freedom of will and responsibility.

When distressing events are known to be under the immediate control of another person, anxiety about them amounts to distrust of him. This social form of anxiety is, of course, extremely important to the topic of free will. If a person's ongoing action is threatening to others, they may interfere with its progress. However, his freedom of will requires that they respond only to the *effects* of his actions, not their appearance. Otherwise their interference will prevent him from shaping his actions for objective effect, and he may be forced to design them for supervisor approval instead. Distrust by important others can stimulate them to arbitrary (subjectively determined) actions and so reduce the possibility of his personal freedom. Accordingly, the creation of trust in those with whom one interacts, the reduction of anxiety or fear in them, is ultimately as necessary to one's freedom of will as the reduction of drive or emotion in oneself.

A person can shape his actions to avoid predictable anxiety-provoking injuries to others and still retain his freedom of will. Indeed it will be shown that if his actions do *not* prevent predictable adverse reactions from others, he will not have gained control over his own fate (even in the apparently exceptional cases of intentional martyrdom). *In this respect, actions in a social situation are strictly comparable to actions in tracing visible mazes or driving automobiles. Freedom of will is evident in behavior that prevents possible misfortune and accidents.* Acting so as to avoid adverse reactions from others amounts, of course, to creating trust of oneself in them. Detailed consideration of the relation between freedom of will and social interaction conveniently begins, therefore, with a review of the determinants of trust and trustworthiness.

TRUST AS A FEATURE OF EFFICACY

Like confidence and anxiety, trust and distrust may develop in a context of nonsocial action when the effects of one's actions respectively promote or impair the well-being of another. Indeed the minimal requirement for a social exchange is that each of two persons can influence each other in this way, as Sidowski (1957) has pointed out. It is not necessary that they know each other, or even that they meet. Such a minimal social exchange can be illustrated in responses to conditions at a solitary picnic site that two parties visit alternately. A tabular representation of this sort of interaction is depicted in Table 9.1.

The structure of act–outcome relations in a situation has been called the "payoff matrix." The sort represented in Table 9.1 has been named "mutual fate control" because each person's actions affect the outcomes of the other. If Party A takes the trouble to leave the site clean, it is B who enjoys it, and vice versa. When such favors are reciprocated, the exchange is cooperative. However, B

TABLE 9.1
Action-Outcome Relations in the Minimal Social Situation of Two Parties Alternating at a Picnic Site[a]

		Actions by party A on quitting site	
		Leaves clutter and garbage	Disposes of garbage, tidies
Actions by Party B on quitting site	Disposes of garbage, tidies	+ / −	+ / +
	Leaves clutter and garbage	− / −	− / +

[a]Positive and negative signs above the diagonals indicate pleasant or unpleasant feelings by Party A, while those below refer to those feelings by Party B.

may not trouble to clean up and accordingly commits A to an unpleasant experience on his next visit. This is a kind of competitive behavior, the sort that induces mistrust.

In situations like this, the development of a series of mutually beneficial, cooperative exchanges is by no means inevitable, even after many exchanges of electric shock as punishment (and its absence as reward). According to a number of experiments since Sidowski's original work, it occurs in only about half of all pairs unless conditions are changed in some way. Fortunately, a common variant of this situation is one in which both parties know that they are interdependent, even though they do not know exactly how they influence one another. Then maybe five-sixths of all pairs ultimately work out a mutually deferential, cooperative pattern of actions. Both this rate of cooperation and the 50% rate of uninformed pairs were observed in experiments by Kelley, Thibaut, Radloff, and Mundy (1962). Those experiments used symbolic rewards and punishments; however later experiments from the same laboratory showed that such symbolic incentives produced essentially the same results as the absence or presence of electric shock (Rabinowitz, Kelley, & Rosenblatt, 1966).

Imagine that you are taking part in a modified version of the experiments by Kelley and associates. Electrodes have been fixed on two of your fingers, and in front of you there is a switch that you can move either to the right or to the left. When your switch is in one of these positions, your partner will get a shock, but you do not know which position has this effect. He is similarly wired and equipped. A light comes on, you push your switch to one side, but feel no shock. With a new signal, you do the same again, but this time you are shocked and the shock continues. What will you do?

What can you do? Your switch has only two positions that count. You must change your choice in an attempt to alter your partner's choice. So you change. His situation, meanwhile, is just like yours. Both of you know that the other's choices determine your state, but neither of you knows how to hurt or help the other. This situation presents a problem, does it not? Perhaps it provokes anxiety?

The problem is not insurmountable. In one of the experiments by Kelley and associates, using a symbolic rewards and punishments, it was ultimately solved by 26 couples although 8 failed to do so. How was it done? Part of the answer is that one partner or the other (and very occasionally both) acted on the realization that, if he were changing his choice after punishment and repeating it after reward, his partner was probably doing the same. This insight occurred in most of the pairs that achieved cooperation, but in very few of those that did not. Its ultility then became clear to some persons.

If one partner repeats any one of his choices for a time, without regard to whether he is simultaneously rewarded or punished, then he can make a reasonable guess about its effect on his partner. If the partner's choices then keep changing, he is presumably being punished. If they stabilize, then presumably he is being rewarded. Accordingly, the insightful person who does this can get a good idea which of his own choices has the rewarding, and which the punishing, effect on his partner. So he can go on to train the partner. If he is right, he will succeed and mutual cooperation will have been attained.

Notice that, in following the "win–stay, lose–shift" rule, one is behaving *reactively,* in accordance with stimuli in the situation. When a person ceases acting this way in order to gather information for controlling those stimuli, he is engaged in *proactive information processing.*

The Effect of Free Will on Social Relations

Four points now have to be made about the development of cooperative behavior in the mutual fate control situation as observed by Kelley and associates:

1. The determinants of the behavior that ultimately created cooperation had become more "abstract." The proactive party had ceased responding with punishment to remove punishment and had begun to seek control of the cause of his fate. When he had solved that problem, his partner gained contingent benefit. In the meantime, he resisted the inclination to immediate action to reduce his current discomfort.

2. The subsequent cooperative behavior of the proactive individual was as much a consequence of his partner's ability to reward or punish him (reactively) as that person's cooperation was a consequence of his more deliberate action. The proactive partner had demonstrated efficacy and freedom of will, but punishment by his partner had created the need to do so.

3. After solution, the cooperative choices of both parties could be described as responsible in the "normative" ("trustworthy") sense of the term, for neither caused discomfort to the other by his acts. However, in the "causal" sense of the term, only the proactive person's actions can be regarded as responsible. His actions alone were "willed"; his partner's were stimulus dependent and reactively determined, and they would remain so unless he, too, developed an abstract construction of the interaction.

4. Finally, each partner may be regarded as having developed trust of the other once the cooperative pattern had become established. Trust is understood to be the expectation that someone will behave in a preferred manner. Being negatively associated with uncertainty (or cognitive incongruity), it should increase with the amount of (uncertainty- and anxiety-reducing) information one gains in a sequence of satisfactory (efficacy-promoting) exchanges. The intentional action that produced the required sequence must, therefore, be accorded credit for the establishment of mutual trust—a condition of mutual efficacy.

PLANFUL BEHAVIOR AND THE "FITTING" RESPONSE

According to H. Richard Niebuhr (1963), responsible behavior is displayed in production of a "fitting" response to events in an ongoing interaction. What is a fitting response depends upon a person's interpretation of "what is happening" and upon his awareness of his social interrelationships and the ethical traditions of his culture (his "sociality"). It is not a simple *reaction,* like escape from unpleasant electric shock. Responsible action is shaped in anticipation of responses to itself, like the proactive behavior of the foregoing experiment. Niebuhr's conception is thus basically compatible with the present analysis. There are differences, however.

What Niebuhr designated a "fitting" response, dependent on interpretation of "what is happening" and upon one's social background, is here analyzed in greater detail, as earlier chapters indicate. Proactive behavior is understood as being shaped to approximate some *(ideal)* conception of *what should be happening.* That in turn is understood to depend upon one's sociality and upon an interpretation of "what is happening." The ideal of what should be happening also involves imagination of preferable events that might be happening but are not, that is of alternatives that are both good and possible. It seems clear, moreover, that both the interpretation and the imagination must be accurate.

The imaginal activity required for development of causally responsible behavior in the foregoing experiment can be described in general terms. The proactive person needed the basic perceptions he presumably shared with his dependent partner, that his action could interrupt his experience of punishment and that reward was preferable to punishment. Besides that, he needed to understand (imaginally) that: (*a*) total absence of punishment was possible and desirable; (*b*) what was happening might be changed if he could discover some further underlying regularity in events; (*c*) such regularity might be found in terms of sequences of reward or punishment although it was not evident in terms of single episodes; (*d*) his partner might have been acting as he himself had been, switching when punished and otherwise not; (*e*) if he were able to resist the inclination to act that way, he could discover which of his own responses punished, and which rewarded, his partner; and (*f*) he would then become able to train that individual. *The "fitting" response here was a planned series of actions, determined by abstract, imaginal, analysis of the situation,* and it brought about a mutually desirable condition in interacting persons. Presumably it came most readily to persons of greater intelligence and higher efficacy.

AMENABILITY TO INFLUENCE

The mutual fate control situation has its counterparts in everyday life, although it is probably unusual in two important features. The first is that neither partner initially understands the act–outcome relations. Neither understands how his actions affect the other. Many adults do have such knowledge about their everyday actions. In addition, some everyday situations involve more conflict of interest than does the mutual fate control situation. Once that payoff matrix was known, it gave the partners no cause for competition. But in commercial situations, or in circumstances where relative status is at issue, one man's gain may be another's loss, and both know it. If cooperative action is also possible, such situations may resemble the "mixed motive matrix," which is illustrated in Table 9.2.

Payoff matrices like that in Table 9.2 have been used in a large number of experiments on the development of trust and cooperation. Choices are simultaneous and the matrix is usually known to both persons. So each one knows that if he picks one of his options both parties may prosper moderately well (depending on the choice of his partner), but that if he picks the other, he may win the highest prize while his partner gets little or loses something. Thus all mixed motive matrices tempt people to compete but threaten them for doing so, and tempt them to cooperate but threaten them for doing that too. They all make it plain, though, that both parties could spend their time collecting rewards if each could rely upon the other to make the cooperative choice. To discover how such conclusions are brought about, is the object of the experimental enquiries.

For the sake of exposition, five styles of "play" in mixed motive "games" can be recognized. A player might (*a*) behave reactively, rerepeating his action when it was rewarded and changing it when punishment ensued. Instead, the

TABLE 9.2
Action-Outcome Relations in an Example
of a Mixed Motive Situation[a]

		Actions by Party A	
		Choice 1	Choice 2
Actions by Party B	Choice 1	6¢ / 6¢	10¢ / 1¢
	Choice 2	1¢ / 10¢	3¢ / 3¢

[a]The numbers of cents above the diagonals are the payoffs to Party A when the indicated coincidence of choices occurs, and those below accrue to B.

player might (*b*) pick the cooperative action consistently, hoping his partner will also act cooperatively. Or he might (*c*) choose the competitive action invariably, hoping his partner will sometimes pick the cooperative option. Another approach (*d*) would be to behave inconsistently, perhaps with a bias in one direction or the other, in the hope of gaining by chance or misdirection. Finally, a player might (*e*) attempt to persuade or train his partner to act cooperatively, for instance by reciprocating with the cooperative option after his partner had chosen it and the competitive one after his partner had chosen that.

The average university student, whose behavior in mixed motive situations has been most frequently studied, does not usually behave reactively. His tendency to do so is quite imperfect, even in two-play sequences. The probabilities of "staying" after a win and "shifting" after a loss range between .60 and .85, according to Rapoport and Chammah (1965). Nor does he choose to cooperate or compete unconditionally. Instead, he operates proactively at least some of the time and follows a strategy somewhat like those just designated (*d*) or (*e*). He is evidently concerned with the future *sequence* of events rather than singular past events.

His attitudes to partners who play various programs as collaborators of the experimenter also imply that the average young person in these experiments is generally striving for control over events. He likes to work with others who use the fifth approach, particularly that of reciprocation (Solomon, 1960), and he quickly develops cooperative exchanges with such persons (Solomon, 1960; Sermat, 1967; Deutsch, Yakov, Canavan, & Gumpert, 1967). By contrast, he does not like partners who cannot be influenced, even those who cooperate unconditionally and whom he consequently profits from. Still less does he like those who compete unconditionally. Such behavior puzzles him and elicits competitive choices, as well as vague feelings of dislike. These responses in turn resemble other reported consequences of powerlessness or perceived external control, and they too seem to depend upon one's expectations. According to some experiments, a partner who can in fact be readily influenced to cooperate, but is understood to be a computer rather than a person, is regarded as rigid and impossible to influence, and elicits defensive competitive behavior (Abric, Faucheux, Moscovici, & Plon, 1967). Amenability and perception of amenability evidently facilitate the development of trust and of solidarity.

Although cooperation with another is impeded when he invariably picks the benevolent choice regardless of your actions, it is not his benevolence that has this effect. According to one experiment (Deutsch *et al.,* 1967), it is his lack of responsiveness. Each player had three choices, one cooperative, one competitive and punishing, and one nonpunitive but unrewarding. When the experimenter's confederate used the first and third options discriminatively, his partners learned to cooperate even more quickly than when he used the first and second (rewarding and punishing) options equally discriminatively. When it is discriminative, benevolent behavior does indeed promote trust in mixed motive situations.

POWER TO PUNISH

Nevertheless, the ability to punish misdemeanors is often necessary to promote cooperation. Among a considerable number of experiments that make this point in mixed motive situations, three are instructive for additional reasons. The first of them is due to Shomer, Davis, and Kelley (1966).

In two related experiments, Shomer *et al.* allowed some pairs the power to punish one another, some others both the power to do this and the ability to threaten to do so, and still other pairs neither. As their measure of cooperation, they used the total of profits by the two players of the game. During initial exchanges, those pairs with power to punish did less well than those without, although they soon learned to cooperate and prospered equally well. However, slightly higher profits were earned by players who could also warn each other of intent to punish. And among them, those pairs who understood the warning to be a signal to cooperate, rather than a competitive ploy, did considerably the best. As one reviewer (Burnstein, 1969) noted about this study, "the communication of an intention to punish conveys not only its possibility, but more important, an understanding of how it can be avoided [p. 387]." This amounts, of course, to a proactive interpretation rather than a reactive one.[1] This demonstration of the value of warnings confirmed earlier evidence (Loomis, 1959).

Some individuals in the earlier experiment had been allowed to pass various types of messages to their partners between plays. One of these asked the partner to make the cooperative choice. Another asked that, and asserted the sender's intention to do likewise, while a third added a threat of retaliation for failure to comply. The latter produced more cooperation than the former two (100% cooperation on the next exchange). This experiment also confirmed that stated trust varied directly with cooperation.

Cooperation in Quasi-Industrial Relations

Even more complex forms of communication were studied in a creative experiment by Thibaut and Faucheux (1965) with conditions analogous to industrial relations situations. These experimenters designed a modified mixed motive game in which one player was given more or less discretion for division of high-payoff outcomes between himself and his partner. With much discretion,

[1]The quoted deduction may not in fact apply to "authoritarian personalities." Kelley and Stahelski (1970) found that such persons attribute competitiveness to others and respond competitively where contrasting personalities infer readiness to cooperate and act accordingly.

he could give his partner less than the partner would have earned if play had ended in a competitive cell, although he could also give him more. This was described as a condition of "high conflict of interest" (CI). In a low CI condition, he could vary the partner's payoff only within narrow limits, such that both were assured relatively high payoffs when cooperative choices were made.

As another modification of the usual mixed motive matrix, Thibaut and Faucheux provided an added option, an "external alternative" (EA). Payoff for this choice was either attractive or unattractive, that is, either higher or lower than the minimum for competitive choices within the matrix. If only one player chose it, the other won nothing.

A final modification permitted the players to discuss the game and work out joint strategies or contracts if they wished. Thus the experiment was designed to reveal the effects on cooperation of differences in two sorts of power, and something of the contracting process.

Before any contracts had come into force, the stronger partner prospered more, relative to his partner, when he had greater discretion over the division of profits. An attractive external alternative reduced the difference due to distributive power, particularly when discretion (and CI) was low. It was, of course, chosen more often by the weaker member, and chosen especially often when CI was high.

Contracts were developed by every pair in which one player had great discretion and the other had benefit of an attractive external alternative. By using the EA, by withdrawing his services as it were, the weaker member could profitably punish the stronger for failure to divide profits equitably. Thus the attractive EA rendered the distributor vulnerable. It made him susceptible to uncertainty and distrust, as his distributive power had presumably done to the weaker member. Both accordingly had motives to negotiate.

The contracts they worked out reflected the fact that each party recognized the threat of the other. Most of the contracts had provisions that the authors called "norms" for both "equity" and "loyalty." They had evidently discovered that it was *good* to have a fair distribution of profits and to stick to the internal choices. The cooperating pairs later made the highest average gains of all, more than twice as large as the average returns to pairs with high CI and an unattractive EA. Only half of the latter had developed contracts, apparently because the weaker member lacked opportunity to profit by an act that would make the stronger amenable to contract.

Looking at all four conditions of this experiment, it is evident that relative power varied between the two pairs of conditions. With the external alternative attractive and the "weak" member relatively strong, a change from low to high CI was a move toward equality of power. When the EA was unattractive and the weak member particularly weak, equalization of power required a change from high to low CI. The results for the whole experiment are consistent with those just described for half its conditions. Cooperation was always improved by increase in the relative power of the weaker member of an interacting pair, presumably because he used it to raise the responsiveness of the stronger to his needs.

The Compatibility of Free Will and Social Regulation

These experiments demonstrate the compatibility of individual freedom with social regulation in simplified settings. They also specify some necessary conditions for it, and provide a factual background for further discussion of responsibility and social accountability. They justify the following interpretive summary.

When experimental circumstances establish an interrelation between two persons such that actions by each promote or retard well-being in the other, each person strives for control over his own state. He does so initially by producing rewarding or punitive reactions to the rewarding or punishing outcomes he experiences in single exchanges. At this stage, incipient recognition of the form of interaction establishes mutual distrust. Later the same actions may be taken in accordance with a plan to establish cooperation, which depends upon understanding the pattern of a sequence of exchanges. Ultimate adherence to a cooperative strategy establishes trustworthiness on the one hand and trust and confidence on the other, and accordingly establishes a state of shared efficacy.

One necessary condition for the development of a cooperative strategy is mutuality of influence, due to appropriate division and appropriate use of power. Presumably it poses the problem that the joint strategy solves, motivating each party to seek it and making each amenable to coordinating signals from the other. Amenability to influence in such situations produces cooperation, trust, and liking. Its absence produces competition, distrust, and dislike. Presumably a weaker person who gains the affection or sympathy of a stronger one thereby gains the needed influence over the stronger. It is probable that efficacy depends upon influence, not necessarily upon power, but there seems to be no direct evidence bearing on this point as yet.

Another necessary condition for the development of cooperation is that at least one person should understand the interdependence and have a plan for a joint strategy of mutual advantage. Verbal requests for action in accordance with such plans will produce some compliance, but they are more generally effective when accompanied by threats of the punitive use of power. Conversely, threats are most effective when interpreted, not as competitive behavior, but as signals to cooperate. Such interpretations, like plans for joint strategy, signify proactive information transfer. When both parties are amenable and joint strategies are developed by negotiation, they specify rules of action for mutual protection, which are analogous to norms or ethics.

Mutuality of influence and effective proactivity in its application by at least one party promote cooperation, solidarity, and trust, which are the conditions of freedom for both from direct control by events or their emotional effects. The absence of either promotes anxiety, competition, mutual distrust, and the domination of behavior by singular events in the environment.

FREEDOM, INDEPENDENCE, AND SOCIAL COHESION

These facts seem to rationalize some of the evidence reviewed in earlier chapters. Differences in mutuality of influence appear to underlie the observed differences in formative social climates and behavior between followers of democratic and autocratic leaders (see p. 112), those between boys who had scored high and low in achievement motivation, and those between open-minded individuals and ethnocentric authoritarian personalities (see p. 111). The original hypothesis on the authoritarian personality contended that it develops when parents who are relatively powerless in their adult world use aggressive disciplinary techniques to "persuade" their even less powerful children to submit to demands that take no account of their needs. These facts and considerations also seem to be consistent with the differences in recollected child–parent interactions between responsible, "internal" college students and irresponsible "externals" (see pp. 117–118). It appears that behavioral independence and freedom from stimulus control develop under the same democratic social influences that promote social cohesion.

All of these facts are inconsistent, however, with a widespread notion that individual freedom operates against social solidarity, and vice versa. That notion seems to have a long history. "Social cohesion and individual liberty . . . are in a state of conflict or uneasy compromise throughout the whole period" of Western philosophical thought, according to Bertrand Russell (1946, p. 12). This notion is also embodied in an old but influential theory due to the psychoanalyst, Erich Fromm (1941).

Freedom arises, according to Fromm, when social conditions marked by solidarity of individual with group give way to conditions that promote individualism. Hence, until the personality develops further, "freedom" means isolation and loneliness for the individual. It also means insecurity and hostility, because separation from the group implies nonentity and powerlessness for the individual. "His relationship to his fellow men, with everyone a potential competitor, has become hostile and estranged; he is free—that is, he is alone, isolated, threatened from all sides [1941, p. 62]."

The insecure, hostile, estranged "individuals" of Fromm's "freedom" seem to resemble authoritarian personalities, presumably relatively powerless persons interacting competitively with more powerful others. It was his thesis that their circumstances create anxiety, from which individuals are compelled to escape—through one of two "escape mechanisms" or drive-reducing *habits*—into subservience to others. He accordingly regarded both the German people's support for Naziism and the tendency he saw among Americans to conform to the demands of public opinion as instances of "escape from freedom." On this hypothesis, compliance and what he called conformity are consequences of low efficacy.

What Fromm called "freedom" may be a condition of competitive relationships as they affect powerless individuals, and it is, of course, antagonistic to social solidarity. However, it is clearly not freedom of will. Nor does freedom of will create such conditions. On the contrary, *as shown here, the development of cooperative strategies, promoting the mutual trust and liking that constitutes social solidarity, are manifestations of freedom of will acting under appropriate influence.* It is doubtful, indeed, whether social solidarity can exist—or ever has existed outside Fromm's imaginary history—without freedom of will. Individuality is biologically given. Both cooperation and competition are learned.

THE FREEDOM CHARTER

Nonetheless there is, of course, a fundamental point about individual freedom that has to be considered in relation to social control. It concerns the conditions under which individual freedom can be attained in a social context. It also concerns the development of cooperation, as in experimental games. Indeed it has already been mentioned in passing.

Assuming he has the necessary abilities, including material resources, what are the minimal conditions under which an individual can achieve freedom of will in a social context? In part, this question inquires into the conditions necessary to establish in a social setting the sort of general environment in which freedom of will is possible—that is one which is predictable and potentially supportive. However, it also inquires into any special characteristics of social environments that may be relevant.

One relevant feature of social environments was assumed, at the outset of this chapter, in connection with the supposition that a person's associates must trust him, if he is to be permitted to act freely. Unlike inanimate situations, human "environments" develop expectancies and anxieties that can motivate defensive actions. To prevent other people from interfering defensively with his actions, a person must either avoid them or cultivate their trust. This, then, is the primary condition for the attainment of freedom in a social setting.

The second and remaining condition is related to this one. Not only must a person be free from interference with his initiatives due to distrust by others (and held accountable only for their effects). He must also be able to trust his associates to avoid initiatives that would injure him. This second condition has to do with predictability in the social environment.

The possibility of freedom in a social context depends ultimately upon cooperation to this end. People *can* be much less predictable than inanimate environments. To a considerable extent, their predictability comes from agreements about what is acceptable human behavior. The attainment of freedom in society accordingly hinges upon joint adherence to standards that restrict the variety of human actions. The realities simulated in the mutual fate control experiments mean that *unrestricted universal freedom is impossible*.

A suitable restriction is represented in the implicit theory of responsibility. It is that people may react punitively to the actions of others without risk of later retaliation, provided that the punished actions had *controllable* adverse effects—provided, that is, injury was presumedly intended or due to carelessness. Such reactions ought, of course, to sanction adherence to this rule. Accordingly, a modified version of universal freedom should be attainable (as a ''right'') by everyone who can gain control over the effects of his own actions in order to avoid such punishment. All that is necessary to avoid interference by others is to take care not to injure others except as the rules permit and prescribe. Anyone who cannot do this cannot be allowed his freedom. He must be treated as either evil or irresponsible. Anyone who can, may pursue his own ends as long as he adheres to the rules.

This is, perhaps, ''the freedom charter'' to which Nicolas Haines (1966, pp. 120–124) has alluded. Hypothetically, it is the very basis of human freedom in a social context. Notice that the obligation it involves may be double-edged. Each social unit must perhaps not only shape its actions to avoid injuring innocent others but also deliver retaliation for deliberate injury by others. And apparently we should also reciprocate benefits that others voluntarily bring us (Gouldner, 1960). Justice must be served.

To follow the ITR rules of conduct is, of course, to cease responding reactively to pleasant or unpleasant states caused by others and to adopt a new set of rules for reciprocation. As illustrated in the mutual fate control experiments, it involves withholding punishment for unintentional injuries and withholding reward for unintentional benefits. Government of one's social actions comes under proactive control. They become intentional deeds, designed in reference to anticipated responses to themselves, and not simple impulsive reactions to the actions of others. It is responsible, rather than compliant, behavior that establishes the social context for freedom of will and social cohesion.

''The freedom charter'' is an agreement to cooperate for the maintenance of freedom. Probably it is not an explicit agreement, like the Magna Charta, but simply an implicit one. It seems probable, also, that its cultural evolution depended, as did the development of cooperation in experimental games, upon mutuality of influence (based on countervailing power) and not solely upon abstract information processing. The importance of the distribution of social power to the attainment of free will is further expounded in the next chapter.

SUMMARY

Trust by others may be a necessary condition of social freedom, permitting one to shape one's actions for their effects, rather than their forms. Distrust of another can arise from anxiety about events under his control. Mutual trust arises from and promotes mutual efficacy, which permits freedom of choice.

The belief that individual freedom and social cohesion are necessarily antagonistic is fallacious. Given mutuality of influence, freedom of will is actually expressed in the creation of mutual trust and affection.

Adverse or interfering reactions by others can be forestalled by proactive processing of the information of social interactions. Cooperative, trust-inducing behavior often develops in experimental situations in which interacting persons share the power to influence one another, but not often otherwise. Its emergence depends upon the discovery and use, by at least one party, of an appropriate, abstract pattern governing the interaction. It can be facilitated by verbal communications and the negotiation of rules or norms. The individuals whose insight and action bring about cooperation and mutual trust have demonstrated freedom of will and causal, as well as social, responsibility.

To follow the rules of conduct that are sanctioned by and enforce the implicit theory of responsibility is to behave cooperatively. Such actions promote development of a predictable social context for individual behavior and thereby enable any competent person to achieve freedom of will. Accordingly, the terms of agreement to do so may be called "the freedom charter."

10

Cultural Determinants
of Freedom and Social Adjustment[1]

SELF-ESTEEM AND SOCIAL ADJUSTMENT

It is convenient to begin this exposition of research specifically directed toward the effects of social and economic conditions upon freedom of will with a discussion that was postponed from Chapter 8. The matter for consideration was the way in which one individual (John Doe) understood the structure of his culture, and this was diagramatically represented in Figure 8.1. As shown in that figure, John had represented himself, by comparison with others, to be "selfish," one of the "bullies," and "in trouble." These terms appear to mean the opposite of labels like "good," "dependable," "clever," and "influential," which connote potency and trustworthiness. The former terms were applied only to people of low social status or prestige—which suggests that John had low self-esteem.

Various theorists have been impressed by the association of self-satisfaction, self-esteem, or positive self-regard with good personal adjustment, and by its absence in people who are "maladjusted." Some have even thought of self-satisfaction as the criterion of good adjustment (Rogers, 1951; Jahoda, 1958). Among the kinds of objections that can be made to this view of a set of social attitudes, two can be discussed with reference to Figure 8.1.

When an individual interacts with his environment, the experiences that tell him about himself are the same as those that inform him about the environment. Some special process is needed if that person is to know himself in any way other than this. The primary lesson to be learned is that one*self* can change some situations, not others; that one is competent where others are incompetent, and

---

[1]This chapter is based on work conducted while the writer was serving as a consultant for New Brunswick Newstart, Inc. Substantial portions of it may appear in a final report on the activities of that organization.

vice versa; that one is comfortable in some situations, uncomfortable in others. From such a general view of oneself and a comparison of one's outcomes with those of other persons in various situations, one might perhaps infer an overall picture of oneself—a "self-concept"—with which of course one may be satisfied or not. Yet a person's basic observations, his raw information so to speak, would inevitably have been found in the interactions by which he had come to know his environment. A self-concept is not only an abstraction. Considered as one of a set of concepts about things, events, and ideas, it is a largely redundant one, because it is based on precisely the same experiences as they are. Satisfaction with oneself is one step removed from satisfaction with one's environment, that is, with one's interactions with it.

The sort of information which might suggest that John is dissatisfied appears in appropriate relational form in Figure 8.1. Certain characteristics that John ascribes to himself are not ascribed to various valued and trustworthy people, and vice versa. These are the characteristics through which John's maladjustment is represented, and through which, it might be argued, he shows dissatisfaction with him*self*. They are also the attributes that differentiate low-status, relatively impotent persons from others of higher esteem, who are clever, dependable, good, and influential. Indeed, John's descriptions imply that being in trouble is due to his lack of the qualities, position, influence, and freedom he ascribes to persons of higher social status or esteem. The implication is that, were his attributes like theirs, he would not be selfish, a bully, or in trouble.

The Relation of Esteem to Freedom

People commonly differentiate one another as John did, in terms of intimacy and status (Brown, 1965). This fact is well known to psychologists and sociologists. Not only do these distinctions appear as basic dimensions in most role construct repertory grids; they are also implicated in the rules that govern our social interactions. Different sorts of rules apply to relations between intimates on the one hand and people of differing status on the other. We use informal speech with our friends ("Hiya Fred!"), but formal address with people of higher status ("Good morning, doctor")—or with strangers. Like John, we would only borrow a comb from an intimate. Though we might wish to have them as friends, we do not invite the high court judge or the university president to dinner; we wait for them to ask us. We give such people places of honor, though we may compete for good seats with our equals.

When we accord higher status to others, we admit their superior power and our readiness to defer to them, and vice versa. So the status differentiations we make represent our freedom of action. John's appears to be restricted, because he is ready to defer or submit to a high proportion of those he knows. His "low self-esteem" means at least this.

Probably it also means dissatisfaction with his situation or, more specifically, with his relation to it. John is not "influential" and able to get what he wants like people of higher status, who perhaps have what he wants. Instead he is "in trouble" and so concerned about personal needs as to justify being called "selfish." This parallel between status and satisfaction is an important one, presumably having to do with personal efficacy.

DETERMINANTS AND CORRELATES OF SOCIAL ESTEEM

People within a culture can generally agree on a ranking of their members from highest to lowest worth or prestige. Socioeconomic status as thus described has specifiable characteristics and determinants. People of higher status have greater power, influence, and respect. Commonly they have superior wealth and a style of life that is generally admired (Brown, 1965). Apparently they excel in efficacy. However, the way that differences in status come about varies from culture to culture. Wealth and title may be inherited in some societies. In others, hereditary physical characteristics are important, and it is probable that physical beauty and strength are universally admired. Personal competence, too, is probably respected everywhere, but it is supposed to justify high status only in so-called meritocracies, such as the United States is supposed to be. The higher a person's status, the greater is the esteem in which he is held and the higher, presumably, are both his efficacy and his freedom of will.

Within British North America, at least, one's status ranking is closely associated with the prestige of one's occupational role or that of one's father. Judges have higher status than unemployed laborers. So it is with financial income and also with education (Brown, 1965). And, in all cases, formal measured intelligence tends to be higher in the higher-ranking occupations. The relations are sufficiently close that differences of informed intelligence can account for about one-quarter of the differences in occupational rank or income (Matarazzo, 1972). Presumably the scale of status cuts obliquely through the axes of Figure 2.2, as do those of responsibility or freedom of will.

The relationship of wealth and education to status and esteem seems clear. They represent the *means,* or the power, to control future situations for personal satisfaction. But the attainment of wealth and education may also be a *sign of* earlier efficacious relationships of oneself or one's parents with the environment.

Status Differences between Societies

What may be an identical relationship, with identical meaning, also applies to status differences between nations. The "more advanced," presumably more

powerful, urbanized, and industralized nations, among 75 studied in one defini-
tive investigation, were also generally the wealthier and better educated, and they
employed more sophisticated economic techniques (Schnore, 1961).

In general, commercial, industrialized, urban economies produce higher per
capita incomes than rural subsistence economies. They are more heavily
capitalized, and their peoples are generally better educated. Accordingly, they
are commonly regarded as economically better developed or "more advanced."
This formulation is probably true, even though one of the more obvious reasons
for believing it can be explained away. That is, it is probably true in spite of the
bias in the statistics that apparently prove it. Such statistics are based on as-
sessments of income in the financial terms of trading communities and do not
count the real goods and services produced by subsistence economies. A synoptic
description of each of these extreme types of socioeconomic systems will provide
the basis for a more accurate justification of their respective characterizations as
"advanced" and "backward."

REACTIVE AND PROACTIVE ECONOMIES

In rural, subsistence economies, the materials for sustaining and enjoying life
are obtained from a given, geographically restricted environment, where perhaps
they are nurtured before being hunted or gathered. Division of labor within these
societies is minimal, though notable. The number of different "roles" a person
may "play" is small. The trading between specialists that reinforces this differentiation is conducted by exchanges of real goods and services. The practical
arts of making and using tools and of converting materials and supplies are
learned from current practitioners when occasions arise. Populations are small
and government is informal. Many natural events are beyond their control. They
produce gluts and famines, good times and bad. So, natural and supernatural
mysteries occupy considerable time and attention, and give rise to practices of
magic and ritual. Such superstitious actions may be intended to placate the fates
and prevent future misfortunes, but few of them have practical preparatory value.
Life, consequently, is short, and may be "mean and brutish" as well.

If life in primitive socioeconomic systems is situation bound and subject to
externally controlled rewards and punishments, the economies of more advanced
cultures are correspondingly abstract and proactive. They are also more extensive, both in time and in space, and affect the lives of larger populations. They
permit regional and personal specialization of economic pursuits, with consequent efficiencies. They require advance planning, record keeping, negotia-
tions, and the advance shipment of goods that must be produced well before the
needs of consumers. In addition to the value of symbols for these purposes, they

have discovered and come to depend upon the benefits of symbolic media to facilitate trading. Increasing proportions of their interactions are accomplished in terms of monetary rewards. Urban concentrations facilitate their communications. They analyze and synthesize materials. They have harnessed nonmuscular sources of power and use them to facilitate manufacturing, transportation, and communications. As in the cases of trade, transportation, and communications, they have evolved new institutions, methods, and occupations to deal with the effects of their specialization and of the increases in population their success has produced. Governments, politicians, public opinion polls, and newspapers are some examples. They have discovered the benefits that are to be gained by planful use of information. Both as cause and as consequence, they have developed, and come to depend upon, stores of detailed theoretical knowledge. They also depend upon the transmission of this knowledge to future generations—by specialists in special settings. Their need for knowledge, especially productive knowledge, has developed because they have proven its benefits for controlling human well-being.

The advantages attained by the evolution of abstract proactive economies are easily specified, independent of the costs of gaining them, which are, of course, considerable.[2] They amount to advances in human security. These economies have proven successful at every stage in their evolution. They have supported increasing populations and the accumulation of increased wealth, particularly as productive equipment and recorded knowledge. They have created conditions in which human life spans have doubled, plagues have been eradicated, and famines reduced. They have improved the nutrition of their citizens, and, as a consequence of this and of their educational systems, have probably increased their intelligence, that is their ability to learn and to solve problems (Matarazzo, 1972). They have become capable of forecasting and defending themselves against droughts, storms, and earthquakes, and of moving needed goods and services by air to other areas that are stricken by natural disasters. They have become able to move mountains. They are efficacious cultures that have enabled increasing number of persons to shape their lives in satisfactory ways.

It may be true that rural, subsistence economies have produced the world's great religions. Yet it was the specialized trading economies of cities that produced the sciences and technologies that have recently doubled world production of human food. Religions may have arisen when human life was most obviously susceptible to external control. The sciences, however, were born as people learned to control natural events, were stimulated by that achievement, and undertook to improve upon the information that brought it about. According to modern knowledge, thus, the free and happy savage is either a temporary acci-

[2]All of the challenges and stresses involved in education for life in mechanized urbanized societies (see, for instance, Toffler, 1970).

dent or a myth. Paradise, it seems, is more often lost through ignorance than through knowledge.

What is valued by human beings seems to vary remarkably with the state of development of the socioeconomic systems in which they live. The determinants of social esteem or status ought to change as human communities shift to the more advanced economic techniques and thereby assume membership in larger socioeconomic systems. As the number of interdependent people in the system rises, the number of competitive outsiders should fall, so that ethnocentrism should decline. The value of established ways and of those (older people) who know them best ought to decline. Possession of capital and information ought to become increasingly valuable, while physical attributes and knowledge of dogma and ritual become less valuable (see references to cross-cultural research by McClelland and associates on p. 88, this volume). Above all, there should be an increase in the value of the symbol-manipulating and information-gathering skills, and of the theoretical knowledge that formal education provides. And all of these changes ought to be reflected in changes in the determinants of social status.

Alternative Interpretations of Social Prosperity

Societies differ in their economic structures and in the sorts of human conduct they accordingly sanction. Moreover, their various forms of organization are not equally effective. Those that have accumulated and use large stores of information and productive equipment (i.e., symbolic and material information) are more successful at using their physical environments to fulfill their needs than are the subsistence economies that own and use less information and capital. This is an exact parallel of some of the differences between individuals of varying socioeconomic status or esteem. The coincidence is remarkable and may be instructive.

One possible explanation of these facts is that the rich have attained their freedom at the expense of the poor, perhaps by exploiting them (as "robber barons" once did and sometimes still do) or perhaps by defeating them in competition for limited supplies (and such events have also been known to occur). This sort of interpretation is important for two reasons. It seems to be a common one. It also implies that the freedom that has been acquired by high-status people and advanced economies *cannot* become available to all.

A different sort of explanation can be found for these facts, however. It is implicit in the foregoing descriptions of trading and subsistence economies. *Success and freedom accrue to individuals and economies that interact proactively with their environments.* In this view, the maladjustments of the poor are due to inferior information-processing procedures, not to either exploitation or competitive defeat by the rich. And they can be corrected, without reducing the wealth and freedom of the more successful, by changing the methods by which the poor deal with events.

Of these two, the latter interpretation may be the better justified. This is not to deny that exploitation and competitive defeat do occur. It is to assert that they occur in particular sorts of socioeconomic environment, which can be altered. Support for this interpretation is provided, together with other important information, by the facts and theories from the sociological research to which the remainder of this chapter is devoted. That material goes beyond a mere demonstration that social potency and success arise from the appropriate, liberating use of information. It weakens the alternate hypothesis by showing that increases in the interactions of the poor with the rich serve to raise, rather than lower, the efficacy, prosperity, and esteem of the poor.

FLUIDITY IN SOCIAL SYSTEMS

The several studies that refer to this question are specifically concerned with differences between social systems in the transmission of information. The first of them distinguishes between societies that are conceived to be *open* to new information and others that are considered *closed*. The central theoretical concepts of *rigidity* and *fluidity* are introduced in the following words:

> A flexible social system as a whole is one which can receive, sort, evaluate, and act upon a wide array of information and make any adjustment that might help maintain its favorable position relative to other societies, from additional specialization to radical change. By its essential openness, it has institutionalized innovation in a variety of ways so that it is not haphazard or serendipitous, but it is valued, regularized, and built into the entire social structure.
>
> It is assumed that the class structure, the economy, and the political structure of a system are relatively separate but closely interacting sub-systems. The social structure has often been termed the integrative and the economy the adaptative sub-system. We might say here that in a society in which all of these sub-systems are flexible, they are loosely coordinated in such a way that change can enter the social system through any channel, and that channel can act with some degree of autonomy apart from other sectors which adapt later. Such terms as dynamic equilibrium suggest our conceptual intent, even though they are difficult to define precisely.
>
> The closed or rigid society, in contrast, is a static equilibrium, where a *status quo* is highly institutionalized and all the forces of the system are focused on the prevention of change. New information is prevented from entering channels and endangering its static state. The rigid or closed society requires a class system based on ascriptive or traditional criteria such as race, religion, caste, or ethnicity, in which mobility is severely restricted and boundaries are tight. It has a centralized political and power system, and both institutions are protected by a traditional ideology and a view of the truth passed on unchanging. Its economic structure also tends to be monolithic in nature, so as to prevent alternate sources of power from arising. Its industry requires a low level of technical training, and this lack of personal competence reinforces the class system and discourages critical feedback. It is not innovative, for sanctions are exercised against theories that challenge the traditional view of the truth. It is simpler or less dif-

ferentiated in organization. The sub-systems of a rigid society are tightly interlocked, and the
pressures exerted on each by the others tend to make all throw up barriers to an outside stimulus
which could endanger the whole rigid system. One might go so far as to say that any change in
a rigid system, for this reason, will tend to be a violent one. In sum, it serves and preserves the
status quo. In the long run of history it is less resilient than the open social system and is subject
to obsolescence, corruption, and revolt from within, and, economic, political, or military con-
quest from without [p. 440].[3]

The research findings reported by these theorists are consistent in a general
way with these conceptions. They further demonstrate how educational achievement and financial income also differentiated between flexible and rigid cultures
among the 48 states of the USA in 1950. And that fact, in turn, suggests that
these determinants of individual efficacy and freedom within society operate also
among societies as determinants of relative flexibility or fluidity in social systems. Perhaps, indeed, that fact means that fluid social systems are the kind that
are created by, and foster the growth of, free individuals, because they respond
appropriately to the constructive actions of their individual citizens.

Correlates of Social Fluidity

As index variables, these sociologists defined two measures of flexibility and
rigidity, that look like indices of social freedom. The first, designated "social
fluidity," refers to the adoption of racially discriminative legislation of varying
kinds by the different state governments. Legislation of this sort restricts the
freedom of a minority by making access to desirable positions and public services
dependent on genetically predetermined characteristics they lack. The relation to
social freedom of the second independent variable, designated "political fluidity," is less obvious. The relevant statistics measured imbalance in the persuasiveness of opposing political parties in recent elections. Where one party has
persistently dominated public affairs for some time, the feasibility of establishing
an alternative power structure by contrary vote is presumably low; but other
reasons for regarding this as a measure of social freedom will be discussed
below. That these independent variables assessed related conditions is shown by
the fact that one-quarter of what was measured by the one proved to be predictable from the other.

The presumption that racially discriminative legislation operates to reduce
social freedom is patently reasonable. It is notable, however, that public acceptance of such legislation may also be a symptom of reduced freedom of will.
It is ignorant, driven persons who are liable to attribute the causes of their
troubles to persons other than themselves. Those are the people who adopt

[3]Reprinted by permission of The University of Chicago Press from R. C. Young and J. A.
Moreno, Economic development and social rigidity: A comparison study of the forty-eight states,
Economic Development and Cultural Change, 1965, *13*, 439–452. © 1965 by The University of
Chicago Press.

stereotyped beliefs and who, under stress, are likely both to support the judgments of group majorities and to adopt oversimplified plans for the solution of
complex problems.

A tendency to shape one's opinions after the expressed judgments of others
and to neglect other relevant facts is also evident in the persistence with which a
single party dominated elections in rigid states. Two statements are justified by
the facts. The first concerns the concentration of votes. It implies that persuasive
power was monolithically distributed in those states, because contrary arguments
and viewpoints had been relatively ineffective there. The second concerns the
persistence of this influence. It implies that factual considerations, which change
from time to time and presumably between elections, must have had little effect
on outcomes at the polls in those states. More durable influences, like party
loyalities or party power, must have been operative instead. Both statements
imply a widespread failure of independent political thinking on the part of many
voters in the less-educated, less innovative, and less prosperous states.

States selected for greater social freedom (or fluidity) according to either
index, were not only more urbanized but had higher proportions of well-educated
people, for instance greater numbers of engineers for every 10,000 factory workers. They were also richer, in terms of average per capita incomes. And they
were more innovative, as indicated by per capita production of new patents and
designs. That is, greater social freedom was found in the presence of greater
economic fluidity (or freedom) and greater technological creativity. Moreover,
the higher education and income levels, which are commonly associated with one
another and with high socioeconomic status, were empirically linked to greater
social freedom, as logically they ought to be.

This study introduced the characterization of social systems as rigid and flexible (or fluid) in response to novel information. The knowledge it provided was
more descriptive than explanatory, however. It showed that differences in education, in attitudes to the unfamiliar, and in innovation were associated with prosperity and freedom in appropriate ways. Although it did not contribute much to
understanding how the different clusters of system attributes come about, it
helped to stimulate a new attack on the problem.

INFORMATION FLOW IN SOCIAL SYSTEMS

The next theoretical contribution to this topic, by the sociologist Paul Eberts
(1971), reversed the assumed causal connections. It argued that the observed
differences between fluid and rigid social systems result from, rather than cause,
differences in information flow into and within them. Those in which information is readily and frequently received and exchanged are supposed to become
"fluid." These systems are expected consequently to discover and solve the
problems of their members quite readily. Where, by contrast, the exchange of

information is restricted to few channels or inhibited by differences in power, "rigidity" exists and many social problems remain undefined and unresolved. Fluid and rigid systems differ in what may be called group efficacy, because they differ in their communication of information.

The concepts of information and communication, as used in this theory, are broader than usual. An order by an employer to an employee is an instance of information flow. So, however, is the employee's reinforcing compliance with that order. So is an exchange of goods for money. Money is recognized to be a symbolic form of power to reinforce the actions of another. Like all reinforcements, as mentioned in Chapter 7, it has to be considered to have both informative and incentive components. Financial incomes and the exchanges that produce them are thus treated as flows of information. In this theory, accordingly, all social interactions involve some communication or transfer of information, and the rate of information flow (per unit time) is variable within systems.

Channels of communication are known in Eberts's theory as "links." Thus the subunits of fluid systems are supposed to have many links with one another. Many sorts of relationships create links, including commercial, instructional, and affectional relationships. A person whose grocer is also his brother-in-law and golf partner has many links with that trader. The more links there are among individuals in a community, and between the individuals and the community's various organizations, the more the individuals are prepared to participate in community affairs. Individual problems are accordingly more likely to gain attention, and individual actions and comments are more likely to influence social affairs in fluid than in rigid communities.

Precisely the same kind of analysis applies to those larger systems in which communities, rather than individuals, are the units. In this case, though, fluidity in the larger systems is due to large numbers of linkages between communities and intercommunity organizations. It also theoretically increases fluidity within the smaller systems. The greater knowledge and prosperity of larger fluid systems (e.g., states) are thus supposed to be due, ultimately, to their more frequent communications with other systems and intersystem organizations. Such communications are also supposed to produce the greater social freedom of their individual members.

Alterations in information flow, due to changes in linkages, are therefore the ultimate causes of the economic, political, and social changes that create changes in knowledge and innovation, as well as prosperity and freedom. Losses of linkages take away people, ideas, and money, while gains add them. Inevitably, too, changes in linkages alter power structures, which tend to become more concentrated when linkages are lost, and less so when they are added. In Eberts's words, referring to the latter case, "The change in linkages will produce changes in the communication patterns of a given local community so that the communication patterns become more fluid, that is more open, as they are between units which are more free and equal with each other [Eberts, 1972, p. 15]." The task of economic development of depressed regions is accordingly that of increasing their fluidity by the creation of new linkages between those regions and others.

Fluid and rigid social systems are thus expected to differ in responsiveness to individual endeavors. Those that reward individual actions sufficiently often to sustain such action reinforcement exchanges will be remarkable for high rates of information flow, that is, fluidity. This presumably occurs when many people have the means to reward one another, that is when power and influence are well distributed (see Chapter 9). And that condition is supposed to be promoted by large numbers of external communications links. Those systems that more often punish, or fail adequately to reward, individual actions suppress internal communications and are accordingly rigid. Following the information in Chapter 9, this presumably occurs when small numbers of people have power and the many with little power are unable to influence them. In Eberts's theory, losses of external linkages bring on this state of affairs, and gains reverse the process. Fluid social systems accordingly promote the efficacy (and consequently freedom of will) of their citizens in greater proportions than do rigid systems.

Economic changes are also predicted to alter the complexity of social systems. Increases or decreases in the linkages of a community with outside social units serve, theoretically, to increase or decrease *community differentiation*. That is, they are predicted to alter the number of different kinds of business activities pursued in the community, the number of different "positions" in its social structure, and the number of different "roles" that need to be filled.

Eberts's theoretical analysis of social fluidity has two kinds of virtue. First, it provides a comprehensive framework into which some earlier theories of economic and social change can be fitted. For instance, Sismondo (1973) has shown how it accommodates anthropological generalizations about "secularization" during change from folk society to modern community, as well as the "central place theory" of growth from economics, and some further theoretical contributions under the general title of "human ecology." Second, however, and most important, it integrates a considerable amount of factual information, which shows that the types of economic development initiatives it suggests for depressed regions lead to the effects it predicts. These facts in turn go a long way toward demonstrating that deprived communities gain potency, prosperity, and freedom as a result of increasing interactions with richer, better-informed, and more potent (well-adjusted) neighbors, rather than losing these benefits as the competition hypothesis demands.

Much of the research that supports Eberts's theory of social and economic change has been developed after the fact, by analysis of changes that had occurred before the research began. The pertinent observations are impressive nevertheless. For instance, one analysis of statistics for the years 1950 and 1960 from 92 counties in the northeastern United States showed (*a*) consistent relations between five different measures of fluidity and two different measures of pros-

perity; (*b*) somewhat higher relations between four measures of (external) linkages and four measures of prosperity; (*c*) higher relations between measures of
linkages and measures of differentiation, urbanization, and population size; and
(*d*) higher relations between the latter and four measures of prosperity (Schmidt,
1973). Impressive as it is, however, such evidence is not as convincing as
experimental evidence of the same sort.

A SOCIOLOGICAL EXPERIMENT

Experimental support for Eberts's theory has also been published (Sismondo,
1973). A research team moved into a depressed region of eastern Canada at the
beginning of a government-sponsored intervention that was intended to promote
economic development. It immediately began preparing for the extraordinarily
difficult tasks that sociological experiments pose. And it immediately began
making predictions in accordance with Eberts's theory.

The New Brunswick Newstart research was concerned with events in 22
different communities in Kent county. It is an indication of the difficulty of this
project that the first task was in fact to delineate these communities. Another
early task was to split them into two sets, matched in population and economy,
one of which would be subject to direct interventions while the other would not
(although theoretically its communities would be influenced indirectly). Here,
incidentally, is another sort of difficulty for experimental sociology. If the effects
of interventions are good, they will be desired by everyone, and the rigorous
requirements of experimentation may become unpopular and subject to modification by political influence. It was also necessary to prepare in advance to assess
fluidity, linkages, differentiation, and levels and distributions of incomes. Finally, detailed interventions that would be consistent with the theory under test
had to be specified and initiated.

The New Brunswick Newstart interventions were diverse, but most of them
involved the stimulation or facilitation of information exchange in the conventional sense. There were, of course, economic impacts and exchanges of money
(as information). The mere accommodation of the corporation's staff put new
money into circulation in the county. And the provision of information on how to
obtain financial assistance in economic enterprises was soon exploited. However, other interventions took the form of information centers, leadership in the
development of economic cooperatives, and instruction of mothers in child-
training techniques, as examples. Such interventions presumably stimulated
problem-oriented, imaginative activities and exchanges of mutual reinforcement.

The measurement of theoretical variables proved complex. For instance, much
of the data had to be collected by vocal questioning of heads of households.
Answers given to surveys of this kind are known to be susceptible to irrelevant
influences, so cannot always be taken at face value. This proved to be the case in

the assessment with Rotter's questionnaire of perceived locus of control, which ought to vary with fluidity. A bias was found, favoring choice of the second statement of any two presented, regardless of its content (Maillet, 1973). Conceivably the same bias influenced responses to other questions in the survey. Consequently the investigators found it necessary, after the fact, to regard some of the information they had gathered as erroneous and to discard it. Such selection of data after the fact is undesirable for the same reason that post hoc definition of measures is undesirable. The development of completely satisfactory methods for experimental sociology will no doubt prove to be a long-term enterprise. So, unfortunately, will the elimination of every minor source of error in the New Brunswick Newstart data.

Nonetheless, a large number of seemingly dependable observations have now been reported. The central hypotheses of Eberts's theory were again confirmed, in some cases with statistics showing very close relationships of the predicted kind. In 1 year, for instance, changes in linkages accounted for about 90% of changes in differentiation and changes of income. A summary of reported relationships is presented in Figure 10.1.

Six sets of findings, most of which are represented in Figure 10.1, merit particular notice:

1. Factor analytic procedures identified three components, or forms, of the concept of fluidity, besides those that were treated as income measures. One was

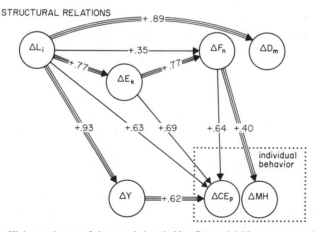

Figure 10.1. Highest estimates of change relations in New Brunswick Newstart research. Reading Δ as "change in," the abbreviations mean: ΔL_i, change in linkage, 1969–1971; ΔE_k, reduction in income dispersion, 1969–1972; ΔF_n, change in fluidity factors, 1971–1972; ΔD_m, change in differentiation indices, 1971–1972; ΔY, income gain, 1969–1972; ΔCE_p, increased consumer expenditures, 1971–1972; ΔMH, increased mental health, 1971–1972. The figures within triple-line arrows are coefficients of multiple correlation; those within single-line arrows are simple correlation coefficients. [Adapted from Sismondo (1973).]

designated "organizational complexity and competition," although the evidence of "competition" might be regarded as evidence of the total volume of particular kinds of business, because this measure was influenced by community size. Another, called "membership," assessed the numbers and proportions of citizens who belonged to local and regional organizations and the numbers and proportions who responded to the annual research questionnaire. A third appraised perceived personal power, in terms of the relative frequencies with which individuals reported participating in community decision making and being able to influence government decisions between elections. This is, of course, the component of fluidity that refers most directly to the generalized expectation of personal control used in Chapter 2 as an index of responsibility and freedom of will. It was increased in communities whose external links had been increased experimentally and in others that gained business links, but not in the remaining communities.

Incidentally, separate experiments established that, when mothers had been taught to shape the behavior of their children by the reinforcement principles of Skinner and associates, their answers to Rotter's questionnaire also revealed increased perception of personal control over the rewards and punishments they, the mothers, received (Goguen, 1972).

2. One measure of "organizational complexity and competition" was the proportional community membership in religious or church-sponsored organizations. Declines occurred in those communities that showed increased participation in community decisions and increased perception of ability to influence governmental decisions. But "no appreciable changes took place in those villages whose linkage structure was not altered [Sismondo, 1973, p. 73]." The same was true of frequency of attendance at the meetings of these organizations. These results complement those on perceived personal power, or internal control. So, at the theoretical level, does the fact that they support the "secularization" hypothesis.

3. As Figure 10.1 shows, increases in community linkages were closely associated with increases in average incomes within the same communities. Presumably these changes also amount to increases in efficacy for some citizens. This conclusion is further supported by the results of separate analyses of half a dozen major types of consumer expenditure.

New installations of oil heating furnaces were related to increases in family incomes for the previous year, to increases in links with the provincial economy, and to changes in perceived personal power. New installations of flush toilets increased as a positive function of increases in the same and other linkages and of changes in perceived personal power as well. New installations of hot water heating equipment and new home improvement expenditures were functions of increased incomes in the previous year and other factors. New installations of telephones were related to changes in certain linkage factors and in perceived personal power. Finally, new purchases of cars or trucks were associated with increases of incomes in the previous years and of linkages 2 years earlier. Each of these instances presumably represents an increase in personal and family efficacy.

4. Inequalities of economic power, as measured by statistics assessing variations of income, were reduced by increases in linkages. They, in turn, were directly associated with increases in those aspects of fluidity that were measured independently of income and that were only weakly associated with changes in linkages.

It is not clear to what degree efficacy depends upon absolute, as distinct from relative, prosperity and success. Presumably, the former is important in reference to primary drives, and comparisons with others are important in reference to secondary drives—like the need for esteem. Reductions of inequalities of income ought, accordingly, to reduce the intensity of secondary drives in previously underprivileged persons. Figure 10.1 shows that such reductions occurred in association with increases in linkages and fluidity. Presumably people like John Doe consequently perceived improvements in their relative power, status, and esteem.

5. In their turn, reductions of inequalities within communities were associated with reductions in the proportions of household heads who reported physical symptoms of distress in answering the research questionnaire on "mental health." In addition to their separate significance, each of the 12 items on this questionnaire seemed to be sensitive to a single underlying factor, presumably anxiety. The relationship of these changes to changes in linkages and fluidity is evidently indirect. However, this evidence suggests that New Brunswick Newstart interventions had produced reductions in anxiety levels. And it supports the notion of this chapter that changes in efficacy can result from changes toward equality in the distribution of power within social systems.

6. Finally, increases in linkages led to increases in differentiation in the structure of relevant communities ("community differentiation"). This was true also of industrial and commercial differentiation a year or so later and of occupational differentiation as well. The complexity of society had increased, so that it had a greater variety of positions to be filled, a greater variety of roles for people to play. Such changes should tend, of course, to increase the complexity of the role construct schemas or systems (such as that shown in Figure 8.1).

This, then, is the kind of evidence that best supports Eberts's theory of fluidity in social systems. Some of it has another value, though. It provides empirical support for the postulated relationship between freedom of will among individuals and flexibility or fluidity in social systems. Social and economic systems, like other environments, must not only permit but also respond appropriately to appropriate actions, before individuals can learn to control what happens to them in those situations. The personal power element of system fluidity is at once a condition and an expression of such responsiveness. Fulfillment of personal needs ought, of course, to be advanced by such actions. The New Brunswick Newstart evidence shows that this was indeed so, at least insofar as financial incomes reduced personal needs. Incomes represent *both* environmental responsiveness *and* the means for reducing some individual needs.

The evidence also shows that changes in these and other aspects of system function were stimulated by changes in information flow between and within systems. Very generally, then, it supports the belief that social environments that respond appropriately to the adaptive activities of individuals by rewarding or reinforcing them promote the development of individual freedom. It also supports the hypothesis that the process of bringing about such conditions in rigid, depressed economies should begin with the creation of new informative and trading relations with external economies and end with reduced inequalities of economic power.

THE INTERACTIONAL CHARACTER
OF FLUID SOCIETIES

The research that supports Eberts's theory refers to the important issue raised on pp. 182–183. By implication, it substantiates the widespread supposition that freedom and esteem are withheld from the poor by defeat in competition with the rich—at least in rigid economies. Explicitly, however, it shows the opposite. The success of prosperity accrues to poorer persons when they become involved in flexible social systems as a result of informative and trading communications with richer others. This research also provides detailed data showing how that comes about. When the flows of information it refers to and the changes it demonstrates are examined in detail, they yield an interesting representation of the social relationships in which the increased freedom and prosperity developed. They were *not* competitive.

Fluid societies are trading societies. That is, they are societies containing large numbers of interdependent subsystems and persons. As conceived, fluidity consists in frequent communications, which may be regarded as reinforced interactions, between units or individuals. If such communications are to continue or be repeated, each party to the interaction must gain something from it—as Goffman has pointed out for the case of individuals (1955) and as the principles of reinforcement require. The applicability of this statement is not restricted to conversations, in which witty or informative sallies are rewarded with laughter, attention, and positive affect. It applies also to the economic interactions that Eberts treats as flows of information, whether they occur between economies or between individuals. Some people, for instance, provide services to others, who reward them with money and are rewarded by those services. They purchase from others, and the process continues. And the same statements can be made for companies or other organizations. *On each of these occasions, each party to a transaction is, of course, reinforcing behavior he desires from the other.* Far from being the bad novelty it was regarded by reviewers of Skinner's book *Beyond Freedom and Dignity,* positive reinforcement of desirable behaviors by others is commonplace and comfortable. Increases of fluidity in a community mean (*a*) that people in it are rewarding and pleasing one another more frequently; and (*b*) that the rewarded behaviors have increased in value as well as quantity.

As participants in trading societies, the citizens and other units of fluid social systems are generally more interdependent than those in rigid systems. The apparent competition of some traders, engaged in similar activities in pursuit of a limited supply of rewards, should not obscure the essential nature of *trading economies*. They *are what they are because their different members perform different kinds of specialized services for one another and are individually rewarded for doing so.* Their mutual dependence is mutually reinforced. Indeed it is this cooperative aspect of the division of labor that might be said to characterize fluid societies, as it characterizes trading societies when contrasted with subsistence cultures.

When a person has found and assumed a "differentiated" role of the sort held by most adults in trading societies, his relationship to his peers is precisely *not* the sort that Fromm associated with individuation (see pp. 173–174, this volume). It is *not* true for individuals with specialized positions, that everyone is a potential competitor. What is true, instead, is that most others are potential trading partners, capable of enriching one if one pleases them. Competition is most likely to occur among persons with similar positions in life. In fact the evidence that gains in linkages bring increased (role or community) differentiation and less inequality also means, by contrast, that competition prevails in rigid societies. Fear of competition may explain the racially discriminative legislation for which the rigid states of 1950 were remarkable (see p. 184, this volume).

A second essential characteristic of fluid, trading societies is that their members have to be prepared to perform their different individual roles. They must accordingly be *educated for informational independence* and creative individuality. If they are to be prepared, as individuals, to resolve the variety of novel problems they will meet in the future, they cannot be persuaded or "trained" in large batches by people who are expert in current problems and techniques. Presumably this accounts for the high value these societies place on education.

Education, as Kelley conceives it, differs in several theoretically interesting ways from persuasion as a technique for shaping the behavior of junior members of an economy. First, of course, the knowledge it transmits is more basic. Instead of providing practical information, it inculcates theoretical and epistemological knowledge and informational independence. Both this knowledge and the initiative its use confers can then be transferred freely to future situations. Second, education amounts to the sharing, rather than the monopolization, of these sources of competence and influence. It is also remarkable, however, that this is a special sort of sharing. The donor loses none of what he shares. Educating another may cost him time, though in the long run it probably costs him less time than repeatedly persuading informationally dependent followers. Education is a cooperative and proactive influence technique. Finally, of course, it is also a more realistic technique. It is more consistent with the facts of social interdependence because it ensures the existence of an independent source of information against future needs.

A third essential feature of fluid trading societies is related to their dependence on education. Their success depends upon their having high levels of information to make accurate predictions and to guide preparatory actions. It depends upon their processing information proactively. So the continuing prosperity of fluid societies depends upon their development of many individuals with high information levels.

Cultural Relativism in Ideals

For all of these reasons, fluid and rigid societies ought to hold quite different conceptions of what is good and valuable in human behavior. Fluid societies ought, for instance, to place greater value on independent proficiency and on informed intelligence, and ought to accord higher social status or esteem to people who produce them. Their ethical standards, too, ought to differ from those of rigid societies; they should be appropriate to cooperative relationships with larger segments of mankind, less egocentric, family centered, ethnocentric, or even nationalistic. Their beliefs about ideal social relationships, and how to create them, ought to differ remarkably from those of people in rigid societies whose relationships with others are less extensively interdependent and more often competitive—and more often subject to the effects of inequalities in power. The ethical systems of people in fluid societies ought to be more comprehensive and better informed because their societies not only display more variety but provide them with greater knowledge and higher personal efficacy. They ought, for instance, to differentiate the good of personal competence or potency from the good of interpersonal virtue, whereas notions like "what has always been done" is the right thing to do should have wider appeal in more rigid economies. And, of course, people in fluid societies ought to place greater value on personal freedom and responsibility. The cultural deprivation interpretation of the authoritarian personality (Kelman & Barclay, 1963) is consistent with these deductions.

People do, indeed, differ remarkably in their conceptions of what are ideal social relationships. And these conceptions in turn differ in reference to both competition and cooperation, and in terms of both inclusiveness and universality. These are matters of fact that must now be examined.

SUMMARY

One's beliefs about and evaluations of people in society commonly represent individuals as differing in potency, prestige, or esteem. Low self-esteem has been regarded as a sign of maladjustment. However, a person's primary evidence for low self-esteem is comparative and arises from unsatisfactory relations with an environment that includes people of higher esteem or status, whose competence or efficacy appears superior to his own.

In many cultural groups, status differentiations are closely related to differentiations of success, assessed in terms of position, wealth, and education. These possessions promote the attainment of personally satisfactory relations with future situations, and they are signs of successful relationships with earlier situations. They represent power and confer freedom of choice.

Comparable characteristics also differentiate the more from the less "advanced" nations. The more powerful and successful of them operate specialized trading economies that process information proactively and control their environments. The less powerful are more vulnerable to influence by natural events and other external forces. Knowledge and wealth seem to have universal value because of their relations to freedom of will.

Wealthier states have displayed greater tolerance for racial and political diversity. Their economies are more urbanized, employ higher proportions of well-educated people, and produce more innovations. They have been described as more open to information, that is more "flexible" or "fluid" than less prosperous "rigid" states in which freedom is restricted in various ways.

A sociological theory about fluidity defines it in terms of information flow along links between social units. The theory predicts that changes in fluidity within social units will follow changes in linkages between them. For instance, changes in economic or trading linkages are expected to produce changes in the flow of money, which is considered as information, and in the differentiation of activities by the subunits in each system (that is, role or community differentiation). The introduction of new linkages of this kind between one community and others is thus predicted to cause increases in the financial incomes of its citizens, to reduce disparities of income, and to increase role-differentiation.

Several investigations using recent historical records, and one experimental study, have confirmed predictions by this theory. Increases in structural linkages between one social system and the outside trading economy are followed by increases in fluidity, increases of income, and increases of structural differentiation within it. The experimental study also discovered changes in communities that presumably demonstrate gains in efficacy by individuals—reductions of income (or financial power) differentials and increases in major expenditures on durable goods, in mental health, and in perceived personal power.

The flow of economic information (or trade) rewards both parties to the exchange. This generalization also applies to similar interactions between individuals, which are mutually rewarding. When the fluidity of a social system rises, cooperation characterizes an increasing proportion of the interactions among its members. More of the interactions in rigid systems are competitive.

Fluid and specialized trading economies seem to produce, and to depend upon, the differentiated activities of informationally independent, responsible individuals. This may account for the high value they place on education.

The different types of social relationships that prevail in fluid and rigid societies are expected also to produce different evaluations of what are "good" and "bad" kinds of human behavior.

Responsibility, Freedom, and Morality

SELF-SERVING ACTIONS AND MORALITY

The tyrannical superegos of Freud's "neurotic" patients in nineteenth-century Vienna seem to have had characteristics Rollo May has labeled "Victorian." Like the dogmatically conventional moral statements of "yielders," "authoritarians," and "externals," they seem to have demanded the *suppression* of *id*-serving impulses in compliance with standards that society pretended to maintain. The ability for such suppression was, in May's view, what Victorian Europeans understood as "will power" (May, 1969, p. 207).

It has been argued, by contrast, that freedom of will depends upon informed intelligence and upon efficacy—that state of satisfactory relations between a person and his environment which is attainable in a fluid society. "Rational" processing of information for consistency of personal experience is supposed to promote development of abstract conceptions of reality that can facilitate the attainment of satisfactory outcomes for self and associates. The assumptions that mutually satisfactory interactions between individual and society are unattainable and that personal needs must be sacrificed to the social good are depicted as consequences of reactive information processing and inadequate knowledge. Personal responsibility, in the moral sense, is represented as not only compatible with personal responsibility in the causal sense but impossible without it.

Is there truly no conflict between the demands of morality and those of individual responsibility and adjustment? According to material reviewed by Fromm (1941), Reformation theologians like Luther and Calvin thought there was. Or are there systems of moral thought compatible with freedom of will which are somehow superior to those that require obedience to the demands of authorities and the suppression of personal needs? Relevant information has been produced by the research work of Lawrence Kohlberg (1969).

197

A STUDY OF MORAL UNDERSTANDING

Influenced by the earlier and similar work of Jean Piaget (1948), Kohlberg spent considerable time collecting, studying, and classifying the explanations ordinary people give for their decisions on hypothetical moral issues. In order to stimulate the thought he wished to study, and because the content of preceding thoughts is not revealed by people who know the right answer, he deliberately constructed problems for which there is no correct answer. His method therefore enabled him to detect *how* decisions are rationalized in terms of beliefs and values; it could *not* produce any useful information on *why* particular choices between equally defensible alternative decisions might be made.

Here, for example, is one of Kohlberg's dilemmas:

> In Europe, a woman was near death from cancer. One drug might save her, a form of radium that a druggist in the same town had recently discovered. The druggist was charging $2,000, ten times what the drug cost him to make. The sick woman's husband, Heinz, went to everyone he knew to borrow the money, but he could only get together about half of what it cost. He told the druggist that his wife was dying and asked him to sell it cheaper or let him pay later. But the druggist said, "No". The husband got desperate and broke into the man's store to steal the drug for his wife. Should the husband have done that? Why? [1969, p. 379].[1]

In this first survey, Kohlberg recorded and analyzed the answers given to 10 such dilemmas by about 100 boys, aged 7 to 17, from various social backgrounds. The analysis of the sort of information obtained in such free verbal responses is an arduous task if the investigator is to prevent his beliefs from influencing his treatment of it. Categories for grouping similar responses together have to be defined and composed with great care. Here, as in other aspects of his research, Kohlberg was able to make use of previous, similar investigations to develop improved methods. He ultimately produced a classification grid composed of 25 columns, each for a different topic of consideration in moral decisions (such as "motive" or "justice") and six rows, each for a different interpretation of, or type of argument about, these considerations. The various answers given by the boys could be sorted quite readily and objectively into the cells of this grid.

The most useful of Kohlberg's findings referred to the row categories. It was established, as a test of objectivity in sorting, that the majority of answers given by any one person and sorted without knowledge of who had produced them turned up in the same row, and most of the others in immediately adjacent rows.

---

[1]This and subsequent quotes cited to Kohlberg, 1969 are from Lawrence Kohlberg, "Stage and Sequence: The Cognitive-Development Approach to Socialization," in David E. Goslin (Ed.), *Handbook of Socialization Theory and Research,* © 1969 by Rand McNally College Publishing Company, Chicago, pp. 376–382. Reprinted by permission.

Then it was shown that the average ages of the authors of interpretations in the different rows made sense, in terms of the moral sophistication suggested by the definitions of those categories. From this evidence, Kohlberg felt he had produced a method for detecting different stages in the development of moral understanding.

In subsequent studies, Kohlberg and his students produced further evidence that the six "row" categories do indeed detect progress in the development of moral reasoning. The answers given by the average child progress from one row to the next, as the children grow older. The same sequence applies in many different cultures, at least through the first four "stages," as he called them. In addition, the rate of a child's progress through these stages is partly a function of his intelligence. Among children of lower measured intelligence, the higher the intelligence, the higher the stage of moral cognition.

The relationship between intelligence and moral development was not found among older persons or brighter children. Kohlberg attributed this fact to the influence on moral reasoning of differences in the moral codes of the groups and cultures in which the interpreters lived. That is, he assumed that there are cultural determinants of moral intelligence and that cultures differ, as do individuals, in the way they understand social and moral issues.

SIX STAGES OF SUPEREGO

The First Stage

At the lowest stage of moral understanding defined by Kohlberg, the criteria for differentiating right from wrong actions have to do with the *appearance* of an action (e.g., a lie and its size) or with its immediate consequences (e.g., damage and its amount). For instance, one response to the drug-stealing dilemma was:

"He shouldn't steal the drug, it's a big crime. He didn't get permission, he used force and broke and entered. He did a lot of damage, stealing a very expensive drug and breaking up the store, too." [p. 379]

Those (children) who construed right and wrong in this way commonly mentioned the necessary risk of punishment by others as an influence in one's choice of action.

"You shouldn't steal the drug because you'll be caught and sent to jail if you do. If you do get away, your conscience would bother you, thinking how the police would catch up with you at any minute." [p. 381]

Kohlberg noted the importance of deference to superior power in the kind of thinking that constitutes this stage, which he named the *"obedience and punishment orientation."*

"Intra-attitudinal consistency," in Rosenberg's sense (see p. 137, this volume) is minimally evident in these views of what distinguishes good from bad actions. Clearly, punishment is negatively valued; certain kinds of acts may lead to punishment; therefore such acts are negatively valued. The latter judgment is consistent with a very small number of beliefs and values. In accordance with generalizations justified earlier, evaluative actions by people who think this way ought often to respond to situational influences. Internal factors should prevail only occasionally, and moral constancy should therefore be minimal. Indeed, it appears from the context of this simple system of values and beliefs that "conscience" here is simply fear of the punishment that certain kinds of act are expected to bring down upon one from outside.

To say that this simple attitude system is short-sighted, self-centered, and premoral is simply to say that it recognizes relatively few entities and has relatively few beliefs and values about things. It is ill-differentiated and shows little understanding of the human interrelationships and interactions that produce wrongs and punishments or good deeds and rewards.

In terms of a conception of "natural law" (see Kant, p. 132, this volume), this understanding of "what is happening" (see Niebuhr, p. 167, this volume) may be expressed as follows: *When a person takes actions of certain manifest forms, or produces certain immediate effects, then other, stronger people punish him. Because it is good to avoid such punishment, one must either avoid such deeds or the supervision of such people.*

The Second Stage

The second most elementary sort of moral understanding defined by Kohlberg is also externally oriented. In this case, however, good and bad deeds are not differentiated according to appearances. They are differentiated in terms of their effects on human needs.

> "He shouldn't steal it. The druggist isn't wrong or bad, he just wants to make a profit. That's what you're in business for, to make money." [p. 379]

Need values also appear, in associated formulations of social sanctions.

> "He may not get much of a jail term if he steals the drug, but his wife will probably die before he gets out so it won't do him much good. If his wife dies, he shouldn't blame himself, it wasn't his fault she has cancer." [p. 381]

In the terms of one of Kohlberg's summaries about this "naively egoistic orientation," "Right action is that instrumentally satisfying the self's needs and occasionally others." There is "awareness of relativism of each actor's needs and perspective, naive egalitarianism and orientation to exchange and reciprocity [p. 376]."

The attitude system, here, has become more complicated. It now recognizes the social context of behavior that is subject to moral judgments. It recognizes, for instance, that actions that have good effects for one person may have bad effects for another and, furthermore, that these may lead the other to actions that have bad effects for the one. And it recognizes, perhaps vaguely, that social harmony and disharmony can develop, and that the one is preferable to the other. It appreciates that it is good to be fair, but it is still, basically, competition-oriented, because its naive egalitarianism shows only an elementary awareness of the possibility that social harmony can be attained cooperatively, by each person's guarding the well-being of others as well as his own. Nonetheless, "conscience" has begun to take note, sympathetically perhaps, of the effects of one's actions upon others. Therefore relevant beliefs and values should sometimes prevail over situational influences and accordingly produce some moral constancy.

Construed as a conception of "natural law," this understanding of "what is happening" in social affairs seems to go somewhat as follows: *Each person has needs that it is good to satisfy, but actions that are good for one person's needs may be bad for another person's and cause the other to punish him; it is good to avoid such frustrations and punishments if possible, but you must be fair, so some losses may have to be incurred for the sake of other gains.*

The Third Stage

In the next stage of moral thinking, according to Kohlberg's information, the criteria of good and bad deeds are not found in the effects of actions, but in the intentions and characters of the actors. Comparably, good behavior is not sanctioned by physical rewards or punishments but by the approval or disapproval shown by other people toward individuals whose intentions and characters they infer to be good or bad.

"He shouldn't steal. If his wife dies, he can't be blamed. It isn't because he's heartless or that he doesn't love her enough to do everything that he legally can. The druggist is the selfish or heartless one." [p. 380]

"It isn't just the druggist who will think you're a criminal, everyone else will too. After you steal it, you'll feel bad thinking how you've brought dishonor on your family and yourself; you won't be able to face anyone again." [p. 381]

In Kohlberg's summation, this "good boy orientation" is characterized by an "orientation to approval and to pleasing and helping others." It involves "conformity to stereotypical images of majority or natural role behavior and judgment by intentions [p. 376]."

Apparently "cooperation" is now positively valued, though still somewhat vaguely apprehended. Articulation of social interactions has progressed to the point at which intentions are recognized and the moral criteria for judging actions are found therein. Intentions of mutually considerate kinds are now positively valued, and are believed to earn the (secondary) reinforcements of social approval; whereas competitive intentions are negatively valued and believed to earn social disapproval. "Characters," too, have come to be recognized as definable entities, and varieties of character have associated values and beliefs. More general incentive mechanisms, involving internal self-reinforcement of actions, have made their appearance, although social approval and disapproval remain potent, if abstract, influences.

What is perhaps most evident at this stage is the use of more abstract categories for construing social interactions and social harmony, and their relation to personal well-being. Intentions and characters now earn approval and disapproval. At lower stages, by contrast, relatively superficial features distinguished actions that were remarkable for effects on the environment or upon more primitive (*id*) needs. The representation of social interactions is not quantitatively more complex than at Stage 2. Yet it is more abstract, and each abstract concept implicates innumerable specific instances. The many specific behaviors, which are thus associated with the valued abstractions of intention and character (and are believed to earn social approval), are of the sort that promote and maintain social harmony. Under these circumstances, the "good boy" who strives for the external reward of approval is striving at the same time for social harmony, however crudely he understands it.

The Stage 3 thinker seems to have become aware of the implicit theory of responsibility and its effects on social interactions. His understanding of "natural law," accordingly, seems to run somewhat as follows: *A person's actions reveal his intentions and dispositions to others so that they think of him as a good person or a bad person. One needs social approval so one must act in ways that earn it.*

The Fourth Stage

The attitude system of Stage 4 moralizers embodies even higher-order abstractions. The integrity of the social system has become explicitly valued, and, because it is believed to be well promoted by dutiful, rule-following behaviors and not sufficiently well promoted by good intentions and good characters, rule-following actions are positively valued and contrary behaviors are negatively valued. For instance:

> "It is a natural thing for Heinz to want to save his wife but it's still always wrong to steal. He still knows he's stealing and taking a valuable drug from the man who made it." [p. 380]

> "You're desperate and you may not know you're doing wrong when you steal the drug. But you'll know you did wrong after you're punished and sent to jail. You'll always feel guilty for your dishonesty and lawbreaking." [p. 381]

More abstract entities are also implicated in the incentives depicted in this system of moral thinking. "Honesty" and "dishonesty," like "honor" and "dishonor," are names for generalized, rule-related, evaluative characterizations of individuals by society. At this stage, one's personal honor seems to have become a valued asset, a matter of pride, and an aspect of conscience. Defense or promotion of a good name seems now to motivate behaviors that are believed appropriate. In addition, because general characterizations of this kind are neither earned nor invalidated by singular instances of praise or blame, the motivational system that refers to them has of course reached a new stage of independence from external reinforcement. Indeed, knowing a system of rules, one is now equipped to assess the validity of specific sanctions that others might apply—to appraise external reinforcement in accordance with internal standards.

Kohlberg has called this an "authority and social-order maintaining orientation." He considers it to involve "regard for earned expectations of others," an "orientation to 'doing duty' and to showing respect for authority and maintaining the given social order for its own sake [p. 376]."

Concepts like trustworthiness and responsibility appear, almost explicitly, in the moral thought of this fourth stage in understanding. A corresponding view of "what is happening" or of "natural law" might therefore take the following form: *The dangers of mutual injury, arising from pursuit of individual goals by members of a community demand that each person follow the rules, both to keep his good name and to maintain social order.*

The Fifth Stage

The conceptions of morality embodied in British common law, as outlined by White (see Chapter 2), resemble those of Kohlberg's fourth stage. Following these rules, though, it is conceivable that a person might cause injury to another and still be exonerated of legal or moral blame, provided that his intentions had been benign and he had followed the rules by taking reasonable precautions against foreseeable harm to others. This is not good enough at the fifth stage of understanding, which accordingly advances beyond the common law.

Stage 5 moralizers recognize that rules do not exist for all situations and that temporal social orders may be wrong. In their "higher" view, the production of morally acceptable behavior depends upon respect for, or concern about, the rights of people—oneself and others. They recognize explicitly what Stage 4 thinkers understand implicitly. Their criteria for good conduct, which are thus superior to rule following, are to be found in unwritten social contracts—such as "the freedom charter" postulated by Haines to account for the freedom people in some cultures accord one another. The maintenance of social harmony, rather than a particular social order, now has paramount value. So, the acceptability of particular forms of social order can now be adjudged against this standard.

> "You can't completely blame someone for stealing but extreme circumstances don't really justify taking the law in your own hands. You can't have every one stealing whenever they get desperate. The end may be good, but the ends don't justify the means." [p. 380]

> "You would lose your standing and respect in the community and violate the law. You'd lose respect for yourself if you're carried away by emotion and forget the long-range point of view." [p. 382]

The sanctions for one's own good conduct are found in emotionally toned personal judgments of one's actions by such standards, and the personal good again seems inextricably bound to the social good.

Moral thought at the fifth stage is characterized by Kohlberg as having a "contractual, legalistic orientation." It is also reported to involve "recognition of an arbitrary element or starting point in rules or expectations for the sake of agreement. Duty [is] defined in terms of contract, general avoidance of violation of the will or rights of others, and majority will and welfare [p. 376]." While the Stage 4 moralizer knows it is good to drive on the right-hand side of the road, one at Stage 5 knows that what matters is that everyone drive on the same side. This attitude system is thus more complex and less culture bound.

Social interactions, in this view, vary according to the expectations of the members of society. Its formulation of the "natural law" in "what is happening" may resemble the following: *The social harmony, which is fundamental to satisfactory life in an interdependent community of human beings, depends basically upon the predictability of individual actions, which everyone has a right to expect. The good of each person depends upon everyone's guarding this right and the other agreed rights of every individual.*

The Sixth Stage

What Kohlberg characterizes as the highest stage of moral thinking is attained by very few people, and each of them has theoretically passed through all the lower stages. From the standpoint of these individuals, Stage 5 thinking is inadequate. It involves ad hoc judgments that may be biased by the ignorance or the inclinations of the judge. This is the fault Kant found in the "subjective principle of action" he designated a "maxim" (Kant, 1785/1910, p. 351, n: 7). The Stage 6 moralizer requires his rules of the road to be logically sound. The orientation he consequently takes is "not only to actually ordained social rules but to principles of choice involving appeal to logical universality and consistency [p. 376]." His criteria of good conduct by self and others are found in such principles.

> "Heinz is faced with the decision of whether to consider the other people who need the drug just as badly as his wife. Heinz ought to act not according to his particular feelings toward his wife, but considering the value of all the lives involved." [p. 380]

> "If you stole the drug, you wouldn't be blamed by other people but you'd condemn yourself because you wouldn't have lived up to your own conscience and standards of honesty." [p. 382]

Adherence to principle is sanctioned by "mutual respect and trust," which of course emphasizes self-respect as well as the respect of others.

The Stage 6 attitudinal system, its construction of "what is happening" in social interaction and of the relevant "natural law," may be described in the following way: *The harmony of an interdependent social community depends upon actions in which each person discharges his duties and so guards the rights of others; but such decisions are liable to error, and may cause wrongs, unless they are based on appropriate, logically consistent and universally applicable principles that can be regarded as absolutely good.* This sort of view is, of course, summarized in Kant's categorical imperative, "Act as if the maxim of thy action were to become by thy will a Universal Law of Nature [Kant, 1785/1910, p. 352]."

SUPEREGO INTELLIGENCE AND SUPEREGO ACTION

Kohlberg's ordering of explanations in moral decisions reveals a related ordering of knowledge about the social interactional bases of moral rules. Increases in the number of beliefs and values consistent with an evaluative judgment are believed, on the basis of research into attitudes, to produce increases in the stability or constancy of such judgments in the face of variations in situational influences. They are believed, indeed, to alter the bases of judgments and to render the whole process increasingly dependent upon the "dispositions" of the judge. Such constancy ought, accordingly, to become increasingly important to a person as he advances through Kohlberg's stages.

Detailed internal evidence from Kohlberg's research supports this deduction. The criteria for good conduct become increasingly *comprehensive* with progress from the lower to the higher stages. They are applied to wider ranges of situation, omitting fewer cases as their scope becomes increasingly general. That is, novel situations are treated, increasingly, as repetitions in essential (abstract) respects of situations previously encountered. Despite (or because of) this increasing generality, references to the possibility of impulsive action or to possible difficulties in impulse control become increasingly rare. And of course the cited loci of relevant sanctions shift progressively from outside to inside the person.

On the assumption that people have no option but to act in accordance with their understanding of how events in the world are related to one another, Stage 1 thinkers ought to act driven in moral situations; they ought to act dependently, like authoritarians, and to shape their actions for appearance, like "yielders." Stage 6 thinkers, on the other hand, should act by principle, autonomously. At least they ought to do so if their conceptions of natural law are the sole determinants of their behavior. They probably are not.

Each person who attains a higher stage in moral development has passed through the lower stages and may accordingly retain, and sometimes act in accordance with, habitlike vestiges of those ways of acting. The ability to act according to "reason independent on inclination" theoretically varies with efficacy, as well as with intelligence. In Kohlberg's terms, it depends on "strength of will" or "ego-strength" (1969, p. 396), a nonmoral determinant of moral behavior. In Kant's terms, when discussing "some qualities which are of service to this good will itself, and may facilitate its action," it depends upon the "moderation in the affections and passions, self-control and calm deliberation [1785/1910, p. 324]," that were represented earlier as aspects of efficacy. Furthermore, according to Kant's practical imperative, it depends upon the degree to which a person's actions in moral situations are designed for compatibility with his own interest: "It is not enough that the action does not violate humanity in our own person as an end in itself, it must also *harmonize with it* [Kant, 1785/ 1910, p. 361]." Freedom of choice among the options one perceives in moral (as in other) situations theoretically depends upon efficacy.

Nonetheless, people do tend to act in moral situations in general accordance with their conceptions of the rules of social interaction, insofar as these are revealed in Kohlberg's studies (1969). Measures of moral maturity are related to ratings by teachers and peers for conscientiousness, fair-mindedness, and moral character. Cheating on tests in grade school and college is three to four times as frequent among the middle as among the upper stages and even more frequent in the lower, premoral stages. Moreover, refusals to comply with morally unacceptable instructions by authority figures are six or more times as frequent among Stage 6 persons as among those at lower stages. All of these facts support the view that one's conceptions of morality constitute a major determinant of the morality of one's actions.

The same relation is evident from the opposite direction, that is, through examination of the moral conceptions of people who act in specified ways. Thus the criteria for good conduct advanced by "yielders," "authoritarians," and "externals" are dogmatic and reveal little understanding of "principles" relating specified kinds of action to specified sorts of outcomes for self or others. For instance, "I believe the moral responsibility for my actions falls upon the government," one American volunteer for military service during the Vietnam War told a group of investigators (cited by Sampson, 1971, p. 442). In speaking so, he unknowingly used the style of explanation Adolf Eichmann had provided for his war crimes against Jews (Kohlberg, 1969). The "law" that counts in such instances assumes the ways of the ingroup to be the correct ways. No universal natural laws of human relations are conceived to justify moral decisions.

Greater rationality, "self-control," and personal responsibility are apparent in the statements of draft resisters examined in the same research. These men, incidentally, were notably less likely than cadets to report having acted impulsively and feeling guilty later. In justification of his defiance of legislation, one of them, for example, said in part: "Everybody knows inside there is no such thing as LBJ's war. The most satisfying thing you can do for yourself is to face squarely your own complicity [cited by Sampson, 1971, p. 443]." His resistance, he said, was a matter of personal responsibility. Other resisters emphasized principles. Thus, when selected for behavioral stands on moral issues, people make the kinds of explanation that are appropriate in terms of Kohlberg's findings; at one extreme they describe external control, at the other, internal control.

MORAL THINKING AND FREE WILL

On Kohlberg's showing, conceptions of natural laws of social interaction develop, from early constructions in terms of physically defined deeds and punishments into or beyond constructions that recognize the possibility of an individual's attaining ends of his own and imposing his own ideals on social affairs. Criteria of, and sanctions for, moral action become increasingly differentiated and abstract. Also, the relation of sanctions to social interaction processes is understood with the increasing comprehension that produces foresight. Individuals are represented as decreasingly subject to unpredicted external events and increasingly capable of governing events by personal action. The latter sort of progress is evident in their behavior, too, within limits set by "strength of will" or efficacy. The development of higher moral conceptions produces increased evidence of freely willed, responsible behavior, when efficacy is sufficiently high. The "good will," like the "free will," depends upon efficacy and informed intelligence.

It appears then, that the advancement of a person through Kohlberg's stages in understanding of moral affairs is due to his development of an increasingly complex and well-informed view of the way the world works. An individual's "world view" becomes progressively less "egocentric," to use Piaget's term for the phenomenon he first described in studies of the growth of intelligence (Piaget, 1952). It is this growth to which Bernstein (1961) refers in his theory about the influence of communications on intelligence. The restricted (or public) code accommodates and theoretically fosters the world view of lower-stage thinkers, while the (formal or) elaborated code is required for higher-level thinking. Theoretically, the formal code promotes an understanding of natural and social events that is progressively less egocentric, being less dependent on immediate sensory impressions. Kohlberg's evidence also indicates that reduced egocentrism in moral thought is accompanied by increased recognition of self-interest in the maintenance of social harmony. The advanced moral thinker sees an identity between what is good for society and what is good for himself. He understands that his responsibility extends to promoting the efficacy of others and to reducing their drives as well as his own.

The limits of this generalization should be recognized. It does *not* say that enlightened self-interest and moral excellence are essentially the same (or even that enlightened self-interest necessarily advances social welfare, as Adam Smith contended). The value or moral worth of an action is certainly not solely due to its advancement of the actor's self-interests as narrowly accounted; benefits to him through others must be counted too. It is not readily apparent, for instance, that starving oneself in nonviolent protest, as Gandhi did, advances one's self-interest directly. To understand such actions in those terms, one must postulate that their authors construe them as promoting some ends that are personally valued (that they constitute self-actualizing behavior). This, however, is very close to the generalization that Kohlberg's work supports.

This evidence indicates that the more intellectually advanced a person's moral thinking, the more he understands his self-interest to be bound up with the interests of his community and fostered by actions that promote social justice and other ideal—that is valued and possible—consequences for all. When ethical behavior is thus understood to be purposive, the action is freely willed and the ethic is "teleological" (Niebuhr, 1963). By contrast, lower-level thinkers understand moral actions to be those sanctioned by external pressures; their behavior is represented as externally controlled, and their ethics are conforming and dutiful (i.e., "deontological," following Niebuhr, 1963).

This is another important aspect of the reduced egocentrism that accompanies increased moral maturity. The advancing person sees himself and others as decreasingly subject to external sanctions and increasingly subject to internal sanctions. The emotional (or affective) component of his own reactions to his own actions changes in a comparable way. Negative self-judgments and remorse increasingly supplant either fear of punishment or total unconcern, according to studies reviewed by Kohlberg (1969). In the terms of learning theory, the reinforcement of moral behavior becomes increasingly independent of the environment, including the behavior of others. The morally advanced person represents people as practicing "self-discipline" and apparently behaves that way himself. However this "self-discipline" evidently depends upon appropriate knowledge, or informed intelligence, and upon the freedom from driving pressures that comes with efficacy.

Individual morality, like other forms of effective, well-adjusted (free-willed and responsible) behavior is not an individual accomplishment, however. It is the representation in an individual of biological, cultural, and economic conditions. Further information on this aspect of the topic must now be examined.

SUMMARY

One conception of moral goodness focuses upon suppression of personal needs in obedience to social standards. Psychological evidence suggests, on the contrary, that self-discipline, resulting from personal efficacy and accurate abstract conceptions of causal relations, is necessary for the production of socially desirable behavior.

People differ in their conceptions of what is morally right and wrong. Six general ways of understanding these issues have been delineated and shown to follow one another in a specific developmental sequence. The most elementary of these is the "obedience and punishment orientation." The most advanced refers to actions based on abstract general principles.

In each of these six stages of moral cognition, moral decisions are justified by reference to social reality. However, these justifications differ in their representations of that reality. They range from the crudely analyzed and superficial to the logically analyzed and abstract.

Different levels of moral understanding are also characterized by differences in representation of the effective sanctions for good conduct. The lower conceptions refer to external sanctions, whereas the higher refer to personal judgments and internal sanctions.

Behavior in moral situations is evidently influenced by moral conceptions, so it appears that everyone tends to obey his understanding of "natural laws" of social interaction. Theoretically, he does so within limits set by personal efficacy. The "goodness" of his will seems therefore to depend upon the accuracy of his understanding, that is, informed intelligence, and upon his efficacy.

Limits to
Freedom of Will

MORALITY AND FREEDOM

Ethical beliefs are oriented to the promotion of freedom for individuals, as
"rights"—to pursue personal goods in a predictable social environment. At the
premoral level, indeed, moral decisions are justified in terms that seem to claim
unrestricted freedom of action for the self as an absolute right. Conventional and
principled moral conceptions recognize, with varying degrees of precision, that
unrestricted universal freedom is impossible. One individual's actions may easily
operate to restrict the freedom of others, who cannot control when they cannot
predict. Moral rules of conduct are accordingly intended to promote *conditional*
freedom for all (see pp. 174-176, this volume). In each of the types of moral
conception described by Kohlberg, cooperative adherence to the rules is supposed (*a*) to reduce the probability of unforeseen injury to or interference by
others; and accordingly, (*b*) to improve the chances that each person can attain
control over his own fate. In each case, too, the rules tend to sanction the
pertinent cooperation, because they stipulate the sorts of deeds that merit reward
and freedom (p. 175, this volume), by contrast with those that justify punishment
and restraint. Ethics, then, is about freedom and adjustment in a social context.

*While the enactment of moral beliefs works to promote freedom of will, their
use in training others also expresses it.* The stimulus-controlled counterparts of
moral sanctions are simple reactive exchanges of rewards and punishments, like
those that initially characterized the mutual fate control games of Chapter 9. Such
behavior is "premoral" of course. None of the moral systems of Chapter 11
advocates punishing those who injure others by impulsive movement or by error.
All of those that reflect upon the issue represent the sanctioning of moral conduct

as "self-controlled," abstract behavior, as proactive processing of the information of social interactions.

People with premoral conceptions of right and wrong find value only in actions that satisfy their immediate personal needs. Higher-level moralizers, however, ascribe value to actions that promote maximization of good outcomes and minimization of bad for larger numbers of people. They apparently understand their own welfare to be promoted thereby (see Chapters 7, 8, and 9). In their view, consideration of the needs and rights of all others is good, regardless of the power of those others. Presumably they value the interactional system such responsibility promotes. These rights include that of a predictable social environment and impose the duty of behaving predictably. To act predictably, so that others may act responsibly, is not only to display proactive responsibility. It is to take the kind of action required to ensure survival of a system that permits people the greatest possible degree of the freedom they evidently value. Morally responsible behavior supports "the freedom charter" (Haines, 1966).

Not only do they promote and express it, moral conceptions also *assume* freedom of will as a generally attainable characteristic of adult human behavior. Their assumptions are consistent with those of the ITR, described in Chapter 2. Thus Kohlberg's various moral conceptions distinguish between actions in terms of intentionality and choice, and they regard social sanctions as appropriate only for deeds that are assumedly both intended and chosen. In these assumptions, they are in fact generally correct when dealing with adults. According to material reviewed, the conditions of the actions that the ITR regards as freely willed are the conditions in which free will is most clearly demonstrated. They are the conditions in which the effects of action are most clearly shaped by the knowledge and ideals of individuals, rather than by situational events or pressures. Chapter 8 showed that evaluative decisions are least subject to situational influences and most clearly appropriate to personal dispositions, that is, personal values and beliefs, when the individuals concerned are most fully informed and free of driving pressures like needs and anxieties. It was also evident in Chapters 3–5 that skillful, enterprising, and creative activities are most likely to occur in these same conditions. When referring to adults, the folk psychology that underlies the ITR and Kohlberg's higher moral conceptions seems to be correct in general outline, although it is undoubtedly open to errors of application.

MAINTENANCE OF THE CONDITIONS OF FREEDOM

Accordingly, cooperative adherence to "the freedom charter" should be self-sustaining in appropriate social conditions—as shown in the experiments on mutual fate control. The benefits attained by successful proactive behavior should be recognized to depend upon the maintenance of social order and so reinforce responsible individuals in the responsible actions that promote it. This seems to be true in the case of people who produce principled moral judgments. Those benefits should be particularly obvious and particularly rewarding to anyone who knows the frustration of a social environment in which reactive exchanges are common. Moral responsibility should also be reinforced in freely willed persons when others punish their lapses or reward their virtues. It should be reinforced vicariously whenever anyone else is seen to be thus punished or rewarded. Given a sufficiently high proportion of responsible individuals, the reinforcement system that maintains the social order required for freedom ought to be self-propagating.

Unfortunately, a necessary social condition is not always met. Before social reactions to irresponsible behavior by any social unit can serve to create responsible behavior instead, that unit must be amenable to influence by those it affects. It must be responsive. This crucial point can be put in other words. To guarantee the survival of an interactive system that is consistent with ''the freedom charter,'' it is necessary to ensure that every unit that is permitted freedom will become and remain (proactively) considerate of the effects of its own actions upon other units. Unless each acts thus responsively, its actions will restrict the freedom of some other units in the system. So, those others must be capable of providing it with ''feedback'' of the effects of its actions on them, in such a way as to motivate reproduction of actions that please them and inhibition of those that do not. This sort of ''feedback'' is known as *justice,* and it is for these reasons that justice is fundamental to the maintenance of universal freedom. High-level moralizers, like the draft resisters of page 207, seem to have reached this conclusion too. Moreover, the hardships and ostracism they encountered demonstrate that it is becoming increasingly difficult for individuals to exercise appropriate influence over large ''impersonal'' social institutions. The survival of ''the freedom charter'' seems to be threatened by powerful and unscrupulous persons or agencies that exploit weaker individuals.

This is the heart of the problem raised in other terms both by Skinner's *Beyond Freedom and Dignity* and by the sociological distinction of flexible from rigid social systems. The maintenance of social freedom depends upon the responsiveness of each unit in the system to the reactions its operations produce in other units. This responsibility is a function of its amenability to influence by means they command. Unless it can be maintained somehow, the interactive system assumed in ''the freedom charter'' will be violated. Some social units will be free while others are not. The charter then will lose general validity. That is, the morally responsible behavior that sustains it will not be reinforced and freedom will ultimately disappear—perhaps in the way democracy disappeared in the economic turmoil of pre-Hitler Germany. In Skinner's terms, this outcome can be prevented by development of appropriate reinforcement schedules. In Eberts's terms, it can be prevented by the stimulation of more frequent and comprehensive communications in a community. However it be understood, the need to cultivate responsibility reflects one of the most important limits to freedom in modern society.

The Skinner–Freedom Controversy

Skinner's proposals for the planned use of rewards to cultivate socially desirable behavior were heatedly attacked by people like those he called "the defenders of freedom" (1971, p. 33). Although their positions were not always clear, many of those writers seemed to believe they were supporting the freedom charter. Apparently they understood that freedom is promoted by maintenance of conditions that merely permit socially uncontrolled access to rewards by enterprising persons or corporations and attempt to ensure mutual responsibility by the cooperative punishment of wrongdoing, as conventionally or legally defined. Moreover, they apparently understood Skinner to be advocating the destruction of a rational and valuable system, seemingly from misunderstanding. Three kinds of issues are raised by this confrontation.

The first issue, perhaps the central one, concerns Skinner's proposition that socially desirable behavior should be shaped by use of positive reinforcement, that is by rewards. By implication it might have seemed to be suggesting that such rewards be withheld by social artifice until supervisors were satisfied that suitable actions had been taken to earn them. Of course Skinner did not suggest any particular mechanism for effecting his proposal. He simply advocated the intelligent use and further pursuit of psychological knowledge. As indicated in Chapter 10, "free" economic interchanges actually correspond to the general pattern he recommended. If all other kinds of desirable behavior were similarly rewarded, his aims would be met. There need be no incompatibility between the preservation of social freedom and the use of rewards for shaping desirable behavior. Of course there could be, if inappropriate methods were employed; there could be, for instance, if governments were allowed to train draft resisters to enjoy military service.

A second issue may be found in the recommendation that the use of punishment as a social sanction should be abandoned. This seems to touch the core of "the freedom charter." Not only is anticipation of retribution for offense supposed to preserve the moral responsibility of free agents. Ability to inflict it is also supposed to enable others to trust them. And this is evidently true for persons of free will, as shown in Chapter 9. On the other hand, behavioral engineers know that the use of punishment is not a very good method for the shaping of desirable behavior. This point can be put in various terms, for instance those of Chapters 4, 6 and 7. In the lexicon of freedom, it means that development of the moral responsibility on which social freedom depends will be inhibited by any regime that punishes errors rather than rewarding successes. Evidence reviewed in Chapters 8, 10, and 11 confirms this generalization.

The third issue is a matter of conflicting assumptions about the basic freedom of will that is causal responsibility. Skinner of course denies its possibility, while "the freedom charter" assumes that essentially everyone has the necessary abilities, at least after a certain age. With some important qualifications the material reviewed in Chapter 3 supports this latter assumption. It is also clear, though, that causal responsibility is a conditional development. This view is supported in every substantive discussion in the foregoing material. Freedom of will is not universally "given." It needs to be nurtured with care, and the unskillful use of punishment seems to stunt its growth.

It is a tenable hypothesis, indeed, that inept application of the same folk psychology that rationalizes "the freedom charter" may actually prevent development of free will in some cases. Punishment and threat of punishment are evidently appropriate treatments for shaping the values of freely willed persons so that their actions defer to the needs of others. However, by the evidence of Chapters 6–8, they may be not only insufficient for that purpose but may even impede the development of free will in children.

Situation-shaping, motivationally independent types of behavior are most likely to be produced by people who have grown up in cultural conditions that accord them freedom of action. However, such individuals seem also to have been assisted by others toward independent reliance upon personal knowledge. Those others seem to have watched their endeavors closely and provided rewards and hintlike information at appropriate points. They seem to have accorded to learners appropriate liberty and respect (or dignity). But they do *not* seem to have followed the strategy the freedom charter and its folk psychology require for responsible adults—simply to allow them to do what they wish and to punish their misdeeds. Rather, they cultivated and rewarded competence.

The confrontation between Skinner and "the defenders of freedom" was a disagreement over how people should treat one another in order to promote social well-being. At the level of values, there may have been little difference of opinion. At the level of recommendations for social action, however, the two viewpoints are mutually inhibitory. The consensus of experts (at least) is a necessary prerequisite for any social action. Social programs aimed at promotion of freedom and personal adjustment for many individuals are not advanced by debates in which neither contender understands the case put by the other. In particular they will not be advanced by ignoring the knowledge of students of behavior.

Construing Adjustment Problems

There are other instances in which the application of psychological knowledge for the cultivation of human freedom is inhibited by inappropriate conventional beliefs. "Neurotic" disorders, for instance, are commonly taken to physicians, because physical distress often accompanies low efficacy or temporary stress. Of course, a physician's competence is generally limited to tending the body's organic condition. That seems appropriate to some driven personalities who construe their problems of adjustment as due to "break down" of the machine (Witkin, 1965) or to other "ego-alien" (Adorno *et al.,* 1950) causes, that is, to influences beyond their control. Unfortunately the causes of the diseases frequently lie elsewhere. On the evidence of many therapeutic experiments (e.g., Franks, 1969), the diseases can commonly be corrected by changes in "reinforcement schedules." They can be corrected, that is, by altering social and economic conditions in accordance with principles discussed by Skinner. The New Brunswick Newstart results of Chapter 10 suggest that they can also be relieved in some people by alterations of social and economic conditions that improve their relative ability to command and confer economic rewards. Some "diseases" are clearly the result of inability to wrest satisfactions from the environment, that is, to find positive reinforcements, even though their symptoms are physiological. In these cases, appropriate treatment is inhibited by construing it as a medical problem, rather than as a social and psychological one.

The misconstruction of adjustment problems that takes anxious people to physicians has a more general counterpart in the methods society at large uses for dealing with such problems. Psychologists and psychiatrists understand that the troubles of many of their patients are traceable to cultural and economic conditions. Yet they are expected to correct these troubles by "psychotherapy." Society, so to say, ascribes these adjustive disorders to individual *psychic* weaknesses, rather than to any malfunction of its own system. This way of thinking about such faulty relations between individuals and society delays more appropriate remedial actions.

What is represented in clinical referrals as psychic "inadequacy" or "impotence," and is commonly regarded as sufficient explanation of some disorders, is treated as "powerlessness" in sociological discussions, where it is considered an explanation for political, economic, and even moral "alienation."

ALIENATION AS CAUSE AND CONSEQUENCE OF IRRESPONSIBILITY

Alienation is a condition plausibly ascribed to social dropouts by contemporary sociologists. It involves dissatisfaction with, and distrust of, many social institutions; and is of course accompanied by reduced interaction with them through conventional means (Seeman, 1972; Blaumen, 1964). As conceived, alienation is the sort of orientation to social affairs that can be caused by "learned helplessness" (p. 49, this volume). It is a special sort of irresponsibility, hypothetically due to repeated frustration in attempts to make the social environment respond to complaints about its actions. The sociopathology it seems to express, and contribute to, is an impairment in the kinds of mutually reinforcing communications that rationalize "the freedom charter."

Possible causes for alienation are not difficult to find. Governmental actions are increasingly resistant to influence by individuals and small groups. Large corporations can act unjustly to individuals and successfully resist claims for redress. They can ignore reactions to the consequences of their misdeeds, apparently protected by monopolistic command of particular markets. Legal processes favor those who can afford the largest expenses and have less need for justice. On the other hand, the individual's rights to protect his own interests have been circumscribed in many ways. In some cases they have been delegated to, or assumed by, new institutions, like police forces and governmental agencies. These however may create as many difficulties in the sanctioning of desirable behavior as they resolve. They are liable to petty bureaucratic stupidities, which arise from ritualistic, habitlike adherence to preestablished, inadequately differentiated rules, and their misdeeds can pass unrectified for the same reasons. The assumption of mutual fate control, which rationalizes "the freedom charter," is commonly violated. Alienated people may feel like children who are tired of trying to play games with stupid giants who have all the marbles!

The term *welfare state* refers to an important class of governmental responses to some causes of powerlessness and alienation. Theoretically these developments should have important and potentially contradictory effects upon freedom. They are, of course, aimed at reducing the biological needs and associated anxieties that restrict freedom of will, as shown in Chapters 4–8. They ought accordingly to promote freedom, as well as personal adjustment. However, in pursuit of this aim, artificial economic environments are being established which may elicit and reinforce behaviors that hamper, rather than help, the larger economy. Deprived persons may learn how to operate the system of rules, regulations, and civil servants that provides for their needs—to the exclusion of socially productive behaviors. Conceivably they might even learn that important rewards come to them regardless of what they do. Such an outcome amounts to "learned helplessness" and may create even greater alienation and reduced responsibility (Seligman, 1973). These grave dangers can only be withstood by development of a system of subsidies that elicits and reinforces socially productive activities.

One aspect of the operations of the welfare state and other new institutions has attracted comment in Nicolas Haines's *Freedom and Community* (1966). The pertinent discussion concerns the obligations of "social servants," a category that expressly includes teachers, physicians, and social workers, as well as civil service employees. In each of these roles, occasions may often present the option of either doing something for the client or of aiding him to help himself (which may be the more difficult course to follow). For those in the teaching profession, the alternatives are illustrated in Kelley's distinction between "persuasion" (or perhaps "training") and education. The one type of action tends to cultivate dependence, whereas the other promotes freedom of will and personal responsibility. It is Haines's point that the latter is the only ethically defensible choice, the only responsible way for professionals to behave. This, of course, is almost an exhortative approach to the project of establishing or preserving the causal responsibility that is assumed in "the freedom charter." With professionals, who are commonly responsible, self-reinforcing persons, it may work—not by creating morally responsible behavior, but by enlightening people in whom a good will is already established.

Large and powerful organizations create feelings of powerlessness among individuals on the inside, as well as on the outside. Employees or members of such groups are obliged to obey their regulations on pain of discharge, for instance. Characteristically these persons neither regard themselves, nor are regarded by others, as responsible for the actions they take in those roles (de Charms *et al.*, 1965). Responsibility tends to be diluted in groups (Wallach *et al.*, 1964; Zimbardo, 1969; Latané & Darley, 1970). No doubt this is true also of what may be called *resistance collectives,* those organizations of workers, consumers, political dissidents, and the rest that are created to combat oppressive monopolies. Tyranny of the majority can occur, even illegal action, when irresponsible yielders support apparent group consensus. All of these facts refer to conditions that reduce the ability of individuals to act with freedom and responsibility in society; and all express their powerlessness. Theoretically their correction will remove important limits on social freedom.

Construing Alienation Problems

Conditions that can alienate individuals from interaction with powerful social institutions can be construed in various ways, with various implications for correcting them. Constructions in terms of powerlessness can lead to efforts by the powerless to coerce or extort respect and responsiveness from the powerful (Baldwin, 1964), and they may culminate in violence, followed by repressive reactions. Constructions in terms of poverty may have helped create "welfare states." Antimonopoly legislation presumably stems from interpretations that refer to market freedom. Philosophical discussions speak in terms of *justice* and *equality* (Haines, 1966). Eberts's theory regards alienating conditions as evidence of social rigidity, due to the effect of concentrations of power and influence upon communications within a social system. These conditions can also be interpreted, in learning theory terms, as malfunctions in the systems by which human beings reinforce one another's actions.

The behavior of a trading corporation that can ignore individual reactions to its misdeeds (or those of its computer) has become independent of reinforcement by its customers as individuals. And of course the dissidence of alienated customers means these corporations have failed to reinforce the right sort of behavior by the customers. By contrast, the harmonious public relations of a popular business reveal reciprocal reinforcement of reciprocally desirable actions. Such interactive relationships induce, as they develop from, mutually responsible communicative actions. Aleination and dissent reveal defects in a people's system for mutual reinforcement.

The same reinforcement analysis can be applied to the many other kinds of social discord that give rise to alienation or violence. The "irresponsibility" shown in these reactions also reveals irresponsibility in the earlier actions of the persons or institutions that shaped them. The causal relations are circular. This at least is the view of a strict reinforcement psychology like Skinner's. The psychology of free will would modify it only slightly, in ways that justify greater optimism. It would contend that it is particularly the behavior of irresponsible, compliant, driven persons that has permitted the development of such social conditions. It would also contend that these conditions can be changed with the application of informed intelligence by other, more efficacious persons.

The development and maintenance of adequate levels of informed intelligence and efficacy are additional serious needs for the preservation of freedom. The increasingly large number of persons who must find their livings from the earth's finite resources poses formidable problems. For millions of illiterate people in overpopulated nations, the provision of basic needs is an enormous task, let alone the provision of the education and social reorganization they will require for personal independence. Their grave problems are already unsolvable by their current techniques. They face the prospect of being driven by circumstances and physical needs, possibly into despotic political organizations and possibly into violent aggression. The solution of these desperate problems demands the application of increasingly more sophisticated scientific knowledge, which they lack. It demands aid from, and therefore changes in behavior by, members of free and wealthy nations, whose technological adaptations are even now proceeding so rapidly as to strain their own capacity to adjust, and may be causing "future shock" (Toffler, 1970). The need for creative intelligence in the service of human freedom seems to have become a matter of desperate urgency on which the very survival of humanity could depend.

CAN PEOPLE SOLVE PROBLEMS?

For readers of B. F. Skinner, the expression "creative intelligence" may seem to beg a question. The question is whether human beings do in fact solve problems or create new environmental conditions.

This *is* a serious question because Skinner raised it in the name of science (see p. 9, this volume). Of course even that way of thinking does not say solutions to human problems are never found, only that the finding of those solutions results from environmental influence. "It is always the environment which builds the behavior with which problems are solved, even when the problems are to be found in the private world inside the skin [1971, p. 195]." Fortunately, this view can be shown to be misleading.

Samples from the body of knowledge that supports Skinner's statement have just been reviewed. Indeed, it has been a major theme of this book that environmental influences determine whether or not a person can display freedom of will. And further information to that effect can be found in the specific context of problem-solving behavior. The facts are not in dispute; their interpretation is.

Skinner's argument—that even the most patently free-willed instances of behavior, such as creative enterprise, are in fact controlled by the environment— uses definitions of freedom and control that conflict with the bulk of the foregoing material. Here, by contrast, creative imagination and abstract knowledge are regarded as liberating humans from control by immediate situational influences. While this view sees the solution of a problem as a triumph of the individual and his knowledge over his current environment, Skinner's sees it merely as another instance of environmental control over individual actions.

One crucial difference between the present perspective and the behavioral engineering view of Skinner is apparent in the interpretation each makes of how "reinforcing" events in the environment effect the "shaping" of "instrumental CRs." According to the evidence and argument of Chapter 4 (especially pp. 58–60), it is not by delivering drive-reducing rewards of this kind that environments control animals, as the behavioral engineering position implies. It is by creating the driven states that these rewards relieve. Thus positive reinforcements are understood as informing individuals and thereby reducing the helplessness, or external control, that drive states attest. Rather than binding individual actions to environmental control, they increase the individual's freedom of choice.

The view that all human actions are controlled by environmental reinforcements is blind to important differences in the determinants of various instances of behavior. The distinction between "autonomous man" and one whose actions are subject to compulsion, impulsion, or restraint must evade anyone who regards them as equally controlled by the environment. That the concept of freedom refers to just this distinction has not altered the Skinnerian way of thinking about behavioral control. It sees reactive responses to current environmental stimulation and the planned application of valid scientific principles to the creation of a new environment as equally controlled by the environment. Nor does the Skinnerian view seem sensitive to whether or not the behavior produces effects that satisfy the individual. In either case, again, it regards the environment as the controlling agent. A method of defining and locating the determinants of behavior that produces such results is quite unsatisfactory, particularly for discussions that refer to freedom.

It should be clear, accordingly, that environments need not be regarded, in the way Skinner imputed to "science," as controlling human actions. It should also be clear that environments sometimes *do* control behavior and that their varying degrees of influence are neatly consistent with the literature on freedom of will.

The Effect of Environments on Problem-Solving Activity

Environments control human thoughts and actions when they create "problems." This may occur when they deny an individual access to supplies he needs, when they impose conditions that upset biological equilibria, or when their actions suggest that either of these conditions are imminent. In these circumstances, individuals become preoccupied with the needs or apprehensions the environment imposes, and with actions that experience shows to have been useful for their reduction. These actions become driven and may be inappropriate to their circumstances if the environment is familiar in some respects and novel in others. They are clearly "controlled" by the "drive" that arises from environmental recalcitrance.

It is true that driven behavior sometimes blunders into "solutions" to simple problems. In the case of human inventions, however, the process of searching for the solution to a problem involves more than random activity or repetition of habitual acts. It involves tests of alternative possible ways of acting, development and use of new discriminations, and application of knowledge that is meanwhile acquired (Humphrey, 1948; Bartlett, 1958). Probably it entails self-reinforcement of progress. It depends upon activities that are impeded by high and rising drive. That, however, is all the problem situation can contribute, in the way of incentive, to the maintenance of search behavior.

Environmental "reinforcement" of problem-solving activities cannot occur until the problem has been solved. The Skinnerian procedure of "shaping" behavior, by reinforcing actions that more and more closely approximate the one the trainer desires, amounts to continuous redefinition of either the problem or the situation. It has few parallels in the real problems presented by physical environments, like those solved by physical innovations. What the problem environment normally contributes to the search process, by way of reinforcement, is entirely negative. It is "drive" and frustration. Indeed it should produce anxiety reactions, not creative reconstructions of the environment.

The occasions that give rise to anxiety, like those that create primary or secondary drives, are also occasions for problem-solving activity. They develop, according to Epstein (see pp. 67–69, this volume), when environments create "primary overstimulation," when they fail to respond appropriately to actions that were expected to change them, when they are different from what they were expected to be, or when they contain signs suggesting that either of these conditions is about to occur. What is observed in anxiety, however, is not the methodical, self-instructing search behavior by which problems are solved. It is, according to Epstein, a disorganized state of energy arousal, which, according to Spence, activates habitual actions. This is precisely the fate that methodical search behavior is likely to suffer under the influence of continuing negative reinforcement from a recalcitrant environment. Of course, a good teacher, knowing the solution to an anxious person's problem, could apply Skinnerian methods for shaping behavior and teach him its solution. This is indeed what Skinner advocates, and advocates correctly. In that case, however, a person with appropriate knowledge would in fact be changing the environment as a means of providing appropriate knowledge to another person. The environment alone would merely have created the problem.

The answer, then, is that people can solve problems, and that environments cannot, except when they are people. However, environmental events can be manipulated so as to teach appropriate behavior to those who are unable to teach themselves. It is important, in the interests of freedom and of human welfare, that this be done where possible and that the necessary information to do it correctly be obtained. This is precisely what Skinner has been advocating. With *Beyond Freedom and Dignity,* unfortunately, he seems to have created unnecessary antagonism to the cultivation and use of knowledge for behavioral engineering. The terms in which one discusses complex and important topics have to be selected and used with great care if such misunderstandings are to be avoided and important limitations on human freedom are to be removed.

THE FREE MIND

According to previous chapters, the persons who succeed in overcoming their problems and controlling their environments, those who deal proactively ("constructively") with stress situations, rather than merely reacting to them, have specifiable characteristics. These are characteristics that behavioral engineers would attribute to the feedback those individuals had been given by their environments. The evidence of preceding chapters seems to indicate that, in large measure, this interpretation is basically correct—basically, but perhaps not completely, because the "causal" relations involved are complex.

Individuals who control their current environments, rather than being controlled by them, are remarkable for informed intelligence and efficacy. In the compliance literature, they show themselves to be "objective" in the government of their actions, with a preference for consistency between their actions and their perceptions over a pretense of agreement with others. Words like "integrity" and "truth" might apply. In the terms of a theoretical analysis reviewed in Chapter 8, they use consistency of personal experience as the criterion of truth. They have appropriate methods for discovering such consistency, including analytic and conceptual skills. They have confidence in their knowledge, because their experience of its validity was the condition of its acceptance. Some information in Chapter 7 supports the assumption of this theory that such "informational independence'' is the culmination of an educational, as distinct from a persuasive, process. When children learn why a given rule is justifiable, rather than merely being persuaded to accept it, they demonstrate greater "self-control."

When interpreting standard pictures of person–environment situations, people who display initiative to change their circumstances give causally connected, analytic accounts of individuals acting with foresight to control events. In experiments, they deal with personal challenges in a like manner, becoming motivationally aroused before the event, rather than reacting emotionally later. They seem to comprehend events in long sequences, in which the present extends well into the past and the future.

Although their energies are easily aroused, enterprising persons are seldom anxious. Presumably their methods of interacting with the world have commonly been successful in preventing "primary overstimulation," cognitive incongruity, and frustration. So their actions are not as readily controlled by threat or negative reinforcement as those of their anxious peers. And they are consequently able to use larger amounts of information, so that their actions are more ("objectively") appropriate to conditions in their environments. That their behavior is autonomously controlled, nonetheless, is evident in their ability to planfully produce the environmental changes they desire.

Their activities are commonly "self-disciplined." They are governed by complex and accurate, though abstract, knowledge of what is desirable and undesirable in human affairs, and of how each comes about. So, concrete environmental conditions and events have little influence over them. They are capable of "self-reinforcement," which means they have vestigial experiences of pleasure when they recognize they have done well, and of displeasure or discomfort when they have not. They are not limited in their recognition of successes and failures by the consequences of external reinforcements; instead their recognition of success or failure initiates internal reinforcements. For all of these reasons, such people are notably "imaginative"—in a special sense of that term.

The Effects of Drive on Imagination

According to the evidence of Figure 2.2, efficacious people are more *disposed* to imaginative activity than are anxious persons, who appear to be disposed instead to concern with concrete, "practical" matters. Comparably, anxious "authoritarian personalities" typically advocated on questionnaires that imaginative activities should be avoided in preference for the practical (i.e., "anti-intraceptive" attitudes, according to Adorno *et al.*, 1950). Men with low achievement fantasy scores, who are also commonly anxious, revealed little imagination of achievement-oriented activity after manipulations to arouse achievement motivation. According to a useful interpretation of practical experience, readiness to think with and elaborate imaginatively upon "hypnotic" suggestions is reduced by anxiety (Barber & de Moor, 1972). An interpretation of evidence on the relation between imagination and creativity has suggested that aversion to imaginative activity may arise from fear of the contents of imagination, and so inhibit creativity (Barron, 1966). This view includes a hypothesis that anxious people avoid imaginative activity because they dislike what they imagine.

The latter hypothesis has additional support. Anxious people can and do have fantasies. When asked to interpret standard pictures of people in various settings, "authoritarian personalities" produced accounts of primitive impulsive aggression and hostility (Aron, 1950). Men with low fantasy achievement scores produced more evidence suggesting fear of failure than hope of success (Clark *et al.,* 1958; Birney *et al.,* 1969). Similar people, similarly motivated, displayed imaginative and attentional "rigidity" on the Luchin's water jar test. What they failed to "imagine" were simpler methods of solving their problems; what they "imagined" were applications of methods they had used repeatedly (Brown, 1953). Anxious persons also display considerable imagination in the clinical setting. Indeed, obsessive rumination or brooding over themes related to their distress are diagnostic signs of acute anxiety and depression (Mather, 1970). What distinguishes efficacious from driven persons is apparently not *that* they imagine so much as *what* they imagine.

It may be true, as in SR theory it should be true, that drive influences imaginative behavior in the same ways it affects overt action. Thus, as indicated in Chapter 4, it should activate thoughts associated with the prevailing emotion, including those concerned with reducing it, to inhibit other thoughts and to reduce the total range of imaginative activities. It should also reduce imaginative discrimination, so the resultant fantasies would display faulty causal analysis like that observed in anxious "externals" and in those entrepreneurial trainees of McClelland and Winter whose enterprise was not improved by training (see p. 90, this volume). To assume that high drive impairs freedom of choice in imagination and reduces the range of imaginative activities would be consistent with its observed effects on overt behavior.

MIND OVER MATTER

What occurs in imagination may influence what occurs in overt action. The evidence on this question from research with fantasy measures of motivation is unclear. The investigators have discussed imaginative activity as the medium by which motives for planned actions are expressed, rather than being the source of such plans. And yet, training to think planfully, as economic entrepreneurs think, seems to increase economic enterprise by men of means (see pp. 89–91, this volume). "Posthypnotic suggestions" also clearly influence overt behavior

(Barber, 1965). In these cases, of course, "imagination" is externally stimulated. In the writing of fantasies, however, the external stimulation is quite as indirect as it is in the production of fiction. The case is similar in human problem solving, where "mental trial and error" is commonly reported during formulation of the hypotheses that are tested in overt action. "Thinking" seems often to precede action and determine its character. Inventions are often first "seen" in imagination (Iles, 1906; Humphrey, 1948).

Assuming that the outcomes of imaginative activity sometimes determine human action, by determining intention and will, the power of "mind over matter" may be quite considerable. Indeed, if the precise form of imaginative contribution to a plan is sometimes due to associations in thought that have no counterparts in experience, the freedom that human will can attain may approach the limit established by its knowledge. The attainment of such freedom would depend, of course, on the liberation of imagination from driving emotions.

The apparent similarity in the effects of high drive on fantasy and overt behavior has a useful counterpart in research on anxiety reduction. Training to extinguish emotional CRs can be conducted in fantasy as well as in fact. The therapist simply directs the thoughts of relaxed patients into slightly frightening versions of situations they fear greatly and then permits the resulting emotion to subside. When it has done so, he stimulates recollection of a situation that was somewhat more frightening, and proceeds in this way until the patient can imaginatively contemplate the most feared situation. This procedure is reported to enable patients thereafter to approach the feared situations in reality with reduced distress (Wolpe & Flood, 1970). The original findings have been confirmed, but whether all features of the original procedure are required is a matter of debate (Wilkins, 1971).

A positive association between relaxation and freedom of imagination has been postulated in discussion of the mechanisms of "hypnosis" (Barber & de Moor, 1972). Such a relationship has, of course, long been claimed by advocates of transcendental meditation. They strive for tranquillity by suitable meditative exercises in pursuit of self-control. The credibility of some of these techniques has been demonstrated by recent research in behavioral science. Many studies, using sophisticated technical aids to provide "biofeedback" to a person (Karlins & Andrews, 1973), have also corroborated and extended similar early findings by Western scientists (Jacobson, 1929). Human beings *can* learn to reduce their own undesirable bodily reactions to frightening events, thereby relieving various physiological symptoms of drive. Conceivably they achieve, at the same time, the freedom of imagination that such self-control is supposed to produce.

When someone has techniques for reducing his own drive level, he has methods for increasing his freedom of will in adverse environmental conditions. If acquisition of such skills were aided by external "biofeedback" displays, or even by external reinforcement of appropriate actions, the resulting freedom would be in no way diminished. Such techniques may remove a most important limitation on freedom of will and promote the realization of human potentialities.

THE GOOD LIFE

The picture is now complete. The people who most often change circumstances to suit their needs are competent and adopt an "abstract attitude" in interacting with their environments. The "good life" they live is not free of difficulties, stresses, and challenges, though they minimize the adverse effects of such circumstances by avoiding some and overcoming others. Nonetheless, it is a life of satisfactions, purpose, and considerable peace and harmony. Low anxiety, or high efficacy, is an essential condition of the competence these people display, and also apparently a consequence of it. This condition summarizes past experience and present expectations. Probably it is an expectation of success, due to previous successes, which prevents efficacious persons from becoming disorganized in discouragement, frustration, or fear of failure when difficulties arise, and so permits them to employ their knowledge and abilities effectively. An old-fashioned word for this valuable outlook toward the future may summarize it conveniently. It is *faith*.

With considerations like this, the discussion of free will and adjustment has taken a turn toward the mystical. This may not be inappropriate. Subjective terms like "tranquillity" and "faith" seem to be applicable to phenomena that can also be described in objective terms like "relaxation" and "efficacy." There are also old fashioned ways of discussing other generalizations suggested in previous chapters. It is interesting, for instance, that the "objectivity" that suggests "integrity" and "love of truth" should be found in association with "faith" and "tranquillity." Objectively determined actions are designed in accordance with valid conceptions of "laws of nature," which may be God's laws. In interdependent groups, personal peace and freedom from adverse reactions by others depend upon acting in consideration of others. Trust of others and benevolence toward others develop together; changes toward equality and justice promote mutual rewards and harmony in social groups; and each of these conditions promotes attainment of the others. These and other implications of what has been reviewed can be put into words that are more familiar in religious contexts.

And they have been. For instance, H. Richard Niebuhr's (1963) understanding of the responsible self, personified in Christ, may be consistent with the free will as represented here. Another religious formulation of the adjustive tendency of free will is to be found in Vivekananda's (reprinted in Vidyatmananda, 1972) conception of a singular ideal in all monotheistic religions. The importance of this shared ideal is so great, he believed, that it is "the whole of religion. Doctrines or dogmas or rituals or books or temples or forms are but secondary

details [p. 1]." The faith of this postulated religion, and the means it follows to the good life, Vivekananda described in the following words:

> *Each soul is potentially divine.*
> *The goal is to manifest this divinity within by controlling*
> *nature, external and internal.*
> *Do this either by work or worship or*
> *psychic control or philosophy—by one or*
> *more or all of these—and be free* [p. 1].

SUMMARY

Social rules governing injury to others restrict absolute freedom of action but render the social environment predictable, so that the universal attainment of freedom of will becomes feasible. Acceptance of these rules accordingly constitutes the fundamental part of an implicit social contract that has been called "the freedom charter."

Causal responsibility in an appropriate social context produces moral responsibility. Common adherence to the rules governing injury to others then establishes and maintains a social order in which freedom of will is more easily attained.

Among adult persons, morality can be sanctioned by the internal reinforcements of conscience. Nonetheless external reinforcement seems to be required to establish basic responsibility and to ensure against injuries due to inconsiderate or careless exercise of freedom by powerful persons or institutions. When such injuries occur unpredictably, the possibility of their prevention disappears, and with it the possibility of individual freedom of will in those circumstances.

So, conditions that inhibit delivery of appropriate reinforcements threaten the survival of "the freedom charter." These include misconstructions of social problems and misunderstanding of the effects of sanctions or reinforcements on behavior. Important practical difficulties also exist due to the relative invulnerability of large corporations to the reinforcements that can be delivered by individuals interacting with them.

Freedom is threatened, too, by economic conditions that imperil the biological well-being of increasing numbers of people.

Contemporary threats to freedom pose serious problems for mankind. These circumstances emphasize the importance of appropriate constructions of knowledge about the conditions that promote or retard creativity and freedom of will. Some faults and virtues of a behavioral engineering philosophy are discussed in this context, in comparison with a few pertinent generalizations about creative imagination that were justified in earlier chapters.

Useful methods evidently exist for training people in autonomous reduction of emotional reactions that constrain freedom of will. A final resumé on "the good life" of responsible freedom alludes to related religious formulations. One of these regards human control of nature, external and internal, as the manifestation of divinity!

References

Abelson, R. P., & Rosenberg, M. J. (1958) Symbolic psycho-logic: A model of attitudinal cognition. *Behavioral Science, 3,* 1–13.

Abric, J. C., Faucheux, C., Moscovici, S., & Plon, M. (1967) Rôle de l'image du partenaire sur la cooperation en situation de jeu. *Psychologie Français, 12,* 267–275.

Achenbach, T. (1969) Cue learning, associative responding and school performance in children. *Developmental Psychology, 1,* 717–725.

Adler, M. J. (1958) *The idea of freedom.* New York: Doubleday.

Adorno, T. W., Frenkel-Brunswick, E., Levinson, D. J., & Sanford, R. N. (1950) *The authoritarian personality.* New York: Harper & Row.

Allport, G. W. (1947) Scientific models and human morals. *Psychological Review, 54,* 182–192.

Allport, G. W. (1954) The historical background of modern social psychology. In G. Lindzey (Ed.), *Handbook of social psychology.* Cambridge, Mass.: Addison–Wesley.

Amsel, A. (1959) The role of frustrative non-reward in non-continuous reward situations. *Psychological Bulletin, 55,* 102–119.

Anscombe, G. E. M. (1958) *Intention.* Ithaca, N.Y.: Cornell University Press.

Argyle, M. (1967) *The psychology of interpersonal behavior.* England: Penguin Books.

Aron, B. (1950) The thematic apperception test in the study of prejudiced and unprejudiced individuals. In T. W. Adorno, E. Frenkel-Brunswick, D. J. Levinson, & R. N. Sanford, *The authoritarian personality.* New York: Harper & Row.

Asch, S. E. (1956) Studies of independence and conformity: a minority of one against a unanimous majority. *Psychological Monographs, 70,* (9).

Ashby, W. R. (1958) *Introduction to cybernetics.* London: Chapman & Hall.

Ashby, W. R. (1960) *Design for a brain* (2nd ed.). London: Chapman & Hall.

Atkinson, J. W. (1958) *Motives in fantasy, action, and society.* Princeton, N.J.: Van Nostrand.

Atkinson, J. W., Heyns, R. W., & Veroff, J. (1958) The effect of experimental arousal of the affiliation motive on thematic apperception. In J. W. Atkinson (Ed.), *Motives in fantasy, action, and society.* Princeton, N.J.: Van Nostrand.

Atkinson, J. W., & McClelland, D. C. (1958) The effect of different intensities of the hunger drive on thematic apperception. In J. W. Atkinson (Ed.), *Motives in fantasy, action, and society.* Princeton, N.J.: Van Nostrand.

Bacon, S. J. (1974) Arousal and the range of cue utilization. *Journal of Experimental Psychology, 102,* 81–87.

Baldwin, J. (1964) *The fire next time*. New York: Dial.

Bales, R. F. (1958) Task roles and social roles in problem-solving groups. In E. E. Maccoby, T. M. Newcomb & E. L. Hartley (Eds.), *Readings in social psychology,* (3rd ed.). New York: Holt.

Bandura, A. (1965) Vicarious processes: A case of no-trial learning. In L. Berkowitz (Ed.), *Advances in experimental social psychology* (Vol 2). New York: Academic.

Bandura, A. (1969a) *Principles of behavior modification*. New York: Holt.

Bandura, A. (1969b) Social learning theory of identificatory processes. In D. A. Goslin, *Handbook of socialization theory and research*. Chicago: Rand McNally.

Bandura, A. (1971) Vicarious and self reinforcement processes. In R. Glaser, *The nature of reinforcement*. New York: Academic.

Bandura, A., & Walters, R. H. (1963) *Social learning and personality development*. New York: Holt, Rinehart, & Winston.

Barber, T. X. (1965) Measuring "hypnotic-like" suggestibility with and without "hypnotic induction;" psychometric properties, norms, and variables influencing response to the Barber Suggestibility Scale (BSS). *Psychological Reports, 16,* 809–844.

Barber, T. X. (1970) *LSD, marihuana, yoga, and hypnosis*. Chicago: Aldine.

Barber, T. X., & de Moor, W. (1972) A theory of hypnotic induction procedures. *The American Journal of Clinical Hypnosis, 15,* 112–135.

Barker, R. G., Dembo, T., & Lewin, K. (1943) Frustration and regression. In R. G. Brown, J. S. Kounin, & H. F. Wright (Eds.), *Child behavior and development*. New York: McGraw Hill.

Barron, F. (1963) *Creativity and psychological health*. Princeton, N.J.: Van Nostrand.

Barron, F. (1966) The psychology of imagination. In S. Coopersmith (Ed.), *Frontiers of psychological research*. San Francisco: Freeman.

Bartlett, F. (1951) Anticipation in human performance. In G. Ekman, T. Husen, G. Johanson, & C. I. Sandstrom (Eds.), *Essays in psychology dedicated to David Katz*. Upsala: Ulmquist & Wicksells.

Bartlett, F. (1958) *Thinking: An experimental and social study*. London: Unwin University Books.

Beck, A. T. (1972) Cognition, anxiety, and psychophysiological disorders. In C. D. Spielberger (Ed.), *Anxiety: Current trends in theory and research*. New York: Academic.

Berger, S. M., & Johansson, S. L. (1968) Effect of a model's expressed emotions on an observer's resistance to extinction. *Journal of Personality and Social Psychology, 10,* 53–58.

Berlyne, D. E. (1960) *Conflict, arousal, and curiosity*. New York: McGraw Hill.

Bernstein, B. (1961) Social class and linguistic development: A theory of social learning. In H. A. Halsey & C. A. Anderson (Eds.), *Education, economy, and society*. New York: Free Press.

Birney, R. C. (1958) Thematic content and the cue characteristics of pictures. In J. W. Atkinson (Ed.), *Motives in fantasy, action, and society*. Princeton, N.J.: Van Nostrand.

Birney, R. C., Burdick, H., & Teevan, R. C. (1969) *Fear of failure motivation*. New York: Wiley.

Blake, R. R., Helson, H., & Mouton, J. S. (1957) The generality of conformity behavior as a function of factual anchorage, difficulty of task, and amount of social pressure. *Journal of Personality, 25,* 294–305.

Blaumen, R. (1964) *Alienation and freedom*. Chicago: University of Chicago Press.

Bogdonoff, M. D., Klein, R. F., Estes, E. H., Jr., Shaw, D. M., & Back, K. W. (1961) The modifying effect of conforming behavior upon lipid responses accompanying CNS arousal. *Clinical Research, 9,* 135.

Bowers, K. S. (1973) Situationalism in psychology: An analysis and a critique. *Psychological Review, 80,* 307–336.

Bramel, D. (1969) Interpersonal attraction, hostility, and perception. In D. Bramel (Ed.), *Experimental social psychology*. New York: Macmillan.

Brehm, J. W. (1966) *A theory of psychological reactance*. New York: Academic.

Brown, R. (1965) *Social psychology*. New York: Free Press.

Brown, R. W. (1953) A determinant of the relationship between rigidity and authoritarianism. *Journal of Abnormal and Social Psychology, 48,* 469–476.

Bruner, J. S., Matter, J., & Papanek, M. L. (1955) Breadth of learning as a function of drive level and mechanization. *Psychological Review, 62,* 1–10.

Bryan, W. L., & Harter, N. (1897) Studies in the physiology and psychology of telegraphic language. *Psychological Review, 4,* 27–53.

Bryan, W. L., & Harter, N. (1899) Studies on the telegraphic language: The acquisition of a hierarchy of habits. *Psychological Review, 6,* 345–375.

Burnstein, E. (1969) Interdependence in groups. In D. Bramel (Ed.), *Experimental social psychology.* New York: Macmillan.

Carmichael, L. (1946) *Manual of child psychology.* New York: Wiley.

Cattell, R. B. (1964) *Personality and social psychology.* San Diego, Calif.: Knapp.

Cattell, R. B., & Eber, H. W. (1967) *Handbook for the sixteen personality factor questionnaire.* Champaign, Ill.: Institute for Personality and Ability Testing.

Chapman, J. J., Chapman, J. P., & Miller, G. A. (1964) A theory of verbal behavior in schizophrenia. In B. Maher (Ed.), *Progress in experimental personality research* (Vol. 1) New York: Academic.

Cheyne, J. A., Goyeche, J. R., & Walters, R. H. (1969) Attention, anxiety and rules in resistance-to-deviation in children. *Journal of Experimental Child Psychology, 8,* 127–139.

Cheyne, J. A., & Walters, R. H. (1969) Intensity of punishment, timing of punishment, and cognitive structure as determinants of response inhibition. *Journal of Experimental Child Psychology, 7,* 231–244.

Christie, R. (1954) Authoritarianism re-examined. In R. Christie & M. Jahoda (Eds.), *Studies in the scope and method of "The authoritarian personality."* New York: Free Press.

Christie, R., & Cook, P. (1958) A guide to published literature relating to the authoritarian personality through 1956. *Journal of Psychology, 45,* 171–199.

Clark, R. A.,Teevan, R.C.& Ricciuti, H. N. (1958) Hope of success and fear of failure aspects of need for achievement. In J. W. Atkinson (Ed.), *Motives in fantasy, action, and society.* Princeton, N.J.: Van Nostrand.

Coch, L., & French, J. R. P., Jr. (1948) Overcoming resistance to change. *Human Relations, 1,* 512–532.

Cohen, J. (1959) The factorial structure of the WISC at ages 7:6, 10:6, and 13:6. *Journal of Consulting Psychology, 23,* 285–299.

Couch, A., & Keniston, K. (1960) Yeasayers and naysayers: Agreeing response set as a personality variable. *Journal of Abnormal and Social Psychology, 60,* 151–174.

Craig, K. D., & Weinstein, M. S. (1965) Conditioning vicarious affective arousal. *Psychological Reports, 17,* 955–963.

Crandall, V. C., Katkovsky, W., & Crandall, V. J. (1965) Children's beliefs in their own control of reinforcements in intellectual–academic situations. *Child Development, 36,* 91–109.

Crandall, V. J., Preston, A., & Rabson, A. (1960) Maternal reactions and the development of independence and achievement behavior in children. *Child Development, 31,* 243–251.

Cromwell, R. (1972) Success–failure reactions in retarded children. In J. B. Rotter, J. E. Chance, & E. J. Phares (Eds.), *Applications of a social learning theory of personality.* New York: Holt, Rinehart, & Winston.

Cross, H. J. (1966) The relation of parental training conditions to conceptual level in adolescent boys. *Journal of Personality, 34,* 348–365.

Cross, H. J. (1970) The relation of parental training to conceptual structure in preadolescents. *Journal of Genetic Psychology, 116,* 197–202.

Crowne, D. P., & Liverant, S. (1963) Conformity under varying conditions of personal commitment. *Journal of Abnormal and Social Psychology, 66,* 547–555.

Curnock, M. (Ed.). (1960) *The journal of the Rev. John Wesley, A.M.* (Vol. 3). London: Epworth.

Davis, W. L., & Phares, E. J. (1969) Parental antecedents of internal–external control of reinforcement. *Psychological Reports, 24,* 427–436.

de Charms, R. (1968) *Personal causation.* New York: Academic.

de Charms, R., Carpenter, V., & Kuperman, A. (1965) The "origin–pawn" variable in person perception. *Sociometry, 28,* 241–258.

Deutsch, M., & Gerard, H. (1955) A study of normative and informational influences upon individual judgment. *Journal of Abnormal and Social Psychology, 51,* 629–636.

Deutsch, M., Yakov, E., Canavan, D., & Gumpert, P. (1967) Strategies of inducing cooperation: An experimental study. *Journal of Conflict Resolution, 11,* 345–366.

Devereux, E. C., Bronfenbrenner, U., & Rodgers, R. R. (1969) Child-rearing in England and the United States: A cross-national comparison. *Journal of Marriage and the Family, 31,* 257–270.

Dewey, J. (1922) *Human nature and conduct: An introduction to social psychology.* New York: Holt.

Diamond, S., Balvin, R. S., & Diamond, F. R. (1963) *Inhibition and choice.* New York: Harper & Row.

Di Caprio, N. S. (1974) *Personality theories: Guides to living.* Philadelphia: Saunders.

Dies, R. (1968) Development of a projective measure of perceived locus of control. *Journal of Projective Techniques and Personality Assessment, 32,* 487–498.

Downing, R. W., Shubrook, S. J., & Ebert, J. N. (1966) Intrusion of associative distractors into conceptual performance by acute schizophrenics: Role of associative strength. *Perceptual and Motor Skills, 22,* 460–462.

Drew, G. C. (1963) The study of accidents. *Bulletin of the British Psychological Society, 16,* 1–10.

Easterbrook, J. A. (1959) The effect of emotion on cue utilization and the organization of behavior. *Psychological Review, 66,* 183–201.

Easterbrook, J. A. (1966) *Redundancy and the measurement of cognitive complexity in the repertory grids of students and psychiatric patients.* Unpublished manuscript.

Easterbrook, J. A. (1972) *The phase-down of coal mining operations in the Grand Lake Basin of New Brunswick.* Department of Psychology, University of New Brunswick.

Easterbrook, J. A., & Fuller, K. T. (1969) *The human effects of some economic development decisions.* Fredericton, N.B.: New Brunswick Department of Labour.

Eberts, P. R. (1971) *A theoretical perspective toward an action-oriented model of community change and development.* Richibucto, N.B.: New Brunswick Newstart Inc.

Eberts, P. R. (1972) *NE-47: Consequences of changing social organizations in the northeast.* Ithaca, N.Y.: Department of Rural Sociology, Cornell University.

Elithorn, A. (1955) A perceptual maze sensitive to brain damage: A preliminary report. *Journal of Neurology, Neurosurgery and Psychiatry, 18,* 287–292.

Elithorn, A., Kerr, M., & Mott, J. (1960) A group version of a perceptual maze test. *British Journal of Psychology, 51,* 19–26.

Elliot, R. (1961) Interrelationships among measures of field dependence, ability, and personality traits. *Journal of Abnormal and Social Psychology, 63,* 27–36.

English, H. B., & English, A. C. (1958) *A comprehensive dictionary of psychological and psychoanalytic terms.* New York: Longmans, Green.

Epstein, S. (1972) The nature of anxiety with emphasis upon its relationship to expectancy. In C. D. Spielberger (Ed.), *Anxiety: Current trends in theory and research* (Vol. 2). New York: Academic.

Estes, W. R. (1944) An experimental study of punishment. *Psychological Monographs, 47* (263).

Eysenck, H. J., & Willett, R. A. (1962) Cue utilization as a function of drive An exploratory study. *Perceptual and Motor Skills, 15,* 229–230.

Eysenck, H. J., & Willett, R. A. (1966) The effect of drive on performance and reminiscence in a complex tracing task. *British Journal of Psychology, 57,* 107–112.

Franklin, J. C., Schiele, B. C., Brozek, J., & Keys, A. (1948) Observations on human behavior in experimental semistarvation and rehabilitation. *Journal of Clinical Psychology, 4,* 28–45.

Franks, C. M. (1969) *Behavior therapy: Assessment and status.* New York: McGraw-Hill.

Freedman, P. E. (1966) Human maze learning as a function of stress and partial reinforcement. *Psychological Reports, 18,* 975–981.

Frenkel-Brunswick, E. (1954) Further explorations by a contributor to "The authoritarian personality." In R. Christie & M. Jahoda (Eds.), *Studies in the scope and method of "The authoritarian personality."* New York: Free Press.

Freud, S. (1927) *The ego and the id.* London: Hogarth.

Freud, S. (1938) *The basic writings of Sigmund Freud.* New York: Random House.

Freud, S. (1950) *Collected papers (Vol. 5).* London: Hogarth.

Fromm, E. (1941) *Escape from freedom.* New York: Farrar & Rinehart.

Fromm, E. (1947) *Man for himself.* New York: Holt, Rinehart, & Winston.

Gaines, J. A., Mednick, S. A., & Higgins, J. (1963) Stimulus generalization in acute and chronic schizophrenics. *Acta Psychiatrica, Scandinavia, 39,* 601–605.

Gardner, R. W., Jackson, D. N., & Messick, D. N. (1960) Personality organization in cognitive controls and intellectual abilities. *Psychological Issues, 2.*

Gardner, R. W., & Long, R. I. (1961) Selective attention and the Mueller–Lyer illusion. *Psychological Records, 11,* 305–310.

Glueck, S., & Glueck, E. (1960) *Unraveling juvenile delinquency,* New York: Commonwealth Fund.

Goffman, E. (1955) On face-work: An analysis of ritual elements in social interaction. *Psychiatry, 18,* 213–231.

Goguen, L. (1972) *Internal–external locus of control: An experiment in behaviour modification through a child-rearing instructional program.* Richibucto, N.B.: New Brunswick Newstart, Inc.

Goldstein, K. (1939) *The organism.* New York: American.

Goldstein, K. (1940) *Human nature.* New York: Schocken.

Gollin, E. S., & Baron, A. (1954) Response consistency in perception and retention. *Journal of Experimental Psychology, 47,* 259–262.

Gollob, H. F., & Dittes, J. E. (1965) Effects of manipulated self-esteem on persuasibility depending on threat and complexity of communication. *Journal of Personality and Social Psychology, 2,* 195–201.

Gorham, D. R. (1956) A proverbs test for clinical and experimental use. *Psychological Reports, 2,* (1-12—Monographs supplement 1).

Gorham, D. R. (1963) Additional norms and scoring suggestions for the proverbs test. *Psychological Reports, 13,* 487–492.

Gouldner, A. (1960) The norm of reciprocity. *American Sociological Review, 25,* 161–178.

Green, H. B., & Knapp, R. H. (1959) Time judgment, aesthetic preference, and need for achievement. *Journal of Abnormal and Social Psychology, 58,* 140–142.

Haber, R. N. (1966) Nature of the effect of set on perception. *Psychological Review, 73,* 335–351.

Haber, R. N. (1970) How we remember what we see. *Scientific American, 222,* 104–112.

Haber, R. N., & Alpert, R. (1958) The role of situation and picture cues in projective measurement of the achievement motive. In J. W. Atkinson (Ed.), *Motives in fantasy, action and society.* Princeton, N. J.: Van Nostrand.

Haines, N. (1966) *Freedom and community.* New York: Macmillan.

Haller, A. O., & Miller, I. W. (1963) The occupational aspiration scale. *The Michigan State University Work Beliefs Check List.* Appendix II. Lansing, Mich.: Michigan State University.

Handlesby, J. D., Pawlik, K., & Cattell, R. B. (1965) *Personality factors in objective test devices.* San Diego, Calif.: Knapp.

Harvey, O. J., & Felknor, C. (1970) Parent–child relations as an antecedent to conceptual function-
    ing. In R. A. Hoppe, G. A. Milton, & E. C. Simmel (Eds.), *Early experiences and the process
    of socialization*. New York: Academic.
Harvey, O. J., Hunt, D. E., & Schroder, H. M. (1961) *Conceptual systems and personality organiza-
    tion*. New York: Wiley.
Hawkes, J. (1973) *The first great civilizations*. New York: Knopf.
Heckhausen, H. (1967) *The anatomy of achievement motivation*. New York: Academic.
Heckhausen, H. (1968) Achievement motive research: Current problems and some contributions
    towards a general theory of motivation. In W. Arnold (Ed.), *Nebraska symposium on motivation
    (Vol. 16)*. Lincoln: University of Nebraska Press.
Heider, F. (1944) Social perception and phenomenal causality. *Psychological Review, 51*, 358–374.
Heider, F. (1958) *The psychology of interpersonal relations*. New York: Wiley,
Henley, W. E. (1908) "Invictus," "Echoes." In *Collected Works*. London: Nutt.
Hess, R. D., & Shipman, V. C. (1965) Early experience and the socialization of cognitive mode in
    children. *Child Development, 36*, 869–888.
Hess, R. D., & Shipman, V. C. (1967) Cognitive elements in maternal behavior. In J. P. Hill (Ed.),
    Minnesota symposia on child psychology (Vol. 1). Minneapolis: University of Minnesota Press.
Hilton, I. (1967) Differences in the behavior of mothers toward first- and later-born children. *Journal
    of Personality and Social Psychology, 7*, 282–290.
Hiroto, D. S. (1974) Locus of control and learned helplessness. *Journal of Experimental Psychology,
    102*, 187–193.
Hodges, W. F., & Spielberger, C. D. (1969) Digit span: An indicant of trait or state anxiety? *Journal
    of Consulting and Clinical Psychology, 33*, 430–434.
Hovland, C. I., Lumsdaine, A. A., & Sheffield, F. D. (1949) *Experiments on mass communication*.
    Princeton, N.J.: Yale University Press.
Hull, C. L. (1943) *Principles of behavior*. New York: Appleton-Century.
Humphrey, G. (1922–1923) The conditioned reflex and the elementary social reaction. *Journal of
    Abnormal and Social Psychology, 17*, 113–119.
Humphrey, G. (1933) *The nature of learning*. London: Kegan, Paul, Trench & Trubnar.
Humphrey, G. (1948) *Directed thinking*. New York: Dodd, Mead.
Hyman, H. H., & Sheatsley, P. B. (1954) "The authoritarian personality: A methodological critique.
    In R. Christie & M. Jahoda (Eds.), *Studies in the scope and method of "The authoritarian
    personality."* New York: Free Press.
Iles, G. (1906) *Inventors at work*. New York: Doubleday.
Inhelder, B., & Piaget, J. (1958) *The growth of logical thinking from childhood to adolescence*. (A.
    Parsons & S. Milgram, trans.). New York: Basic Books.
IPAT Staff, *Interim manual for form E, sixteen personality factor questionnaire*. Champaign, Ill.:
    Institute for Personality and Ability Testing.
Irwin, R. W. (1971) *Intentional behavior and motivation*. Philadelphia: Lippincott.
Jacobson, E. (1929) *Progressive relaxation*. Chicago: University of Chicago.
Jahoda, M. (1958) *Current concepts of positive mental health*. New York: Basic Books.
James, W. (1890) *Principles of psychology*. New York: Holt.
Janis, I. L., & Feshbach, S. (1953) Effects of fear-arousing communications. *Journal of Abnormal
    and Social Psychology, 48*, 78–92.
Janis, I. L., & Feshbach, S. (1954) Personality differences associated with responsiveness to fear-
    arousing communications. *Journal of Personality, 23*, 154–166.
Janis, I. L., & King, B. T. (1954) The influence of role playing on opinion change. *Journal of
    Abnormal and Social Psychology, 49*, 211–218.
Janisse, M. P., & Palys, T. S. (1976) Frequency and intensity of anxiety in university students.
    Journal of Personality, 40, 502–515.

Joe, V. C. (1971) Review of the internal–external control construct as a personality variable. *Psychological Reports, 28,* 619–640.

Jones, E. E., & Davis, K. (1965) From acts to dispositions: The attribution process in person perception. In L. Berkowitz, *Advances in experimental social psychology* (Vol. 2). New York: Academic.

Jones, M. C. (1924a) The elimination of children's fears. *Journal of Experimental Psychology, 7,* 383–390.

Jones, M. C. (1924b) A laboratory study of fear: The case of Peter. *The Pedagogical Seminary and Journal of Genetic Psychology, 31,* 308–315.

Kagan, J. (1966) Developmental studies in reflection and analysis. In A. H. Kidd & J. L. Rivoire (Eds.), *Perceptual development in children.* New York: International Universities.

Kanfer, F. H. (1970) Self-monitoring: Methodological limitations and clinical applications. *Journal of Consulting and Clinical Psychology, 35,* 148–152.

Kant, I. (1785/1910) Fundamental principles of the metaphysic of morals. (T. K. Abbot, trans.) In C. W. Eliot (Ed.), *The Harvard classics (Vol. 32).* New York: Collier.

Kant, I. (1785/1959) *Foundations of the metaphysics of morals* (L. W. Beck, trans.). Indianapolis: Bobbs-Merrill.

Karlins, M., & Andrews, L. M. (1973) *Biofeedback: Turning on the power of your mind.* New York: Warner.

Katz, E. (1957) The two-step flow of communication: An up-to-date report on an hypothesis. *Public Opinion Quarterly, 21,* 61–78.

Kelley, H. H. (1967) Attribution theory in social psychology. In D. Levine (Ed.), *Nebraska symposium on motivation* (Vol. 15). Lincoln: University of Nebraska Press.

Kelley, H. H. & Stahelski, A. J. (1970) Social interaction basis of cooperators' and competitors' beliefs about others. *Journal of Personality and Social Psychology, 16,* 66–91.

Kelley, H. H., Thibaut, J. W., Radloff, R., & Mundy, D. (1962) The development of cooperation in the "minimal social situation." *Psychological Monographs, 76,* (19).

Kelly, G. A. (1955) *The psychology of personal constructs* (Vol. 1). New York: Norton.

Kelman, H. C., & Barclay, J. (1963) The *F*-scale as a measure of breadth of perspective. *Journal of Abnormal and Social Psychology, 67,* 608–615.

Kiesler, C. A. (1969) Group pressure and conformity. In J. Mills (Ed.), *Experimental social psychology.* New York: Macmillan.

Kimble, G. A. (1968) *Hilgard and Marquis' Conditioning and learning.* New York: Appleton-Century–Crofts.

King, B. T., & Janis, I. L. (1956) Comparison of the effectiveness of improvised versus non-improvised role playing in producing opinion change. *Human Relations, 9,* 177–186.

Knapp, R. H., & Garbutt, J. T. (1965) Variation in time descriptions and n-achievement. *Journal of Social Psychology, 67,* 269–272.

Kohlberg, L. (1969) Stage & sequence: The cognitive developmental approach to socialization. In D. A. Goslin (Ed.), *Handbook of socialization theory and research.* Chicago: Rand McNally.

Kozma, A., & Easterbrook, P. (1974) Effects of baseline self-reinforcement behavior and training level on posttraining self-reinforcement behavior. *Journal of Experimental Psychology, 102,* 256–259.

Krech, D., Crutchfield, R. S., & Ballachey, E. L. (1962) *Individual in society.* New York: McGraw-Hill.

Kubie, L. S. (1954) The fundamental nature of the distinction between normality and neurosis. *Psychoanalytic Quarterly, 23,* 167–204.

Kubie, L. S. (1961) *Neurotic distortion of the creative process.* Toronto: Ambassador.

Kulpe, O. (1919) *Outlines of psychology* (E. B. Titchener, trans.) (3rd ed.). New York: Macmillan.

Latané, B., & Darley, J. W. (1970) *The unresponsive bystander: Why doesn't he help?* New York: Appleton-Century-Crofts.

Lazarus, R. S. (1974) *The riddle of man*. Englewood Cliffs, N.J.: Prentice-Hall.

Lee, D. (1965) *Freedom and culture*. Englewood Cliffs, N.J.: Prentice-Hall.

Lefcourt, H. M. (1966) Internal versus external control of reinforcement: A review. *Psychological Bulletin, 65,* 206–220.

Lefcourt, H. M. (1973) The function of the illusions of control and freedom. *American Psychologist, 28,* 417–425.

Leger, G. L. (1972) *Maze performance as a function of experimental instructions and measured beliefs about personal control of outcomes*. Unpublished M.A. thesis, University of New Brunswick.

Leventhal, H. (1967) Fear—For your health. *Psychology Today, 1,* 54–58.

Leventhal, H., Singer, R., & Jones, S. (1965) Effects of fear and specificity of recommendation upon attitudes and behavior. *Journal of Personality and Social Psychology, 2,* 20–29.

Lewin, K., Lippitt, R. O., & White, R. K. (1939) Patterns of aggressive behavior in experimentally created "social climates." *Journal of Social Psychology, 10,* 271–299.

Lewinsohn, P. M., & Riggs, A. (1962) The effect of content upon the thinking of acute and chronic schizophrenics. *Journal of Abnormal and Social Psychology, 65,* 206–207.

Locke, E. A., Carteledge, N., & Koeppel, J. (1968) Motivational effects of knowledge of results. *Psychological Bulletin, 70,* 474–485.

Long, R. I. (1962) Field articulation as a factor in verbal learning and recall. *Perceptual and Motor Skills, 15,* 151–158.

Longnecker, E. D. (1962) Perceptual recognition as a function of anxiety, motivation and the testing situation. *Journal of Abnormal and Social Psychology, 64,* 215–221.

Loomis, J. L. (1959) Communication, the development of trust, and cooperative behavior. *Human Relations, 12,* 305–315.

Lowin, A. (1967) Approach and avoidance: Alternative modes of selective exposure to information. *Journal of Personality and Social Psychology, 6,* 1–9.

Luchins, A. S. (1942) Mechanization in problem solving: The effect of Einstellung. *Psychological Monographs, 54* (6).

Lynn, R. (1966) *Attention, arousal and the orientation reaction*. London: Pergamon.

McClelland, D. C. (1961) *The achieving society*. Princeton, N.J.: Van Nostrand.

McClelland, D. C. (1965) Toward a theory of motive acquisition. *American Psychologist, 20,* 321–333.

McClelland, D. C., Atkinson, J. W., Clark, R. A., & Lowell, E. L. (1953) *The achievement motive*. New York: Appleton-Century-Crofts.

McClelland, D. C., Atkinson, J. W., Clark, R. A., & Lowell, E. L. (1958) A scoring manual for the achievement motive. In J. W. Atkinson (Ed.), *Motives in fantasy, action, and society*. Princeton, N.J.: Van Nostrand.

McClelland, D. C., Clark, R. A., Roby, T. F., & Atkinson, J. W. (1958) The effect of need for achievement on thematic apperception. In J. W. Atkinson (Ed.), *Motives in fantasy, action, and society*. Princeton, N.J.: Van Nostrand.

McClelland, D. C., & Friedman, G. A. (1952) A cross-cultural study of the relationship between child-training practices and achievement motivation appearing in folk tales. In G. E. Swanson, T. M. Newcomb, & E. L. Hartley (Eds.), *Readings in social psychology*. New York: Holt.

McClelland, D. C., & Winter, D. G. (1969) *Motivating economic achievement*. New York: Free Press.

McCord, W., & McCord, J. (1956) *Psychopathy and delinquency*. New York: Grune & Stratton.

MacDonald, A. P. (1971) Internal–external locus of control: Parental antecedents. *Journal of Consulting and Clinical Psychology, 37,* 141–147.

McGinnies, E. (1966) Cross cultural studies in persuasion. III: Reactions of Japanese students to one-sided and two-sided communications. *Journal of Social Psychology, 70,* 87–93.

McGuire, W. J. (1962) Persistence of the resistance to persuasion induced by various types of prior belief defenses. *Journal of Abnormal and Social Psychology, 64,* 241–248.

McGuire, W. J. (1966) Attitudes and opinions. *Annual Review of Psychology, 17,* 475–514.

McGuire, W. J. (1968) Personality and susceptibility to social influence. In E. F. Borgatta & W. W. Lambert (Eds.), *Handbook of personality theory and research.* Chicago: Rand McNally.

McNamara, H. J., & Fisch, R. I. (1964) Effect of high and low motivation on two aspects of attention. *Perceptual and Motor Skills, 19,* 571–578.

McNulty, J. A., & Walters, R. H. (1962) Emotional arousal, conflict, and susceptibility to social influence. *Canadian Journal of Psychology, 16,* 211–220.

Maillet, L. (1973) *Toward the refinement of a measure of internal–external locus of control.* Richibucto, N.B.: New Brunswick Newstart, Inc.

Malmo, R. B. (1966) Studies of anxiety: Some clinical origins of the activation concept. In C. D. Spielberger (Ed.), *Anxiety and behavior.* New York: Academic.

Maltzman, I., Fox, J., & Morrisett, L., Jr. (1953) Some effects of manifest anxiety on mental set. *Journal of Experimental Psychology, 46,* 50–54.

Mandler, G., & Sarason, S. B. (1952) A study of anxiety and learning. *Journal of Abnormal and Social Psychology, 47,* 166–173.

Mann, R. D. (1959) A review of relationships between personality and performance in small groups. *Psychological Bulletin, 56,* 241–270.

Maslow, A. H. (1954) *Motivation and personality.* New York: Harper.

Masserman, J. H. (1943) *Behavior and neurosis.* Chicago: University of Chicago Press.

Matarazzo, J. D. (1972) *Wechsler's Measurement and appraisal of adult intelligence.* Baltimore: Williams & Wilkins.

Mather, M. D. (1970) Obsessions and compulsions. In C. G. Costello (Ed.), *Symptoms of psychopathology.* New York: Wiley.

May, R. (1969) *Love and will.* New York: Norton.

Meichenbaum, D., & Goodman, J. (1969) Reflection–impulsivity and verbal control of motor behavior. *Child Development, 40,* 785–797.

Miller, G. A. (1967) Professionals in bureaucracy: Alienation among scientists and engineers. *American Sociological Review, 32,* 755–768.

Miller, G. A., Galanter, E., & Pribram, K. H. (1960) *Plans and the structure of behavior.* New York: Holt.

Miller, N. E. (1951) Learnable drives and rewards. In S. S. Stevens (Ed.), *Handbook of experimental psychology.* New York: Wiley.

Mischel, W., & Staub, E. (1965) Effects of expectancy on working and waiting for larger rewards. *Journal of Personality and Social Psychology, 2,* 625–633.

Morse, N. C., & Reimer, E. (1956) The experimental change of a major organizational variable. *Journal of Abnormal and Social Psychology, 52,* 120–129.

Moulton, R. W. (1958) Notes for a projective measure of fear of failure. In J. W. Atkinson (Ed.), *Motives in fantasy, action, and society.* Princeton, N.J.: Van Nostrand.

Moulton, R. W., Raphelson, A. L., Kristofferson, A. B., & Atkinson, J. W. (1958) The achievement motive and perceptual sensitivity under two conditions of motive arousal. In J. W. Atkinson (Ed.), *Motives in fantasy, action, and society.* Princeton, N.J.: Van Nostrand.

Mowrer, O. H. (1953) Neurosis, psychotherapy, and the two factor learning theory. In O. H. Mowrer, *Psychotherapy theory and research.* New York: Ronald.

Mowrer, O. H., & Viek, P. (1948) An experimental analogue of fear from a sense of helplessness. *Journal of Abnormal and Social Psychology, 43,* 193–200.

Murphy, I. C. (1964) Serial learning, conditionability, and the choice of an independent measure of anxiety. *Journal of Abnormal and Social Psychology, 69,* 614–619.

Nauss, D. (1972) *Generalized expectancies of internal–external control in persons with high and low reading comprehension scores on the Dvorak-Van Wagenen examination.* Research report to UNB Department of Psychology, Fredericton, N. B.

Niebuhr, H. R. (1963) *The responsible self.* New York: Harper & Row.

Osgood, C. E., Succi, G. J., & Tannenbaum, P. H. (1957) *The measurement of meaning.* Urbana, Ill.: University of Illinois Press.

Parke, R. D. (1969) Effectiveness of punishment as an interaction of intensity, timing, agent nurturance, and cognitive structuring. *Child Development, 40,* 213–235.

Parsons, O. A., Maslow, H. I., Morris, F., & Denny, J. P. (1964) Trail Making Test performance in relation to certain experimenter, test, and subject variables. *Perceptual and Motor Skills, 19,* 199–206.

Phillips, B. N., Hindsman, E., & McGuire, C. (1960) Factors associated with anxiety and their relation to the school achievement of adolescents. *Psychological Reports, 7,* 365–372.

Phillips, B. N., Martin, R. P., & Meyers, J. (1972) Interventions in relation to anxiety in school. In C. D. Spielberger (Ed.), *Anxiety: Current trends in theory and research.* New York: Academic.

Piaget, J. (1948) *The moral judgment of the child.* (M. Worden, trans., 1st ed., 1932) Glencoe, Ill.: Free Press.

Piaget, J. (1948) *The language and thought of the child.* (M. Worden, trans., 1st ed., 1926) London: Routledge,

Piaget, J. (1952) *The origins of intelligence in children* (M. Cook trans.). New York: International Universities.

Pizer, S. A. (1969) Scoring manual for sense of efficacy. Appendix I of D. C. McClelland & D. G. Winter, *Motivating economic achievement.* New York: Free Press.

Porteus, S. D. (1950) *The Porteus maze test and intelligence.* Palo Alto, Calif.: Pacific.

Rabinowitz, L., Kelley, H. H., & Rosenblatt, R. M. (1966) Effects of different types of interdependence and response conditions in the minimal social situation. *Journal of Experimental Social Psychology, 2,* 169–197.

Raphelson, A. C. (1958) The relationships among imaginative, direct verbal, and physiological measures of anxiety in an achievement situation. In J. W. Atkinson (Ed.), *Motives in fantasy, action, and society.* Princeton, N.J.: Van Nostrand.

Rapoport, A., & Chammah, A. M. (1965) Sex differences in factors contributing to the level of cooperation in the prisoner's dilemma game. *Journal of Personality and Social Psychology, 2,* 831–838.

Razran, G. H. S. (1938) Conditioning away social bias by the luncheon technique. *Psychological Bulletin, 35,* 693. (Abstract)

Razran, G. H. S. (1940) Conditioned response changes in rating and appraising socio-political slogans. *Psychological Bulletin, 37,* 481. (Abstract)

Reitan, R. M. (1955) The relation of the Trail Making Test to organic brain damage. *Journal of Consulting Psychology, 19,* 393–394.

Riesman, D. (1955) *The lonely crowd.* Garden City, N.Y.: Doubleday.

Roe, A. (1953) *The making of a scientist.* New York: Dodd Mead.

Roff, M. (1952) A factorial study of tests in the perceptual area. *Psychometric Monographs, 8.*

Rogers, C. R. (1951) *Client centered therapy: Its current practice, implications and theory.* Boston: Houghton-Mifflin.

Roget, P. M. (1939) *Roget's thesaurus of English Words and Phrases.* London: Longmans Green.

Rosen, B. C. (1958) The achievement syndrome: A psychocultural dimension of social stratification. In J. W. Atkinson (Ed.), *Motives in fantasy, action, and society.* Princeton, N.J.: Van Nostrand.

Rosen, B. C., & D'Andrade, R. G. (1959) The psychosocial origin of achievement motivation. *Socimetry, 23,* 185–218.

Rosenbaum, M. E., & Bruning, J. L. (1966) Direct and vicarious experience of variations in percentage of reinforcement. *Child Development, 37,* 959–966.

Rosenberg, M. J. (1968) Hedonism, inauthenticity, and other goads toward expansion of a consistency theory. In R. P. Abelson, E. Aronson, W. J. McGuire, T. M. Newcomb, M. J. Rosenberg, & P. H. Tannenbaum (Eds.), *Theories of cognitive consistency: A source book.* Chicago: Rand McNally.

Rosenzweig, M. R. (1966) Environmental complexity, cerebral change, and behavior. *American Psychologist, 21,* 321–332.

Rosner, S. (1957) Consistency in response to group pressures. *Journal of Abnormal and Social Psychology, 55,* 145–146.

Rotter, J. B. (1954) *Social learning and clinical psychology.* Englewood Cliffs, N.J.: Prentice-Hall.

Rotter, J. B. (1966) Generalized expectancies for internal versus external control of reinforcement. *Psychological Monographs, 80* (809).

Rotter, J. B. (1971) External control and internal control. *Psychology Today, 5,* 37–42 and 58–59.

Rotter, J. B., Chance, J. E., & Phares, E. J. (Eds.) (1972) *Applications of a social learning theory of personality.* New York: Holt, Rinehart, & Winston.

Russell, B. (1946) *A history of western philosophy.* London: Allen & Unwin.

Ryan, T. A. (1970) *Intentional behavior: An approach to human motivation.* New York: Ronald.

Salter, A. (1949) *Conditioned reflex therapy.* New York: Creative Age.

Samelson, F. (1958) The relation of achievement and affiliation motives to conforming behavior in two conditions of conflict with a majority. In J. W. Atkinson (Ed.), *Motives in fantasy, action, and society.* Princeton, N.J.: Van Nostrand.

Sampson, E. E. (1971) *Social psychology and contemporary society.* New York: Wiley.

Sarason, I. G. (1972) Experimental approaches to test anxiety: Attention and the uses of information. In C. D. Spielberger (Ed.), *Anxiety: Current trends in theory and research.* New York: Academic.

Schacter, S. (1959) *The psychology of affiliation.* Stanford, Calif.: Stanford University Press.

Schacter, S. (1966) The interaction of cognitive and physiological determinants of emotional state. In C. D. Spielberger (Ed.), *Anxiety and behavior.* New York: Academic.

Scheerer, M. (1954) Cognitive theory. In G. Lindzey (Ed.), *Handbook of social psychology.* Cambridge, Mass.: Addison Wesley.

Schmidt, F. E. (1973) *Economy, polity, and public outcomes: An exploratory analysis in counties of the northeastern United States, 1950 to 1970.* Ithaca, N.Y.: Department of Rural Sociology, Cornell University.

Schnore, L. F. (1961) The statistical measurement of urbanization and economic development. *Land Economics, 1961, 37,* 229–245.

Scott, W. A. (1957) Attitude change through reward of verbal behavior. *Journal of Abnormal and Social Psychology, 55,* 72–75.

Scott, W. A. (1959) Cognitive consistency, response reinforcement, and attitude change. *Sociometry, 22,* 219–229.

Sechrest, L. C., & Wallace, J. (1967) *Psychology and human problems.* Columbus, Ohio: Merrill.

Seeman, M. (1972) Social learning theory and the theory of mass society. In J. B. Rotter, J. E. Chance, & E. J. Phares (Eds.), *Applications of a social learning theory of personality.* New York: Holt, Rinehart, & Winston.

Seligman, M. E. P. (1968) Chronic fear produced by unpredictable shock. *Journal of Comparative and Physiological Psychology, 66,* 402–411.

Seligman, M. E. P. (1973) Fall into helplessness. *Psychology Today, 7,* 43–48.

Seligman, M. E. P., & Maier, S. F. (1967) Failure to escape traumatic shock. *Journal of Experimental Psychology, 74,* 1–9.

Sermat, V. (1967) The effect of an initial cooperative or competitive treatment upon a subject's response to conditional cooperation. *Behavioral Science, 12,* 301–313.

Shipley, T. E., Jr., & Veroff, J. (1958) A projective measure of need for affiliation. In J. W. Atkinson (Ed.), *Motives in fantasy, action, and society.* Princeton, N.J.: Van Nostrand.

Shomer, R. W., Davis, A. H., & Kelley, H. H. (1966) Threats and the development of coordination: Further studies of the Deutsch and Krauss trucking game. *Journal of Personality and Social Psychology, 4,* 119–126.

Sidowsk1, J. B. (1957) Reward and punishment in a minimal social situation. *Journal of Experimental Psychology, 54,* 318–326.

Sismondo, S. (1973) *The measurement of development: Selected findings for rural communities in Kent county.* Richibucto, N.B.: New Brunswick Newstart, Inc.

Skinner, B. F. (1971) *Beyond freedom and dignity.* New York: Knopf.

Smith, C. P., & Feld, S. (1958) How to learn the method of content analysis for *n* achievement, *n* affiliation, and *n* power. In J. W. Atkinson (Ed.), *Motives in fantasy, action, and society.* Princeton, N.J.: Van Nostrand.

Smith, M. B. (1969) *Social psychology and human values: Selected essays.* Chicago: Aldine.

Solley, C. M. (1969) Effects of stress on perceptual attention. In B. P. Rourke (Ed.), *Explorations in the psychology of stress and anxiety.* Don Mills, Ont.: Longmans, Canada.

Solomon, L. (1960) The influence of some types of power relationships and game strategies upon the development of interpersonal trust. *Journal of Abnormal and Social Psychology, 61,* 223–230.

Solomon, R., & Wynne, L. C. (1953) Traumatic avoidance learning: Acquisition in normal dogs. *Psychological Monographs, 67* (354).

Solomon, R., & Wynne, L. C. (1954) Traumatic avoidance learning: The principles of anxiety conservation and partial irreversibility. *Psychological Review, 61,* 353–385.

Spence, K. W. (1958) A theory of emotionally based drive (D) and its relation to performance in simple learning situations. *American Psychologist, 13,* 131–141.

Spence, K. W. (1960) *Behavior theory and learning: Selected papers.* Englewood Cliffs, N.J.: Prentice-Hall.

Steiner, I. D. (1970) Perceived freedom. In L. Berkowitz (Ed.), *Advances in experimental social psychology* (Vol. 5). New York: Academic.

Stotland, E., & Canon, L. K. (1972) *Social psychology: A cognitive approach.* Toronto: Saunders.

Thibaut, J. W., & Faucheux, C. (1965) The development of contractual norms in a bargaining situation under two types of stress. *Journal of Experimental Social Psychology, 1,* 89–102.

Thurstone, L. L. (1944) A factorial study of perception. *Psychometric Monographs, 4.*

Titchener, E. B. (1908) *Lectures on the elementary psychology of feeling and attention.* New York: Macmillan.

Toffler, A. (1970) *Future shock.* New York: Random House.

Tolman, E. C. (1948) Cognitive maps in rats and men. *Psychological Review, 55,* 189–208.

United States Employment Services Staff (1967) *Manual for the general aptitude test battery,* Sections II & III. Washington, D.C.: United States Department of Labor, Manpower Administration.

Veroff, J. (1958) Development and validation of a projective measure of power motivation. In J. W. Atkinson (Ed.), *Motives in fantasy, action and society.* Princeton, N.J.: Van Nostrand.

Vidyatmananda, Swami (1972) *What religion is in the words of Swami Vivekananda.* Calcutta: Advait Ashrama.

Walker, E. L., & Atkinson, J. W. (1958) The expression of fear-related motivation in thematic apperception as a function of proximity to an atomic explosion. In J. W. Atkinson (Ed.), *Motives in fantasy, action, and society.* Princeton, N.J.: Van Nostrand.

Wallach, M. A., Kogan, N., & Bem, D. J. (1964) Diffusion of responsibility and level of risk taking in groups. *Journal of Abnormal and Social Psychology, 68,* 263–274.

Walster, E., & Walster, B. (1963) Effect of expecting to be liked on choice of associates. *Journal of Abnormal and Social Psychology, 67,* 402–404.

Walters, R. H., Marshall, W. E., & Shooter, J. R. (1960) Anxiety, isolation, and susceptibility to social influence. *Journal of Personality, 28,* 518–529.

Walters, R. H., & Ray, E. (1960) Anxiety, social isolation, and reinforcer effectiveness. *Journal of Personality, 28,* 358–367.

Weckowicz, T. E., & Blewett, D. B. (1959) Size constancy and abstract thinking in schizophrenic patients. *Journal of Mental Science, 105,* 909–934.

White, A. R. (1964) *Attention.* Oxford: Blackwell.

White, R. K., & Lippitt, R. O. (1960) *Autocracy and democracy.* New York: Harper & Row.

White, R. W. (1959) Motivation reconsidered: The concept of competence. *Psychological Review, 66,* 297–333.

White, R. W. (1972) *The enterprise of living.* New York: Holt, Rinehart, & Winston.

Wilkins, W. (1971) Desensitization: Social and cognitive factors underlying the effectiveness of Wolpe's procedure. *Psychological Bulletin, 76,* 311–317.

Willis, R. H. (1965) Social influence, information processing, and net conformity in dyads. *Psychological Reports, 17,* 147–156.

Wine, J. (1971) Test anxiety and direction of attention. *Psychological Bulletin, 76,* 92–104.

Witkin, H. A. (1965) Psychological differentiation and forms of pathology. *Journal of Abnormal Psychology, 70,* 317–336.

Witkin, H. A., Dyk, R. B., Faterson, H. F., Goodenough, D. R., & Karp, S. A. (1962) *Psychological Differentiation.* New York: Wiley.

Witkin, H. A., Faterson, H. F., Goodenough, D. R., & Birnbaum, J. (1966) Cognitive patterning in mildly retarded boys. *Child Development, 37,* 301–316.

Wolosin, R. J., Sherman, S. J., & Till, A. (1973) Effects of cooperation and competition on responsibility attribution after success and failure. *Journal of Experimental Social Psychology, 9,* 220–235.

Wolpe, J. (1958) *Psychotherapy by reciprocal inhibition.* Stanford, Calif.: Stanford University Press.

Wolpe, J., & Flood, J. (1970) The effect of relaxation on the galvanic skin response to repeated phobic stimuli in ascending order. *Journal of Behavior Therapy and Experimental Psychiatry, 1,* 195–200.

Woodward, P. M. (1953) *Probability and information theory, with applications to radar.* London: Pergamon.

Woodworth, R. S. (1938) *Experimental psychology.* New York: Holt.

Wright, D. (1971) *The psychology of moral behavior.* Harmondsworth, Middlesex: Penguin.

Young, R. C., & Moreno, J. A. (1965) Economic development and social rigidity: A comparative study of the forty-eight states. *Economic Development and Cultural Change, 13,* 439–452.

Zaffy, D. J., & Bruning, J. L. (1966) Drive and the range of cue utilization. *Journal of Experimental Psychology, 71,* 382–384.

Zeaman, D., & House, B. J. (1963) The role of attention in retardate discrimination learning. In N. R. Ellis (Ed.), *Handbook of mental deficiency.* New York: McGraw-Hill.

Zimbardo, P. G. (1969) The human choice: Individuation, reason, and order versus deindividuation, impulse, and chaos. In W. J. Arnold & D. Levine (Eds.), *Nebraska symposium on motivation* (Vol. 17). Lincoln: University of Nebraska Press.

Name Index

Numbers in italics refer to the pages on which the complete reference is listed.

243

Subject Index

H

Habit(s), 55–56, 59–67, 69–72, 78, 85, 108, 109, 174, 206, 217, 220–221, *see also* Conditional responses
Habituation, 65–66
Helplessness, *see* Control, locus of
Hidden Figures Test, 24, 43
Hope, *see* Expectancy; Expectation
Hostile
   actions, *see* Aggression
   feelings, *see* Feelings
Hunger, 51–63, 65, 67, 71, *see also* Drive
Hypnotic suggestion, *see* Suggestion

I

Ideal(s)
   components of attitude systems, *see* Attitude systems
   standards for action, 14, 32–39, 48–49, 57–58, 71, 76–77, 98–99, 113–114, 123–127, 131, 133, 135, 156, 167, 208, 212
Ideomotor action, 104–105
Imagination, *see also* Freedom
   contents of (images), 75–77, 80, 167
   mental activity, 24–26, 41, 54, 83–84, 167, 188, 223–226, *see also* Fantasy
   "the possible" in determination of behavior, 6, 18–19, 22, 24, 41, 45–50, 73–93, 121, 167, 221
Imitation, 101, 111–112, 123–126, 153, *see also* Models for action
Impetuosity, *see* Impulsiveness
Implicit theory of responsibility, *see* Responsibility
Impotence, *see* Helplessness
Impulse control, 33, 57, 66–67, 85, 120–123, 127–128, *see also* Independence
Impulsive (impelled) action, 5, 18, 22, 27, 33, 48–50, 57, 65, 69, 72, 85, 120–123, 127–128, 206–207, 211, 220–221, *see also* Reactive movement; Stimulus bondage
Inadvertence, *see* Cue utilization
Incentive(s)
   gain of possible pleasure, 18–22, 25–27, 34, 75–77, 109, 121–133, 135–140, 156, 158–159, 201–205, 221–223
   relief from stress, 18–22, 25–27, 34, 75–77, 103–109, 123–124, 144–147, 156, 158, 200–201, 220–222, *see also* Aversion

Inclinations, *see* Desires
Income, 12–13, 103, 116, 179–180, 187–196
Independence, autonomy, 7, 13, 24–25, 41, 46–47, 49–50, 52–53, 56–58, 61, 67–71, 92–93, 100–101, 113, 115–133, 136–159, 166, 169, 172–174, 177–178, 192–194, 207–209, 215–219, 222–225, 227, *see also* Freedom
Individuality, individuation, 173–174, 193–194
Influence(s), *see also* Control
   amenability to, *see* Event sequences
   social, 21, 45–47, 97–133, 139–140, 144–149, 152–155, 163–196, 211–219, 222
Information
   flow in society, *see* Economies, fluid/rigid
   instrumental, in reinforcement, *see* Reinforcement
   level, 23–26, 154–159, 193–194, 222–223
   processing, proactive/reactive, 30–35, 47–50, 57–58, 61, 73, 75–80, 83, 86–93, 105, 111, 113, 121, 165–167, 172–173, 175–176, 180–184, 194–196, 197, 211–213, 220, 222–223
   processing capacity, 37–38, 44–45, 50, 58–61, 63–65, 73, 81–83, 105–107
   seeking, 85, 145, 166–167, 182–185
   transfer, behavioral, 48–49, 58
Inhibition, 48, 49, 53–55, 66–67, 81–83, 105–108, 120–122, 131–133, 224, 227
Innovation(s), 183–184, 221, *see also* Creativity
Inoculation against brainwashing, *see* Persuasion
Insecurity, *see* Anxiety
Insight (self knowledge), 100
Instincts, 3
Instructions, *see* Commands
Instrumental activities, *see* Conditional responses; Intentional/unintentional action
Insult, *see* Approval/disapproval
Integration
   of personality, 7, 123
   temporal or serial, 31–40, 49–50, *see also* Information processing, proactive
Integrity, *see* Consistency
Intelligence
   educated or informed, 23–25, 91, 110, 125, 156–157, 179, 194, 197, 207, 209, 222
   perceptual, 24, 36, 43, *see also* Perceptual proficiency
   unqualified, 25–27, 35–36, 44, 52, 70, 73,